Matthew
THY KINGDOM COME

JOHN F. WALVOORD

moody press
chicago

©1974 by
THE MOODY BIBLE INSTITUTE
OF CHICAGO

Library of Congress Card Catalog Number: 74-15342

ISBN: 0-8024-5189-6

Second Printing, 1975

Printed in the United States of America

CONTENTS

INTRODUCTION

THE GOSPEL OF MATTHEW has commonly been considered one of the most important books of the New Testament, and properly a gospel to be placed first in the New Testament. Although the order of the books came from human choice rather than divine inspiration, this gospel, a bridge between the Old and New Testaments, fittingly introduces the books that follow. Matthew deals primarily with the life of Jesus Christ as fulfilling Old Testament prophecies relating to the coming King, and, on the other hand, it explains why the prophecies relating to the kingdom of Christ on earth are delayed in fulfillment until the second coming. Anyone desiring to master the New Testament may, accordingly, well begin with the gospel of Matthew, which fulfills the divinely intended purpose of being an introduction to New Testament truth.

History uniformly testifies that the first gospel was written by Matthew, one of the twelve disciples. All of the early copies of Matthew are headed by the phrase "according to Matthew," and the testimony of the early Fathers is unanimous on the authorship of this gospel.

The authorship and authenticity of the gospel, however, are complicated by two factors: (1) the question of whether Matthew is a translation of an earlier Hebrew work; (2) the question of whether Matthew is heavily indebted to the gospel of Mark for most of his facts. The genuineness of the gospel, however, is not questioned except by some liberal critics.

The early church Fathers refer to a book of "The Sayings" (Gr. *ta logia*) written in contemporary Hebrew (Aramaic) by Matthew and supposedly translated by an unknown translator into the gospel of Matthew. Although this explanation of the gospel of Matthew is questioned by many capable scholars today, it seems to have been held by such early Fathers as Papias, who is quoted by Eusebius, and supported by others such as Irenaeus, Epiphanius, Origen, Jerome, and later Fathers, such as Gregory Nazianzen, Chrysostom, Augustine, and others.[1]

Papias, bishop of Hierapolis in Phrygia early in the second century, is quoted by Eusebius in the middle of the second century to the effect that Matthew had written the sayings of Christ in Hebrew. Papias does not seem to be aware of a Greek gospel. Irenaeus affirms that Matthew was written in Matthew's native Hebrew tongue, in connection with his preaching to his own people. Jerome also refers to this Hebrew version, affirming that it was the first gospel to be written and that he was uncertain as to who translated it into Greek. Based on these early traditions, there has been speculation as to whether these sayings in Hebrew, which are now lost, form the entire gospel, or whether it was merely the basis of it. Also, the concept that it is translated from Hebrew into Greek by an unknown translator raises questions about the inspiration of the Greek text.

The testimony of the early Fathers has some minor contradictions but is uniform on the existence of such a Hebrew version of the gospel. Although the opinion of the early Fathers is considered to have some weight, many twentieth-century scholars question whether the story is accurate. An examination of the Greek gospel of Matthew does not substantiate the idea that it is a translation, as there are none of the characteristics of a translated work. For instance, the gospel of Matthew uses a number of original Aramaic terms which are left without translation. These would be intelligible to Jewish Christians, but if Matthew was translated from Aramaic into Greek for the benefit of Gentile Christians, these terms would require an explanation. The fact that the terms are not translated tends to prove that the gospel of Matthew was originally written in Greek, even though intended for an audience that also understood Aramaic. Lenski, who gives an exhaustive list of the various arguments, concludes, "But these few instances are scarcely sufficient to convince the thoughtful reader that Matthew's Gospel as we now have it is a translation and not an original production."[2]

Almost invariably, modern writers who claim that the Greek version of Matthew was a translation of an earlier Aramaic work do not accept the concept that Matthew is the inspired Word of God and usually question whether Matthew wrote it at all. For instance, *The Anchor Bible,* after long discussion which leaves the whole question in uncertainty, states, "The reader has already been warned that there are no firm conclusions to be drawn as to the authorship of our present gospel of Matthew."[3]

Conservative scholarship has agreed that whether or not there was an earlier Hebrew version, the present Greek version was Matthew's own work and that it is the inspired Word of God. Whatever earlier materials Matthew may have produced in his native tongue, the point is that the Greek gospel was inspired of God and bears the authority of being the Word of God.

The early Fathers are quite clear in their testimony that Matthew was the first gospel to be written and was followed in order by Mark, Luke, and John. This is the order which is observed in the Scriptures as now published. Some today, however, prefer the order of Matthew, Luke, Mark, and John. Modern liberal scholarship, however, is generally united that Mark's gospel was first and that Matthew had Mark before him when he wrote the gospel. W. C. Allen, representing the liberal point of view, states, "Almost the entire substance of the second Gospel has been transferred to the first."[4] William R. Farmer, however, although a liberal critic, holds to the priority of Matthew, a conclusion based on extensive research.[5]

Many conservative interpreters, like R. C. H. Lenski, generally hold with the early Fathers that Matthew was first,[6] but the question remains open even among conservatives.

A theory also advanced by many scholars that both Mark and Matthew had a common source of written material called Q (Ger. *Quelle,* source) also is rejected by many conservative expositors. After all the discussion and various views are considered, the monumental and original character of the gospel of Matthew stands out. Even Allen, who holds so strongly to the early writings of Mark, has a long list of materials in Matthew which are not found in Mark.[7]

Actually, while many similarities between the synoptic gospels exist, the proof that one is dependent on the other is not convincing, as there are so many variations. The gospel of Matthew has many evidences of being written independently, both in the order of the narrative and in the addition and subtraction of details. However, the inspiration of Matthew would not be affected if he had chosen to use some of Mark's material, if Mark was written earlier. Matthew probably wrote his gospel in Greek some time before the fall of Jerusalem in A.D. 70 and possibly as early as A.D. 44, during the persecution of Agrippa I.

More important than discussion on the sources of the gospel is its self-evident unique character which has caused this gospel to be placed first in the New Testament. Its position is assured because its subject matter serves as a bridge between the Old and New Testaments. Matthew's purpose obviously was to demonstrate that Jesus Christ was the promised Messiah of the Old Testament, that He fulfilled the requirements of being the promised King who would be a descendant of David, and that His life and ministry fully support the conclusion that He is the prophesied Messiah of Israel.

The gospel of Matthew, accordingly, presents Christ's royal genealogy and the early recognition that He was indeed the King of the Jews. These historical materials are followed by the Sermon on the Mount, stating the moral principles of the kingdom, given more extensively in Matthew than in the other gospels. The theme is continued by presenting the sayings and the miracles of Christ as His credentials prophesied in the Old Testament.

Having laid this broad base, Matthew then proceeds to account for the fact that Christ did not bring in His prophesied kingdom at His first coming. The growing rejection of Christ, His denunciation of the unbelief of the Jews, and His revelation of truth relating to the period between the two advents (Mt 13) serve to support this point.

Beginning in Matthew 14, the growing line of rejection leads to the Olivet discourse in Matthew 24 and 25, describing the course of the age between the two advents, with special reference to the great tribulation just preceding His second coming to the earth. Having set forth the rejection of Christ in the context of ultimate glorification, the gospel of Matthew then records the facts of His death, resurrection, and postresurrection ministry.

As a whole, the gospel is not properly designated as only an apologetic for the Christian faith. Rather, it was designed to explain to the Jews, who had expected the Messiah when He came to be a conquering king, why instead Christ suffered and died, and why there was the resulting postponement of His triumph to His second coming. The gospel of Matthew, with its many quotations from the Old Testament, is the proper platform on which the later books of the New Testament were erected. The magnitude of Matthew's contribution as he wrote, guided by the Spirit of God, fully justified the attitude of the early church, which regarded Matthew as the most important gospel and its contents as fundamental to the Christian faith.

In writing this commentary, my indebtedness to the extensive literature on the gospel of Matthew is self-evident, although some independence in interpretation serves to provide fresh insights. The Bibliography includes works consulted frequently. Inclusion of a work in the Bibliography does not indicate approval of its theological interpretation, which, in some instances, differs considerably from the conservative position.

The King James Version is used as a basis for exposition, corrected as necessary by reference to other versions and the original Greek.

In adding this commentary on the important first gospel to my previous works, I hope to make another contribution to the understanding of Scripture, which will be helpful to all students of the Bible.

PART ONE

THE ORIGIN OF
JESUS CHRIST

1

The Genealogy and Birth of Jesus Christ

Royal Genealogy, 1:1-17

THE FIRST GOSPEL opens by presenting the evidence that Jesus Christ is indeed the true Son of David, the Son of Abraham, the Son of God, and is the true Messiah of Israel and the Saviour of the world. Such a far-reaching claim must be supported by the best evidence. Accordingly, Matthew presents in an orderly way first the genealogies establishing legal claim of Jesus Christ to be the King of Israel. Then it accounts for the supernatural conception and deity of Jesus Christ by explicitly detailing the virgin birth. In the process, the genuineness of His claim to be the King of Israel is demonstrated, and the damaging suspicion that Christ was illegitimate, a slander propagated by unbelievers, is completely answered. This material, as well as the rest of Matthew 1-2, is found only in this gospel.[1]

The opening words, "The book of the generation of Jesus Christ, the Son of David, the Son of Abraham," are intended to provide an introduction to the genealogy, not to the book as a whole. This introduction clearly demonstrates that Matthew's purpose in writing the gospel is to provide adequate proof for the investigator that the claims of Christ to be King and Saviour are justified. For this reason, the gospel of Matthew was considered by the early church one of the most important books of the New Testament and was given more prominence than the other three gospels.

As presented by Matthew, the genealogy begins with Abraham and concludes with Joseph, described as the husband of Mary but explicitly excluded from being the actual father of Jesus Christ. In the phrase "of whom was born

17

Jesus," *whom* is a feminine pronoun, referring to Mary. By contrast, the genealogy of Luke 3:23-38 is usually interpreted as giving the genealogy of Mary.

The genealogy is divided into three divisions of fourteen generations each. In making this division, some names are omitted, such as the three kings, Ahaziah, Joash, and Amaziah, who are included in the line in 1 Chronicles 3:11-12. Also of interest is the fact that the names recorded in Matthew 1:13-15 are not found in the Old Testament but may have been recorded in the registers of families available at the time of Christ. The deliberate editing of the genealogy to provide three divisions of fourteen generations each was by design, probably for literary symmetry, although some have pointed out that the numerical value of the Hebrew consonants in the word *David* add up to fourteen. A further problem appears because the last section has actually only thirteen names. Complicated explanations are not wanting.[2] Suggested answers include a textual omission of Jehoiakim or the possibility that Jesus is considered the fourteenth.

The threefold division is explained by Matthew himself in 1:17. The first division is the generations from Abraham to David, including Abraham as the first in the line of promise and culminating in David as the king. The second group of fourteen are kings who trace the line from David to Jeconiah, and the third division, the continuity of the line through the captivity to Jesus Christ.

An unusual feature of the genealogies is the prominence of four women who normally would not be included. Each of these had an unusual background. Tamar (1:3) got in the line by playing a harlot (Gen 38:11-30). Rahab, a harlot rescued from Jericho because she delivered and sheltered the spies (Jos 2:6; 6:25), is declared by Matthew to have been the wife of Salmon, the father of Boaz. There is no Old Testament support for Matthew's statement.

Another Gentile was included in the Messianic line in the person of Ruth, the subject of the beautiful book in the Old Testament. She, alone of the three women, although a Gentile, had an unspotted record. The fourth was Bathsheba, the mother of Solomon, who had formerly been the wife of

Uriah, whose relationship to David began with adultery and resulted in the murder of her husband (2 Sa 11:1—12:25).

No explanation is given for the emphasis of these facts in the genealogy which many Jews would love to have forgotten. Possible reasons include the preparation for the prominence of Mary as the culmination of the line and also to put Jewish pride in its place for having falsely accused Mary. Taken as a whole, genealogies support the conclusion that Christ is a genuine son of David and Abraham through Mary, a King with a right to rule, with His legal title through Joseph, and His deity supported by His supernatural conception without a human father.

Supernatural Conception and Birth of Jesus, 1:18-25

To put to rest any question or false accusations against the virtue of Mary or the nature of the origin of Christ, Matthew explicitly describes the relationship between Joseph and Mary. Joseph was legally betrothed to Mary and is described as her "husband" in Matthew 1:16. Betrothal was legally equivalent to marriage, and the relationship could only be broken by divorce or death. The relationship preceded actually living together as man and wife.

In this waiting period, according to 1:18, Mary was found pregnant. She had not revealed her experience with the angel, recorded in Luke 1:26-38. Obviously, Joseph knew nothing about it, and possibly Matthew himself, when writing this account, did not have this information, as the gospel of Luke was probably written later than the gospel of Matthew. Joseph considered the consummation of the marriage impossible and contemplated a quiet divorce rather than a public disclosure and scandal.

At the beginning of the narrative, Matthew at once declares that the child is "of the Holy Ghost" (1:18) and then describes how this fact was revealed to Joseph. An angel sent by God appeared to him in a dream, addressing him as "Joseph, thou son of David." He is instructed not to be afraid of taking Mary as his wife, as the child had been conceived by the Holy Spirit. Further, Joseph is informed that when

Mary's Son is born, He should be called Jesus, meaning Saviour, "for he shall save his people from their sins."

Matthew goes on to support the doctrine of the virgin birth by quoting Isaiah 7:14, which prophesied that a virgin, literally, "the virgin," should bear a son whose name would be Immanuel, meaning "God with us." Matthew clearly claimed not only that Christ was born of a virgin but that this was anticipated by the prophecy of Isaiah as being the method by which God would become man.

In obedience to the angelic vision, Joseph took Mary as his wife but "knew her not" until after Jesus was born. Normal interpretation of this expression would indicate that Joseph and Mary did not have physical union until after Jesus was born, but that thereafter, they had a normal married life with children born to them. The alternate explanation, that the brothers of Christ were children of Joseph by an earlier marriage, while possible, is less probable. The perpetual virginity of Mary was not necessary to the divine purpose, although a useful device in exalting Mary beyond what the Scriptures justify.

Although liberal critics have spared no efforts to assail the account given in this first chapter of Matthew, unquestionably, the record as given was accepted literally by the early church and is supported by the rest of the New Testament, including the account of Luke. Every reason ever advanced for denying the historicity of Matthew has carried with it the premise of rationalistic rejection of the supernatural and determined prejudice against the claims of Jesus Christ to be the God-man. Faith in the accuracy of such a record induced early believers to die as martyrs rather than renounce their faith in the virgin-born Son of Mary.

2

The Divine Protection of the Child Jesus

WORSHIP OF THE MAGI, 2:1-11

FROM THE MANY INCIDENTS relating to the birth and childhood of Jesus, Matthew mentions only three highly significant events (cf. Lk 1:26—2:52). The first is the visit of the Magi. Many misconceptions have arisen concerning the visit. These Magi were students of astrology who searched the heavens for significant movement in the stars. They were not magicians in the evil sense, as liberals have charged; neither were they kings, even though they brought kingly gifts to the child King, Jesus. Their number is not told, but it probably was more than three. The time of their arrival was not the night of the birth of Jesus but some weeks later.

In Matthew's account, they appeared in Jerusalem, where they inquired concerning the birth of the King of the Jews. At this time, there was widespread expectation of the coming of a great ruler, a truth which was inherent in Jewish prophecy and spread by Jews as well as others over the Roman world. The Magi probably came from Babylon, which, for centuries, was a center of the study of astrology, as both Lenski and Allen observe.[1] Allen, after citing a dozen or more instances in ancient literature referring to Messianic expectation, comments, "The whole world was expecting the Savior King."[2]

The wise men, or the Magi (Gr. *magio,* from a Persian word for those who were expert in the stars), told inquirers that their interest was aroused by seeing an unusual star in the East, which signified to them that the King had come. These tidings, when reported to King Herod, troubled him, for Herod knew all too well the Jewish aspiration of throw-

21

ing off the Roman yoke and his own rule over them. Herod was an Edomite, a people hated by the Jews, and there was always the possibility that Jewish hope, aroused by the arrival of a supposed Messiah, could inflame them to rise up against him. The tidings of the Magi are reported by Matthew as troubling Herod and all Jerusalem with him.

Herod, having called an official meeting of the Sanhedrin —including all its three classes of members, the high priest, scribes, the elders—demanded of them a formal statement where the Messiah was to be born. This was common information, as it was stated in Micah 5:2, and Herod may have known the answer, but he wanted it officially from the Jewish leaders. They replied by paraphrasing Micah 5:2, with some additional facts from other Scriptures, or at least translated the Hebrew freely.[3] They named Bethlehem in Judea, which, although a small town, would distinguish itself as the birthplace of the one who would rule over Israel. Matthew adroitly answers Jewish unbelief concerning Jesus Christ by quoting their own official body to the effect that the prophecy of His birth in Bethlehem was literal, that the Messiah was to be an individual, not the entire Jewish nation, and that their Messiah was to be a King who would rule over them.

In the cunning mind of Herod, a plot had already formed to nip this growing bud of Messianic hope before it got out of hand. Having dismissed the Sanhedrin, he called the wise men to him privately and, with skill, inquired when the star appeared. He did so to pinpoint the age of the child. He further urged them to find the child and then bring him word that he also could worship Him. It is an amazing thing that Herod did not send his servants with them, and that the Jews themselves, stirred up as they were by the report, apparently did not lift a finger to search out the young child. As Richard Glover expresses it, "It is strange how much the scribes knew, and what little use they made of it."[4] Such is the appalling gulf between religious belief and practice.

The wise men, however, immediately set out for Bethlehem. To their amazement and delight, the star in the East reappeared and guided them so unmistakably that it even designated the house where the child was. The most probable explanation is that the star in the East as well as the star that guided them to Bethlehem were supernatural rather than natural phenomena. No star in the distant heavens could provide such accurate guidance.

With joy unbounded, they went to Bethlehem and found the young child with Mary, His mother. To Him, they made obeisance and worshiped in Oriental style, and presented their gifts of gold, frankincense, and myrrh. Unquestionably the gifts were chosen appropriately: gold for His deity and majesty, frankincense for the fragrance of His life and His intercession, myrrh for His sacrifice and death.

FLIGHT INTO EGYPT, 2:12-15

That fateful night, God spoke both to the wise men and to Joseph. The wise men were instructed not to return to Herod, and they lost no time returning to their country by another route. In the night also, Joseph was warned by an angel of the Lord to take Mary and Jesus and flee to Egypt to avoid the murderous intent of Herod. Quietly, both the Magi and Joseph and his family stole away in the night. More details are not given. Artists picture Mary riding on an ass, holding the baby, and being led by Joseph. No Scripture is found as to where they stayed in Egypt. Matthew, however, anticipating the charge that Christ picked up magical arts by a long stay in Egypt, specifies that they were there only until the death of Herod, which occurred within three years of His birth.

Why was Joseph directed to Egypt? Why not to Babylon with the Magi, or some other direction? Matthew (2:15) cites Hosea 11:1, "Out of Egypt have I called my Son," referring to the exodus of Israel from Egypt to the promised land. Matthew draws the contrast between Israel, as the Son of Jehovah going to Egypt and returning, to Christ, the greater Son who also came from Egypt. In both cases, the descent into Egypt was to escape danger. In both cases, the return was important to the providential history of the nation Israel.

CHILDREN IN BETHLEHEM KILLED, 2:15-18

The reason for the departure to Egypt becomes all the more evident in Matthew's subsequent account. Herod, discovering he had been tricked by the Magi, ordered all the male children in Bethlehem, approximately two years old and under, to be killed. The number of children thus slain has been estimated to be from six to as many as thirty.[5] It, accordingly, was an outrage too small to be mentioned by historians, such as Josephus, who records many other murderous crimes of Herod.

The ruthless act, performed no doubt by soldiers who accomplished their horrible deed in the presence of the mothers, fulfilled the prophecy of Jeremiah 31:15-16. This prophecy referred to the captivity in Babylon and the slaying of children in the conquest of Judea by Babylon. The parallel in Bethlehem is all too evident. Rachel represents mothers in Israel who mourn their children. In both cases, sorrow came in a time when Israel religiously was in apostasy and under the heel of the oppressor. A later Roman ruler was to order this same Jesus nailed to a cross, the ultimate rejection of Israel's Messiah.

Death was also to overtake Herod shortly thereafter. Josephus, in his *Antiquities,* records Herod's horrible end, his body rotting away and consumed by worms.[6] His grandson, Herod Agrippa, was to die a similar death (Ac 12:23).

THE RETURN TO NAZARETH, 2:19-23

The death of Herod made possible the return of Joseph from Egypt to Palestine (cf. Lk 2:39-40). Instructed in a dream by the angel of the Lord that he could return home because Herod was dead, Joseph began the long journey. Approaching Judea, however, he heard that Archelaus, the son of Herod, was on the throne. One of the first acts of Archelaus was to murder some three thousand people in the temple because some of their number had memorialized some martyrs put to death by Herod. Like father, like son. Instead of going back to Bethlehem, which Joseph probably considered a suitable residence for his royal Son, Joseph went instead to Nazareth in Galilee. Matthew declares this also was a fulfillment of prophecy: "He shall be called a Nazarene" (2:23). Endless explanations have been made of this, as no express passage in the Old Testament declared that Christ should be a Nazarene. The most plausible explanation is that it may be an oblique reference to Isaiah 11:1 where Christ is declared to be a rod (Heb. *netzer*) out of the stem of Jesse. Just as a rod has an insignificant beginning, so Nazareth was an insignificant city from which the Messiah would come. There is always the possibility that Matthew referred to an oral prophecy not recorded in Scripture.

The incidents of the worship of the Magi and the flight to and return from Egypt serve to emphasize Matthew's purpose not to give a complete life of Christ, but to record those incidents which significantly support the conclusion that Jesus Christ is the Messiah, the Son of David, the Son of God. Having skillfully painted this picture, Matthew picks up the narrative thirty years later with John the Baptist.

PART TWO

THE EARLY MINISTRY OF JESUS

3

The Introduction and
Baptism of Jesus

FOR FOUR HUNDRED YEARS since the close of the Old Testament, no prophetic voice had been raised in Israel. To be sure, God had spoken by angels to Zacharias and Elizabeth, to Joseph and Mary, and to the Magi, but no human voice had spoken for God, except that of the child Jesus in the temple (Lk 2:41-50). Suddenly, seemingly out of nowhere, came John the Baptist preaching in the wilderness of Judea (cf. Mk 1:1-8; Lk 3:1-20). Clothed in a long garment made of rough camel hair, bound with a leather belt, and eating locusts and wild honey, John's garb was appropriate to his office and was similar to that of Elijah (2 Ki 1:8) and which, apparently, was the customary dress for prophets, even those who were false prophets (Zec 13:4). As Tasker points out, Matthew assumes that his readers are familiar with John the Baptist and does not give his background as Luke does (Lk 1:5-25, 57-80).[1]

The message of John was like that of Elijah, as he heralded his exhortation to Pharisees as well as Sadducees and to all who came: "Repent; for the kingdom of heaven is at hand." His role was that of a herald coming before the king. Matthew finds John fulfilling the prediction of Isaiah 40:3-5, that there would be a voice crying in the wilderness to prepare the way before the Lord. Like the servants of a king who would smooth out and straighten the road in preparation for their sovereign's coming, so John was preparing the way spiritually for the coming of Christ.

John's message was a stern rebuke of the hypocrisy and shallow religion of both the Pharisees and the Sadducees.

Unquestionably, he was attacking the established religion of his day and demanding sincerity and repentance instead of hypocrisy and religious rites. His call to repentance is backed up by the succinct announcement, "The kingdom of heaven is at hand."

What did John mean by "kingdom of heaven"? While the precise phrase is not found in the Old Testament, it is based on Old Testament terminology. Nebuchadnezzar, for instance, referred to God as the "King of heaven" (Dan 4:37). Daniel had predicted that the climax of world history would come with the advent of the Son of man, who would be given an everlasting kingdom. This was likewise to be fulfilled by the prediction of Daniel 2:44 that "the God of heaven" would "set up a kingdom, which shall never be destroyed." Matthew, alone of New Testament writers, uses "the kingdom of heaven" and rarely uses "the kingdom of God," which is often used in parallel passages in the other gospels and throughout the New Testament. Most expositors consider the two terms identical.

Although the kingdom of heaven and the kingdom of God are similar, there seems to be some distinction. The kingdom of heaven refers to that which is obviously in its outer character a kingdom from above and seems to include all who profess to be subjects of the King. The kingdom of God is more specific and does not seem to include any but true believers who are born again. In Matthew 13, the kingdom of heaven seems to include both the good and bad fish caught in the net and the wheat and the tares in the same field, whereas Nicodemus is informed that the new birth is necessary to enter the kingdom of God (Jn 3:5). All agree that those in the kingdom of God are also in the kingdom of heaven, however.

Eschatologically and dispensationally, a threefold distinction must be observed in the use of the term "kingdom of heaven." First, in John the Baptist's ministry, it is announced as at hand, meaning that in the person of the King, Jesus Christ, the kingdom was being presented to Israel and to the world. Second, in Matthew 13, the kingdom in its present mystery form is revealed, that is, the rule of God over the earth in the hearts of believers during the present age when the King is absent. These are mysteries because they were not anticipated in the Old Testament doctrine of the kingdom. The third and climactic form of the kingdom will be when Christ returns to set up the kingdom of heaven on earth, in fulfillment of Daniel's prophecies and countless other passages of the Old Testament that picture a golden age, when the Son of David will reign over the entire world in righteousness and peace. Only the premillennial interpretation of the concept of the kingdom allows a literal interpretation of both Old Testament and New Testament prophecies relating to the future kingdom.

The ministry of John the Baptist signaled a spiritual crisis in Israel. Would they accept their King, or would they reject Him? The ministry of John the Baptist was to prepare the way by calling Israel to repentance.

The phenomenal success of John's ministry is evident in the thousands that came out to see him. Estimating that between 200,000 and 500,000 must have responded to his call for repentance and baptism,[2] Lenski, in keeping with his Lutheran concept of baptism, argues that the very numbers of those who repented make impossible baptism by immersion of all of them.[3] He interprets baptism as referring to Jewish rites of washing rather than immersion. The number of those baptized, however, is not given in Scripture, nor is it confirmed by other evidence. And this issue of immersion versus affusion depends on the definition of baptism itself, that is, whether it is used in its primary sense of immersion or submersion, or in its secondary sense of placing in or initiation.

The more important question than the mode of baptism, however, is the meaning of the baptism of John. It is clearly not Christian baptism, as it does not signify initiation into the body of Christ; neither is it symbolic of a work of the Holy Spirit, as John himself refers to it as a work of Christ. It is rather a religious rite, signifying their confession of sins and commitment to a new holy life, such as was proper for Jews in the old dispensation.

The ministry of John the Baptist was very pointed. He

challenged the prevailing Jewish concept that they were
saved simply because they were descendants of Abraham.
He declared that God is able to raise up children unto
Abraham from the stones of the earth, certainly a dramatic
picture of supernatural, spiritual resurrection. He declared
that the ax is already in hand to cut down every tree that
does not bring forth fruit. By this he meant individual Jews
as well as Judaism as a dead ritual.

The climax of John's thundering message was that he
was only the forerunner. After him was to come a greater
Prophet whose shoes he was unworthy to remove. This
coming one would baptize with the Holy Spirit and with
fire and would bring judgment on the nation like one who,
in threshing, separates the wheat from the chaff. In thus
describing Jesus Christ, John was speaking prophetically.
Although he knew Jesus, as his mother, Elizabeth, was a
cousin of Mary, at this time he had not identified Jesus
as the Messiah, although he may have had some knowledge
of His call as a Prophet.

In this third chapter of Matthew, three baptisms are
mentioned: (1) that of John the Baptist, a baptism of repentance; (2) a baptism of the Holy Spirit, which would
be brought and administered by Christ; (3) a baptism with
fire. These should not be confused. The baptism of repentance, administered by John, was in preparation for the
coming of Christ and was succeeded by the baptisms administered by the apostles. The baptism of the Holy Spirit
was not initiated until Acts 2 and the day of Pentecost
and symbolized entrance into the body of Christ (1 Co
12:13). The baptism with fire seems related to the second
coming of Christ, for only then will the wheat and the
tares be separated and the tares, like the chaff mentioned
by John the Baptist, burned with fire (cf. Mt 13:30, 38-42,
49-50).

All of the baptisms signify initiation into a new situation of separation to God for the righteous or separation
unto judgment for the wicked. The apt figure of the threshing floor, where the wheat and the chaff are tossed into
the air with a wooden shovel to allow the wind to separate

the two (the wheat falling to earth while the chaff blows away), is symbolic of the coming separation between that which is true and that which is false in religion.

BAPTISM OF JESUS, 3:13-17

All four gospels give the account of the baptism of Jesus (cf. Mk 1:9-11; Lk 3:21-22; Jn 1:31-34). When Jesus came to Galilee to be baptized by John, He was immediately identified, according to John 1:29, as "the Lamb of God, [who] taketh away the sin of the world." John alone records the announcement before His baptism that Jesus was the one of whom John had been preaching: "This is he of whom I said, After me cometh a man which is preferred before me: for he was before me" (Jn 1:30). Matthew alone records John's protest that Jesus did not need to be baptized, and John consents only when Christ says, "Thus it becometh us to fulfil all righteousness" (3:15). When Jesus was baptized, Matthew, along with all the other gospels, records how the Spirit of God descended like a dove upon Christ and how the Father's voice from heaven identified Jesus, "This is my beloved Son, in whom I am well pleased."

The tendency to identify the baptism of Jesus as one of repentance or as one similar to Christian baptism can be justified only on superficial connection. The baptism of Jesus Christ was unique, an initiatory right, setting Him apart to His role as Prophet, Priest, and King, and anticipating His death on the cross. No other, before or after, can share this baptism.

This chapter of Matthew is noteworthy, first, because Matthew passes over all the incidents of Christ's childhood, including His appearance in the temple at age twelve (Lk 2:41-50). His presentation is thematic, not biographical. He is introducing Jesus as the Messiah King of Israel, fulfilling the anticipatory prophecy of the Old Testament and confirmed by the voice of the Father from heaven as God's beloved Son. Those who accept this testimony must respond by worship and obedience.

4

The Temptation of Jesus and the Call of His First Disciples

TEMPTATION OF JESUS, 4:1-11

THE TEMPTATION OF JESUS, recorded also in Mark 1:12-13 and Luke 4:1-13, occurred immediately after the testimony to His deity from John the Baptist and God the Father. The Spirit of God, seen descending like a dove upon Him at His baptism, led Him into the wilderness to be tempted of Satan. Mark speaks of the devil "driving" Him into the wilderness. The thought is that Christ is impelled in the will of God into this period of testing which God Himself has recognized as necessary. It was not against the will of Christ but also not of His human choosing. The English word *tempted* is stronger than the Greek word, *peirazo*, meaning to "try" or "test," and does not imply any inward cooperation with Satan's proposals. Unlike sinful man, Christ has no temptation from within.

The time of trial consisted of forty days of fasting, during which there undoubtedly was constant provocation by Satan. Although Lenski insists that Christ's fast involved no weakening of His power to resist,[1] the physical weakness induced by fasting coupled with the wearing persistence of Satan is better understood as setting up circumstances conducive to Satan's temptations. As Tasker points out, the tempter is described simply as "the devil" (Gr. *diabolos*), his name meaning, "the slanderer" or the "adversary."[2] The devil is mentioned in Scripture from the Garden of Eden to his being cast into the lake of fire in Revelation 20. The corrupter of Adam and Eve and the opposer of every good work and person, Satan was here attempting to corrupt the Son of God. Satan, by nature and program, is com-

34

mitted to usurp God's place, to oppose God's will, and to corrupt all that is holy and good. He could do no other than to attempt here what is absolutely impossible, that is, to induce Christ to sin, even though he knew before he began that such was impossible.

In this temptation of Christ, Satan followed the well-established pattern of temptation revealed in the Garden of Eden and illustrated throughout Scripture. It is defined in 1 John 2:16 as being temptation along three lines: (1) the lust of the flesh; (2) the lust of the eyes; (3) the pride of life. The order of the temptation in 1 John 2:16 is the same as the serpent's temptation of Eve in Genesis 3:6, where the fruit was (1) good for food, the lust of the flesh; (2) pleasant to the eyes, the lust of the eyes; (3) to be desired to make one wise, the pride of life. Luke 4:1-13 presents it in the same order as in Genesis and 1 John. Matthew chooses to present it in what was probably the actual historical order, with the offer of the kingdoms of the world last.

The first temptation was to turn stones into bread. Under other circumstances, this might not have been sinful, but to do it at Satan's suggestion and to make satisfaction of His hunger primary was contrary to the will of God. Christ replied by quoting Deuteronomy 8:3, declaring the priority of the Word of God. Lenski is unrealistic in declaring that the hunger of Christ had nothing to do with the temptation.[3] The experience of Moses on Sinai (Ex 34:28, Deu 9:9, 18) and that of Elijah going forty days without food (1 Ki 19:8) are perhaps not entirely parallel but illustrate the character of the temptation of Christ.

The second temptation, in order, states that the devil took Jesus into Jerusalem to a pinnacle of the temple, that is, a wing of the temple towering above the rocks and the valley below. This may have been on the south wall or possibly the east wall of the temple building.

Satan's proposal was that Jesus, as the Son of God, should cast Himself down and, by His miraculous preservation, demonstrate His deity. It was the subtle temptation to do miraculous works and thus gain recognition. In support of this, Satan quoted Psalms 91:11-12, significantly omitting the promise that God would keep Him "in all thy ways." Lenski holds that the main point was not the omitted Scripture but its misapplication.[4] In either case, the Scripture is deceitfully used.

In this temptation, as in the first, the temptation is introduced, "If thou be the Son of God," literally, "If thou be Son of God." While the omission of the article must not be pressed, and some, like Tasker, consider this a first-class condition which could be translated, "Since thou art a Son of God," there was obviously a subtle challenge to prove His deity.[5] In reply, however, Jesus did not argue but cited Deuteronomy 6:16, forbidding testing God in this way.

In the final temptation, the devil took Him to a high mountain. Lenski argues here, as in the second temptation, that Jesus was actually transported first to the temple and then to the high mountain.[6] Tasker regards it more as a mere vision or mental transfer.[7] Matthew's account states that the devil took Him to both places, and probably a literal understanding of the passage is better.

In the third temptation, Jesus was shown supernaturally "all the kingdoms of the world, and the glory of them" (4:8). Here was the temptation to become King of kings without a cross and without a struggle. That Satan could offer them temporarily seems to be supported by his role as the god of this world, but Satan had no right to offer them as a kingdom forever. To accept would have made Jesus his slave, not his victor. Again, Jesus quoted Scripture, this time Deuteronomy 6:13 and Deuteronomy 10:20. Significantly, all three scriptural quotations come from Deuteronomy, the object of great attack by the higher critics. This time, Jesus not only quoted Scripture but commanded Satan to go. This supports the conclusion that in the historical order of events this was the last of three temptations.

Satan had failed in every avenue of temptation open to man, the lust of the flesh, the lust of the eyes, and the pride of life. Jesus, because of His humanity, could be tested, but the perfect God-man could not be made to sin.

Ordinary men, subject to similar temptations, can anticipate Satan's strategy of attack, the temptation to indulge the flesh, the temptation to doubt God, and the temptation to attain divine goals by worldly means, which encourages human pride. Believers are always promised a way of escape (1 Co 10:13).

Although Satan later continued, in subtle ways, to tempt Christ to turn to the left or right from the path that led to the cross, after being vanquished in this encounter, Satan never recovered from his defeat. Once Satan had left, it was fitting that the angels would come and minister to Jesus, undoubtedly providing food to restore His physical strength and prepare Him for the task ahead.

JESUS MOVES FROM NAZARETH TO CAPERNAUM, 4:12-16

While Jesus was engaged in the activities described in Matthew 3-4, John the Baptist continued his ministry. In his fearless preaching, John had attacked Herod the Tetrarch for his adulterous relationship to his brother Philip's wife, with the result that Herod had imprisoned him, probably in the fortress of Machaerus on the east side of the Dead Sea (cf. Lk 3:19-20). The report that John had been imprisoned indicated an unfriendly atmosphere in Jerusalem for a prophet, and was probably the occasion for Christ's departing into Galilee. Instead of returning to Nazareth, His childhood home, He established residence in Capernaum at the north end of the Sea of Galilee, referred to as "the sea coast, in the borders of Zabulon and Nephthalim" (Mt 4:13).

Ruins of Capernaum are visible today, a testimony to the scathing judgment of Christ on this city for not recognizing its day of opportunity. In Matthew 11:23-24, Jesus pronounced a solemn judgment on Capernaum, declaring that it would "be brought down to hell." His sojourn there was anticipated by Isaiah 9:1-2, and quoted by Matthew to still the criticism of Jews that Jesus was a Galilean (4:16). The quotation attests both that Isaiah was a prophet and that God spoke through him. As in other instances, the

quotation is not word for word, but gives the substance
of the prophecy. Characterizing the people as those who
sit in darkness correctly anticipated the mixed character of
this population, partly Gentile, partly Jewish, but living
in spiritual darkness.

The message of Jesus to Capernaum was similar to that
of John the Baptist, "Repent; for the kingdom of heaven
is at hand." This was the theme of His ministry until it
became evident that He would be rejected. The kingdom
being at hand meant that it was being offered in the person
of the prophesied King, but it did not mean that it would
be immediately fulfilled.

CALL OF FIRST DISCIPLES, 4:17-22

Because of Capernaum's proximity to the Sea of Galilee,
it was natural for Jesus at this time to call His disciples
who were fishermen (cf. Mk 1:16-20; Lk 5:1-11; Jn 1:35-
42). To Peter and Andrew, fishing in the sea, He extended
the invitation, "Follow me, and I will make you fishers of
men" (Mt 4:19). In like manner, He called James and
John, the sons of Zebedee, who were mending their nets.
They too left their occupation and their father and followed
Christ. Matthew here records the early call of these disciples.
Lenski, because of the disparity between this account and
that of Luke 5:1-11, holds that between this first call of
Matthew and the call in Luke, the early disciples continued
to fish for a time and not until the call in Luke 5 did they
forsake all.[8] While Matthew's gospel indicates that they
followed Jesus, there is no clear statement that they left
their fishing occupation for good.

EARLY PREACHING MINISTRY OF JESUS IN GALILEE, 4:23-25

In the days which followed, ceaseless activity characterized
the ministry of Jesus (cf. Mk 3:7-12; Lk 6:17-19). Going
from one synagogue to the next, He preached the gospel
of the kingdom, performed countless acts of healing, and
was followed by great multitudes, who came not only from

Galilee but from Jerusalem in the south and from the territory of Decapolis and Perea on the east of Jordan. His
miracles dealt not simply with trivial diseases but with in-
curable afflictions, such as epilepsy, palsy, and demon possession. No affliction was beyond His healing touch. The kingdom blessings promised by Isaiah 35:5-6, due for fulfillment
in the future kingdom, here became the credentials of the
King in His first coming.

PART THREE

THE PRINCIPLES OF
THE KINGDOM:
THE SERMON ON
THE MOUNT

5

The Moral Principles of the Kingdom

THE PURPOSE OF MATTHEW to present the truth relating Jesus as the King and the message of the kingdom is the guiding principle in placing the Sermon on the Mount here so early in Matthew's gospel. Many events recorded later in the gospel actually occurred before the Sermon on the Mount. The Sermon on the Mount is given priority because it is a comprehensive statement of the moral principles relating to the kingdom which Jesus proclaimed. As Kelly comments, it was designed "to counteract the earthly views of the people of Israel."[1]

Some, like Tasker, consider this sermon a collection of various sayings of Jesus delivered on different occasions.[2] This opinion, although common, is mere conjecture. Preferable is the view that Jesus delivered this sermon as Matthew indicated, although probably He repeated many times the truths in the Sermon on the Mount, or delivered the same sermon more than once to different groups (cf. Lk 6:20-49). Here, however, He spoke directly to His disciples, probably the inner circle. But during the discourse, apparently many others joined the crowd, as there is reference to "the people" in Matthew 7:28, which would imply a large crowd.

In placing this discourse early in Matthew, the intent is plainly to set forth the main principles of Christ's teaching, which are subsequently rejected in Matthew 8-12. This rejection in turn led to the second major discourse in Matthew 13 on the mysteries of the kingdom, or the age intervening between the first and second advents of Christ. Matthew's third major discourse, in Matthew 24-25, dealt with the end time preceding the second coming. These three major discourses should be contrasted to the fourth discourse found in John's gospel, 13-17, dealing specifically with the spiritual character of the present age in which God would call out His church. Matthew's gospel is, therefore, comprehensive in presenting the three major discourses relating to kingdom truth, and is, as Kelly expresses it, given in "dispensational" order.[3]

Few passages in the gospel have occasioned more disagreement as to their essential character than the Sermon on the Mount. Some, who regard the Christian message mainly as an ethic, hail it as the summary of the whole gospel. Even Lenski considers the Sermon on the Mount as presenting the gospel in its fundamental content.[4] Kelly states the matter correctly: "The sermon on the mount treats not of salvation, but of the character and conduct of those that belong to Christ—the true yet rejected king.[5]

That the Sermon on the Mount presents ethical content all agree. That it delineates the gospel that Jesus Christ died and rose again, that it presents justification by faith, or is suitable to point an unbeliever to salvation in Christ is plainly not the intent of this message.

Others have gone to the other extreme of considering the Sermon on the Mount hypothetical; that is, Jesus is saying, "If you want me as King, these are rules under which I will operate." This would make the entire sermon eschatological, that is, applying to the future millennial kingdom but having no bearing upon the present church age. While it is clear that the epistles are more precise in delineating the particular responsibility and privilege of Christians in the present age, it would hardly be fitting for Matthew, writing this gospel many years after the death of Christ, to introduce material which would be irrelevant to his contemporaries.

The Sermon on the Mount, as a whole, is not church truth precisely. A. W. Pink holds, "Its larger part was a most searching exposition of the spirituality of the Law and the refutation of the false teaching of the elders."[6] It falls short of presenting the complete rule of life expounded at a greater length in the epistles, and it is not intended to delineate justification by faith or the gospel of salvation. On the other hand, the Sermon on the Mount is clearly intended to be a definitive statement of Christ's teaching and should not be pushed aside lightly by unnecessary stricture which would relegate it to unimportant truth. If these various limiting approaches are inadequate, what is the true approach?[7]

As in every text of Scripture, the truth presented must be first of all seen in its context. In the gospels, Jesus was presenting Himself as the prophesied King, and the kingdom He was offering is the prophesied kingdom. Those who are premillenarian can understand this as referring to the earthly kingdom predicted in the Old Testament. Although Jesus, in His teaching, did not spell out all that was revealed in the Old Testament, He clearly presented Himself as the prophesied King, the Son of David, who had the right to reign on earth. It is quite evident that the Jews, while they wanted deliverance from the Romans and fulfillment of the material blessings promised in the millennium, were quite unprepared to accept the view that the millennial kingdom has spiritual implications. It was to be a rule of righteousness as well as a rule of peace. It demanded much of subjects as well as providing much for them. The political character of the kingdom was not seriously questioned by the Jews, who anticipated that their Messiah would bring deliverance to them. Because of their neglect of the spiritual and moral principles involved, Christ necessarily emphasized these in the Sermon on the Mount. The Sermon accordingly must be understood in this eschatological context.

A careful reading of what Christ said makes it obvious, however, that the principles of the kingdom are far more than merely rules for a future millennium. Proceeding as they do from the nature of God and nature of morality and spiritual truth, many of the statements of Christ in the Sermon on the Mount are general in character, and the appeal is that inasmuch as these general truths must be accepted, their particular application to the kingdom may be taken for granted. In the progress of this narrative, Jesus not only proclaimed lofty general principles, but also made particular applications to current situations. This address can hardly be viewed as only prophetic, and it is clear that Jesus expected immediate response from His hearers, not simply acquiescence that He was telling the truth. Accordingly, the study of the Sermon on the Mount yields its treasures to those who analyze each text, determining its general meaning, its present application, and its relation to the future kingdom program. Problems of interpretation in most instances vanish easily when viewed from this prospective.

Chapter 5, after describing the setting as a place in the mountains, presents first the Beatitudes (vv. 3-12), then the spiritual influence of true disciples (vv. 13-16). Beginning with Matthew 5:17, the laws and the principles of the kingdom are unfolded and are related to the Mosaic law, to contemporary problems, and to the future judgment of God as well. The ethical teachings of chapter 5 are summed up in the last verse, "Be ye therefore perfect, even as your Father which is in heaven is perfect."

BEATITUDES, 5:2-12

The introductory verses, picturing Jesus seated, imply, as Tasker points out, Christ's role as a Lawgiver or Rabbi.[8] The Beatitudes pronounce those blessed, or happy, who fulfill these six standards of the kingdom in character and experience: those poor in spirit, or consciously dependent on God; those who mourn; those who are meek, or humble; those who thirst after righteousness; those who are merciful; pure in spirit; and who are peacemakers, although persecuted for righteousness' sake, are proper disciples and subjects of the kingdom. Through verse 10, these are addressed as "they," in contrast to "ye" in verses 11-12. Here is illustrated present application of general truth. The disciples were to experience persecution and false accusation. They are exhorted to rejoice in that day because they share persecution similar to that of prophets of old and because they will have great reward in heaven. It is of interest that these words addressed to those living in that generation promised them reward in heaven rather than in the future millennial kingdom. This is realistic, of course, because they would ultimately move into the church with its heavenly destiny and reward.

INFLUENCE OF TRUE DISCIPLES, 5:13-16

In verses 13-16, disciples are compared to salt and a lamp. Salt, which has lost its salty character, is utterly useless. While salt can preserve and flavor almost any food, it is useless to add good salt to bad, and salt without flavor should be thrown away. So disciples, without true moral character and spiritual commitment to the King, are useless in the kingdom of heaven. It also implies the rottenness of the world, which needs the preservative of the salt, as D. Martyn Lloyd-Jones points out.[9]

Likewise, disciples should be like a light or lamp, which, if it is going to fulfill its function, must be on a lampstand and not hidden under a bushel. The disciples were to be like a city set on a hill, and to let their light shine. The result would be that they would not attract men to themselves but would glorify the Father in heaven.

The implication of this passage is that only those who have experienced conversion and transformation by the grace of God can be true citizens of the kingdom of heaven. The same thought was expressed to Nicodemus in John 3, when Jesus said, "Except a man be born of water and of the Spirit, he cannot enter into the kingdom of God" (Jn 3:5). What John describes as casual, new birth or new life, Matthew considers as result, new morality, new character, new witness. Both demand genuineness to be a true subject of the kingdom of heaven.

LAWS AND PRINCIPLES OF THE KINGDOM, 5:17-48

In Matthew 5:17-48, the details of the moral principles of the kingdom are outlined, and the following subjects are mentioned: the relation of the law of the kingdom to the Mosaic law and the prophets (vv. 17-19); the righteousness of the kingdom as compared to the righteousness of the scribes and Pharisees (vv. 20-32); laws relating to perjury (vv. 33-37); laws relating to injustice and unfair advantage (vv. 38-42); and laws relating to enemies (vv. 43-48).

In introducing the laws of the kingdom, Jesus paid full respect to the Mosaic law. He declared that He had not come to destroy it or replace it, but to fulfill it. Although the Mosaic law, as a dispensation, was to end at the cross, its moral and spiritual implications were to be fulfilled in later dispensations, including the kingdom. While it is not accurate to say that the kingdom period when Christ reigns on earth will be under the Mosaic law any more than the present age of grace is, it is obvious that the future kingdom is more legal in its government as directed by an absolute Ruler, who rules with a rod of iron (Rev 19:15). Jesus called, however, for a righteousness which would exceed that of the scribes and Pharisees. The scribes and Pharisees were attempting to fulfill the letter of the law, but were actually breaking the spirit of the law. They not only fell far short of the Mosaic law but fell even shorter of the law of the kingdom. Just as Jesus was to fulfill the law Himself, so His disciples also would share in the fulfillment of the law of righteousness.

According to Jesus, not one jot, that is, the smallest Hebrew letter, *yod,* or one tittle, that is, the smallest part of a letter that would change the meaning, would be left unfulfilled. Clearly, Jesus upheld the inerrancy of the Scriptures in their entirety, not simply their moral sense. The kingdom rule which He was presenting had the highest moral standards, and His disciples were expected to obey.

The morality of the kingdom, in many respects, was to exceed that of the Law of Moses. Beginning with Matthew 5:21, He brought up case after case where morality in the kingdom is more precise and exacting than their customary interpretation of the Mosaic law. Whereas Moses said they should not commit murder, in the kingdom it was wrong to be angry with a brother without cause. One who called his brother Raca, or "empty headed" (i.e., a numbskull), would be in danger of the Sanhedrin. Even worse would be to call him a fool, which would place him in danger of eternal punishment, literally, the fire of Gehenna. While this does not necessarily mean that a person who carelessly calls another a fool today is in danger of hell, it involves an attitude of superior wisdom which does not take into consideration the sinful state of everyone who is saved. The order of reference in verse 22 is climactic, but all is contrasted to murder in verse 21.

In keeping with this, if one would bring a gift to the altar of God and would there remember that he had something against a brother, Jesus exhorted him to leave the gift in order to be reconciled to his brother and then to return to offer the gift. The series of exhortations, beginning in verse 20, is addressed to the second person, making it direct exhortation.

Expanding the problem of reconciliation to a brother, in verses 25 and 26, He took up the matter of an honest debt which must be cared for, lest the debtor be hailed into court and imprisoned until the last farthing is paid. The adversary of verse 25 is certainly not the devil, as Morgan suggests, but an ordinary human creditor.[10] The point is that God demands perfect righteousness and what we owe a brother, we owe God.

Proceeding from matters which offend a brother, or debts which are owed a brother, He then took up the matter of adultery and lust and its relationship to divorce. In contrast to the law which forbade adultery, Jesus charged that anyone looking on a woman in lust had already committed adultery. He charged them that if their right eye offend, they should pluck it out, or if their right hand offend, it should be cut off. There is no scriptural support that Jesus meant that lust would be conquered by doing this literally, as there still would be the left eye and the left hand, but rather that the severity of the sin required severe self-judgment. If the choice were to lose a member or to be cast into the eternal damnation of Gehenna, obviously it would be better to be maimed.

With this as a background, He contrasted divorce in the

kingdom to divorce in the Mosaic law. In the Old Testament, it was comparatively easy to secure divorce. According to Deuteronomy 24:1, a woman no longer in favor with her husband could be given a bill of divorcement and sent away. If in the meantime, however, she married another, she was under no circumstances to return to her first husband, indicating that the divorce was real and final. In the kingdom, the only justifiable cause is that of fornication, or unfaithfulness. Although the matter of divorce in the teaching of Jesus is subject to various interpretations, the tenor of this passage is to recognize divorce as real and final when there is fornication after the marriage relationship has been established. This was more strict than the Mosaic law but less strict than an absolute prohibition of divorce.

In the kingdom, it was not only true that they should not perjure themselves by failing to perform their oath, which was prohibited in the Mosaic law (Num 30:2), but in the kingdom they were not to swear at all, especially in view of man's limited ability to fulfill his oath. Accordingly, he could say yes or no, but he could not pledge beyond this. This indicates care should be used in giving solemn promises but should not be construed as completely prohibiting entering into a pledge or a promise in this age.

Again, the kingdom standards are in contrast to the Mosaic law with its demand for an eye for an eye and a tooth for a tooth. Those in the kingdom were exhorted not to resist evil, but if smitten on the right cheek, they were to turn the other also. This principle was further expanded by the instruction that if a man be sued at law, he should allow his adversary not only to take his coat or tunic but his cloak or robe also; if compelled to go a mile, he should volunteer to go two; and should give to those that borrow and not turn them away. In the millennial kingdom, such high standards could be literally enforced.

It is not clear whether Jesus expected immediate compliance. Jesus Himself was unresisting as He went to the cross. Paul, however, claimed his rights as a Roman citizen when falsely accused. The principle should probably be construed as being illustrated here but not applicable to every conceivable situation. What might work with the King present in the millennial kingdom might not work in the mystery form of the kingdom with the King absent.

Although some might deduce from the principles of the kingdom expounded here that the Bible supports pacifism, most interpreters would not draw this conclusion. In dealing with publicans, John the Baptist instructed them not to abuse their power (Lk 3:13-14). Jesus here was not trying to give hard and fast principles that are applicable under all circumstances, but was stating the ideals which govern His kingdom.

The principle that our acts should be by unselfish love is clear. This is brought out in the closing passage of Matthew 5, where, in contrast to the law, which exhorted men to love their neighbor but permitted them to hate their enemy, Jesus laid down the principle that citizens of His kingdom should love their enemies, bless those that curse them, do good to those that hate them, and pray for those who persecute them. In this, they would emulate the love of God, which causes His sun to shine upon both the evil and the good and sends rain both for the just and unjust. He pointed out that even the world, with its tax collectors, rewards those that reward them and greets those that greet them. Morgan notes love is "the principle of life that crowns everything," and that love is the guiding principle of this entire chapter.[11] The standard of conduct in all areas should be God's attitude of love.

Chapter 5 concludes with the exhortation to be perfect, as God the Father in heaven is perfect. Perfection here refers to uprightness and sincerity of character with the thought of maturity in godliness or attaining the goal of conformity to the character of God. While sinless perfection is impossible, godliness, in its biblical concept, is attainable.

6

The Life of Faith in the Kingdom

IN CONTRAST TO CHAPTER 5, dealing mostly with moral issues, chapter 6 delineates the life of faith. Important in this life of faith are four main elements: (1) performing alms in secret and trusting God for open reward (vv. 1-4); (2) praying in secret and trusting God for open reward (vv. 5-18); (3) laying up treasures in heaven rather than on earth (vv. 19-24); (4) seeking the kingdom of God today and trusting God for His supply tomorrow (vv. 25-34).

GIVING ALMS, 6:1-4

In the opening four verses, Jesus called attention to the ostentatious almsgiving which often characterized Jewry. In the kingdom, alms should be given secretly, but God would reward openly. The reference in verse 1 to "your Father which is in heaven" (cf. also 6:4) is one of seventeen references to God as Father in the Sermon on the Mount, and as Pettingill notes, this "must surely have sounded strange to Jewish ears," accustomed to thinking of God "as The Great and Dreadful God."[1]

INSTRUCTIONS CONCERNING PRAYER, 6:5-18

In like manner, instead of praying publicly in the synagogue and on the corners of the street, as was customary for the Pharisees, they were exhorted to pray in secret, trusting God to answer their prayers openly. Likewise, their prayers were not to be repetitious, as if repetition gained merit, but instead they were to pray simply.

As an illustration, in verse 9, He gave them a sample

prayer often called the Lord's Prayer. It is more properly, however, the disciples' prayer, that is, a prayer for beginners. As Ironside points out, "Jesus Himself could not pray it, for it includes a request for forgiveness of sins, and He was ever the Sinless One."[2] There is no indication that this prayer ever was repeated from memory in the early church or considered a part of its ritual. The same prayer, found in Luke 11, has minor variations and additions, including the closing clause in Matthew 6:13, which is not found in the more ancient manuscripts. According to Jesus, prayers should be addressed to God as the Father who is in heaven, thereby recognizing the disciples' relationship to God as His children. Worship of God is the essence of prayer, and the first petition is that God's name be hallowed or revered. In keeping with the context, the next petition is "Thy kingdom come," certainly including the future millennial kingdom but broad enough to include the contemporary spiritual kingdom. This is followed by that which would be in keeping with the kingdom, that is, that God's will should be done in earth as it is in heaven. The first three petitions are all aorist imperatives in the Greek text, pointed commandments to be fulfilled in full.

In verse 11, the petitions are changed to the first person, relating to human need. Included in the prayer was the petition for daily bread, representing all necessary temporal needs. Second, forgiveness is sought, assuming that the petitioner also forgives, although the reverse order is observed in the epistles; that is, we should forgive because we are already forgiven. In the family relationship, the other aspect is also true. The Christian already forgiven judicially should not expect restoration in the family relationship unless he, himself, is forgiving. Verse 12 does not deal with salvation but the relationship of a child to his father. This is followed by the petition not to be led into temptation, that is, into unnecessary enticement into sin, but rather to be delivered both from evil temptation and succumbing to it. The King James Version includes the doxology that to God belonged the kingdom, the power, and the glory forever, certainly proper ascriptions, whether included in the original text or not.

In the verses which follow, further exhortation is given concerning the necessity of forgiveness in human relationships if we expect God the Father to forgive us. Again, this must not be interpreted as relating to the issue of personal salvation but rather to proper fellowship between the child and his father.

Contriteness of heart, however, should not be a matter of outward appearance which Jesus attributed to hypocrites, or those who are merely acting sad and who disfigure their outer appearance to indicate that they are fasting. Rather He exhorted them that if they want to fast, they should hide this from men by anointing their head and washing their face and doing their fasting in secret that God may reward them openly. The life of faith depends upon God and not men for recompense. Fasting today is neither commanded nor forbidden, and is beneficial only if practiced under the guidance of the Holy Spirit.

TREASURES IN HEAVEN, 6:19-24

Important in Jewish thinking was material wealth. In His public ministry, Jesus repeatedly rebuked them for the prominence they gave to material wealth. A true subject of the kingdom, Jesus said, would lay up his treasures in heaven, where they would be impervious to the moth which would eat his beautiful silk fabrics, the rust that would corrupt his jewelry, and would be beyond the grasping fingers of thieves. The principle involved was that their heart would be where their treasure was. If their eyes were in an evil way coveting money and wealth, their whole body would be full of darkness, but if penetrated by the revealing light of eternal values, their whole body would be full of light.

The contrast between the darkness of covetousness and the light of faith and treasure in heaven carries over to the concept of two masters. Necessarily a choice must be made, and they must either regard a master with love and obedience or with hate and disobedience. So, similarly, a choice must be made between God and mammon, or money. As Tasker notes, "Men cannot *serve* (i.e. 'be slaves of') *God* and mammon (Knox 'money') at once, for single ownership and full-time service are of the essence of slavery."[3] In the kingdom, they must live for God and not for material gain, and in committing their treasures to heaven, they would put their trust in the God of heaven.

CURE FOR ANXIETY, 6:25-34

The place of material gain in life carries over into the problem of anxious care. Because they could trust God for time as well as eternity, they were not to spend their time worrying about their provision of food and drink and raiment for the body. Like the fowl of the air, they were to trust divine provision; and like the lilies of the field, God would care for them. The argument was advanced that if God can care for the grass of the field, existing only for a day and then used for fuel for the oven, how much more will He clothe and care for those who are the objects of His great salvation? Although concern for earthly things characterized the unbelieving Gentile world, Christ reminded them that their Father knows their needs and that they should seek first His kingdom and His righteousness, and that God would add the necessary temporal things to them. The chapter concludes, accordingly, on the note that they should not have anxious care about tomorrow but rather concern themselves with serving God today.

7

Doing the Will of the Father

JUDGING OTHERS, 7:1-6

THE FINAL CHAPTER recording the Sermon on the Mount
contrasts the true and false way, that is, doing the will of the
Father or not doing the will of the Father.

Morgan calls this chapter "a summary of principles of action."[1] The chapter begins by forbidding hypocritical judgment of others. Those desiring to judge their fellow men are
warned that as they judge so they will also be judged. Too
often, the one judging, who is able to see a mote or a small
speck in his brother's eye, overlooks the fact that he has a
beam, or a splinter in his own eye, which is much larger.
Such judgment is hypocrisy, and Jesus declared one should
first cast out the beam from his own eye in order to be able
to see clearly to help his brother. However, in helping others,
care should be exercised to do that which will be really ap-
preciated and helpful. Something holy should not be cast
to dogs because they would not appreciate it; and pearls
would only be trampled under the feet of swine, and they
might turn and injure their benefactor. Help to others should
be thoughtful and deliberate.

ENCOURAGEMENT TO PRAY, 7:7-11

Earlier, Jesus had given them a model prayer. Now assurance was given that God welcomes prayer. They were, accordingly, exhorted to ask, seek, and knock, with the assurance
that those who ask, receive; those who seek, find; and those
who knock shall find the door open. As Tasker points out,
the force of the present imperative in these commands is
iterative: the petitioner should be persistent, keep on asking,
seeking, knocking.[2] If a son asks bread, would a father give

him a stone? Or if he should ask for fish, would he receive
a poisonous serpent? In like manner, if men, who naturally
are evil, can give good gifts to their children, how much more
can God the Father in heaven, who is infinite in His good-
ness, give good things to them that ask Him? In the kingdom, there is the reassuring fact that God the Father cares
for those who are His.

GOLDEN RULE, 7:12

The moral principles outlined in the Sermon of the Mount
are summarized in Matthew 7:12 in what is often called the
golden rule, which has no exact parallel anywhere else in
literature. The principle is laid down that what men would
ordinarily want others to do to them, so they should do to
others, and this rule is the sum of the law and the prophets.
As Morgan expresses it, "That is the whole thing." Morgan
goes on to quote Hillel, Socrates, Aristotle, and Confucius
as expressing similar sentiments, but concludes, "These are
negative and passive; Christ's comment is positive and
active."[3]

TWO WAYS, 7:13-14

Entering into the kingdom is likened to going through a
narrow gate, in contrast to going through the gate which is
wide and broad, leading to destruction. Jesus gave no assurance that the majority will enter the kingdom; He declared
that few find the gate leading to life and righteousness. There
have been many attempts to soften this hard fact, to deny
that few are saved, and to affirm that all will eventually be
reconciled to God. There is no justification for ignoring these
plain words of Christ. The way is indeed narrow, and only
one Saviour is offered the world (cf. Ac 4:12).

TRUE AND FALSE TEACHERS, 7:15-20

Jesus warned against false prophets who are like wolves
clad in sheep's clothing, preying upon the flock. Tasker holds

that false teachers are part of the cause for the way being narrow and hard to find.[4] False prophets can be known by their fruits. Just as a good tree brings forth good fruit and a bad tree brings forth bad fruit, so it is with prophets. In the orchard, trees that do not bear good fruit are cast into the fire, and disciples of Jesus can expect God, in His time, to deal with those that are false.

TRUE AND FALSE PROFESSION, 7:21-23

Not only are there false prophets but there is false profession on the part of some who claim to follow Jesus. Not every one who addresses Him as Lord will enter into the kingdom of heaven, even if they have prophesied in the name of Christ and have cast out demons and have performed wonderful works. The ultimate test is whether they are obedient to the Father and characteristically do His will. This principle does not mean that salvation in the kingdom is secured by works, but it does teach that works are the fruits, or evidences, which are found in a true disciple.

TRUE AND FALSE FOUNDATIONS, 7:24-29

The Sermon on the Mount concludes with a parable. Those who hear and respond in obedience to the sayings of Jesus were declared to be like a wise man building his house upon a rock. The storms which beat and the rains which came did not destroy the house because of its solid foundation. The foolish man, however, who built his house upon the sand, in time of storm, discovered that his house would fall, because he had not built upon that which is eternal and true. As Ironside points out, Christ is the rock, the only sure foundation (Is 28:16; 1 Co 3:11; 1 Pe 2:6-8).[5]

This masterful address, comprehensive and authoritative in its pronouncement, astonished the people. As Ironside expresses it, "Never had such words as these been heard in Israel."[6] The teaching of Christ was in great contrast to the way the scribes taught and clearly showed that this was the truth of God.

The expression "and it came to pass" (Mt 7:28) is a characteristic transitional expression of Matthew (cf. 9:10; 11:1; 13:53; 19:1; 26:1). A similar expression is found much more frequently, however, in Luke and Acts than it is in Matthew, but it serves to introduce a summary of the reactions to what Jesus said and did.

PART FOUR

THE CREDENTIALS OF THE KING

8

The Authority of the King Over Disease and Nature

FOLLOWING THE PRONOUNCEMENT of the principles of the kingdom in chapters 5-7, chapters 8-9 present the supporting mighty works of Jesus as credentials of the Messiah King.

Three groups of miracles may be observed. In Matthew 8:1-17, the healing of the leper (vv. 1-4), the healing of the servant (vv. 5-13), and the healing of Peter's wife's mother (vv. 14-15), are followed by an evening of many miraculous healings (vv. 16-17).

A second group of miracles is found in 8:23—9:8 with the stilling of the storm (vv. 23-27), the casting out of demons (vv. 28-34), and the healing of the paralytic and the forgiveness of his sins (9:1-8).

The third group of miracles is found in 9:18-38 with the healing of the ruler's daughter (vv. 18-19, 23-26), the healing of the woman with the issue of blood (vv. 20-22), the healing of two blind men (vv. 27-31), the healing of the demoniac (vv. 32-34), followed by a general statement of many instances of healing (v. 35).

In between these accounts of miracles, which are not necessarily in chronological order, are other instances of significant events which took place in Christ's ministry. The purpose of Matthew in these two chapters is to offer the credentials of the Messiah as predicted in the Old Testament. The order of the presentation deals with Christ's power over disease in the first group; His power over nature, demons, and authority to forgive sins in the second group; with His power over death and other miscellaneous human needs in the third group. In 8:17, the whole picture is related to Isaiah's prophecy of a suffering Messiah who would bear the sickness and the sins of Israel.

LEPER HEALED, 8:1-4

Coming down from the mountain with great multitudes following Him, Jesus was confronted suddenly by a leper (cf. Mk 1:40-45; Lk 5:12-14). The crowd undoubtedly surrounded the leper at a safe distance, afraid of his terrible disease. The leper addressed Jesus, "Lord, if thou wilt, thou canst make me clean" (Mt 8:2). This is the first instance in Matthew where Christ is addressed as Lord (Gr. *kyrios*). The word means "master," but as used of Jesus, it is a recognition of His authority and deity. The leper had confidence in the power of Jesus; he was not sure whether Jesus was willing to heal.

Jesus first touched the leper, which amazed the crowd, for lepers were not touched (cf. Lev 13). With this loving gesture, Jesus said, "I will," and immediately the leper was healed. The leper was instructed not to tell anyone but to go to the priest, fulfilling the procedure of Leviticus 14 in regard to the cleansing of a leper. Commentators like Wrede and R. H. Lightfoot have strained at the command not to tell others and questioned the purpose of going to the priest. The command not to tell others was probably to avoid gathering ever greater crowds, which by their size were getting out of hand, as Tasker has observed.[1] The command to tell the priest was first of all an act of obedience to the law, but Jesus probably wanted to have a genuine case of healing certified in a formal way. Telling the priests would not increase the problem of the large crowds and did not contradict Christ's instructions to "tell no man." The effect on the priests must have been electrifying, as they had never before in their memory had a leper healed. Significantly, in Acts, many of the priests are recorded to have believed in Jesus.

CENTURION'S SERVANT HEALED, 8:5-13

As Jesus was entering into Capernaum, a centurion, a Roman soldier, besought Him to heal a servant, sick with palsy and in great suffering (cf. Lk 7:1-10). The servant is called in Greek, a *pais,* meaning a child, but the word is sometimes used of adult servants. Jesus immediately responded to the centurion with a promise that He would come and heal him. In reply, the centurion declared himself unworthy for Jesus to come into his house, and besought Him to speak the word only, saying that he too was a man in authority who could command and have instant obedience. Jesus marveled at his faith, greater than any He had found in Israel, and commented that in the future kingdom, the children of the kingdom would be cast out and others, that is, Gentiles, would be admitted instead. Jesus then brought the encounter to a close, saying to the centurion, "Go thy way; and as thou hast believed, so be it done unto thee. And his servant was healed in the selfsame hour" (Mt 8:13).

HEALING OF PETER'S MOTHER-IN-LAW, 8:14-15

In Capernaum, Jesus went to Peter's house, which was located there, and finding his wife's mother sick of fever, He healed her. Then she rose and ministered to them (cf. Mk 1:29-31; Lk 4:38-39). The best texts indicate that she ministered to Him (singular) rather than to "them," although she probably ministered to the others also. In healing first the leper—an outcast—then a Gentile centurion, and finally a woman, Jesus was dealing with those either excluded or unimportant in Jewish thinking. As Morgan expresses it, "He began with the unfit persons for whom there was no provision in the economy of the nation."[2] Jesus was uncontaminated by contact with leprosy and disease, and He was not bound by Jewish narrowness from those whom the world despised.

EVENING OF HEALING, 8:16-17

Matthew brings to a close this group of miracles by stating that that evening, many afflicted with demons and all others who were sick were healed, in fulfillment of Isaiah 53:4-5 (cf. Mk 1:32-34; Lk 4:40-41). Matthew, having made his point that Jesus fulfilled the Old Testament prophecies of these miraculous works, is content to summarize many incidents in one short statement.

PRICE OF DISCIPLESHIP, 8:18-22

Two instances of would-be followers of Jesus are mentioned, typical of the multitude, attracted by the miracles, who
wanted to be disciples (cf. Lk 9:57-62). The first to be introduced is a scribe who promised to follow Jesus wherever
He went. Jesus replied by pointing out that while foxes have
dens and birds have nests, the Son of man did not have a
home. Following Jesus would be difficult. Another person is
described in Matthew 8:21-22 as desiring to follow Jesus
but wanting first to bury his father. Evidently, he meant that
he wanted to live with his father until he died. Jesus replied
by showing the priority of His claims.

JESUS STILLS THE STORM, 8:23-27

Beginning a second group of miracles, the account is given
of the stilling of the storm on Galilee, also given in Mark
4:35-41 and Luke 8:22-25. While Jesus and the disciples
were in the boat on Galilee, a sudden storm overtook them
and was filling the boat with water, while Jesus Himself
was asleep. The disciples awoke Him with the urgent petition,
literally translated, "Lord, save, we are perishing." Jesus,
thus awakened, first rebuked them for being fearful and of
little faith; then, He rebuked the winds and the sea, and suddenly there was a great calm. The disciples, accustomed to
miracles, were amazed at the suddenness of the change and
the evidence of the power of Christ, and, speaking in awe,
said, "Even the winds and the sea obey him."

HEALING OF TWO DEMONIACS, 8:28-34

After the instance of stilling the storm on Galilee, as they
arrived on the other side of the lake, they were met by two
men who were demon possessed and lived in a graveyard,
which, because of their presence, was considered so dangerous that others avoided passing that way (cf. Mk 5:1-21;
Lk 8:26-40). The demons, speaking through the men, recognized Jesus as the Son of God, and expressed the fear that

He had come to torment them before their time. The King James translation "devils" is better rendered "demons" and refers to fallen angels who are Satan's agents. Their ultimate judgment is assured and is apparently simultaneous with Satan being cast into the lake of fire (Rev 20:10).

As an alternative to being cast out completely, the demons requested permission to enter the herd of swine feeding nearby. Jesus gave the simple, abrupt command, "Go." The demons, entering the herd of swine, caused them to run violently down a steep cliff into the sea, where they perished. The demons' foolish request demonstrated their limited knowledge, as they were just as much cast out after the swine perished as if they had been cast out of the demoniac without entering any other being.

The report of the keepers of the swine brought out the whole city of Gadara, about six miles from Galilee, a preferred reading to Gergesenes, a town some thirty miles south and east of Galilee.[3] When the people of the town saw Jesus, they urged Him to leave their country. Keeping swine was, of course, forbidden to Israel, and their destruction was a justifiable judgment from God, which should have shown the people their spiritual need. Their choice of swine, rather than Christ, dramatically illustrated their blindness. They preferred pigs and money to Christ and spiritual riches. As the next chapter reveals (Mt 9:1), Jesus obliged them and left. The creature is able to reject the Creator in time, but will render account in eternity for his lost opportunity.

While Matthew does not record it, in the parallel account in Mark 5:1-20, the man delivered from demons is instructed to go to his home and testify to his friends, the only instance where Jesus told one healed to testify to his own people (cf. vv. 19-20).

9

The Authority of the King to Forgive Sin

HEALING OF THE PARALYZED MAN, AND HIS FORGIVENESS, 9:1-8

AFTER BEING REJECTED by the people of Gadara, Jesus returned by boat to the other side of the lake to Capernaum. There, a man, paralyzed and lying on a bed, or couch, was brought to Him (cf. Mk 2:3-12; Lk 5:18-26). Recognizing the faith of his friends who had brought him, Jesus first said, "Son, be of good cheer; thy sins be forgiven thee" (Mt 9:2). This was done deliberately by Jesus, knowing the unbelief of the scribes who were watching and who, in their hearts, thought that He committed blasphemy.

Replying to the unspoken objection, Jesus posed the question as to whether it was easier to say, "Thy sins be forgiven thee," or to say, "Arise and walk." Obviously, merely to say either was easy. In the case of forgiveness of sins, there would be no way to demonstrate whether it had been accomplished, but to say, "Arise and walk," would have the testimony of immediate healing. To demonstrate His power to do both, however, Jesus then said to the man, "Arise, take up thy bed, and go unto thine house" (9:6). Before them all, the man arose from his sick bed, taking up the portable couch on which he was lying, and departed as the multitude marveled. This miracle closes the second group of three, demonstrating Christ's control over nature, the demon world, and His power both to heal disease and to forgive sin.

CALL OF MATTHEW, 9:9-17

Before introducing the third group of miracles, Matthew records briefly his own call to the ministry (cf. Mk 2:14;

Lk 5:27-29). In the parallel accounts in Mark and Luke, he is called Levi; but here, he refers to himself as Matthew. As an official in the tax office, he left his lucrative position in order to follow Christ. This tax office, located at Capernaum, probably had the responsibility of collecting taxes from those who were on the caravan route from Damascus to the East, which passed through Capernaum. As a tax collector, he probably knew Greek well, which qualified him for writing this gospel in the Greek language.

The incident which followed, according to Luke 5:29, was a feast, which Matthew held in his own house for Jesus. It possibly was Matthew's way of introducing Jesus to his fellow tax collectors. To eat with publicans or tax collectors, however, was frowned upon by the Pharisees, who considered tax collectors as the enemies of their people and as those who were compromising morally. As W. H. Griffith Thomas notes, "A tax-gatherer was one who elicited intense animosity on the part of the Jews who strongly opposed this work of Roman domination."[1] The Pharisees, complaining to the disciples, drew from Jesus the reply, "They that [are] whole need not a physician, but they that are sick" (Mt 9:12). He then cited to them Hosea 6:6, which brings out that God prefers mercy to sacrifice, a point mentioned only by Matthew. In the process, Jesus declared, "I am not come to call the righteous, but sinners to repentance" (Mt 9:13).

Objections were also raised by the disciples of John, who, perceiving Jesus attending a feast such as this, wanted to know why the disciples of Jesus did not fast like the Pharisees. To them, Jesus replied that it is unfitting to mourn during a wedding feast, implying that this was not the time in Christ's ministry to mourn. He prophesied, however, that the time would come when the Bridegroom would be taken away and they then could fast. In this, He anticipated His own death and ascension into heaven.

This attempt to apply the standards of the Pharisees to the new dispensation, which Jesus was introducing, was, in His words, like adding new cloth to an old garment or putting new wine into old wineskins. The Pharisees' religion, in-

cluding its fasting, was quite inadequate for what lay ahead,
whether it be the dispensation of the church or the dispensation of the kingdom. As Ironside expresses it, "He had not
come to add something to the legal dispensation but to super-
sede it with that which was entirely new. . . . The new wine
of grace was not to be poured into the skin-bottles of
legality."²

Two Women Healed, 9:18-26

As Jesus was discussing His answer to the question of the
disciples of John, a ruler of the Jews came and, having done
obeisance, petitioned Him to raise his daughter whom he
declared to be already dead (cf. Mk 5:21-43; Lk 8:40-56).
As Jesus followed him, a woman in the crowd, afflicted with
an issue of blood for twelve years, touched the hem of His
garment, believing that if she could but touch His garment,
she would be made well. In Mark 5:30, Christ is recorded
to have asked the question, "Who touched my clothes?" In
response to the question, the woman identified herself. Matthew does not include these details but records the comfort-
ing words of Christ that her faith had made her whole.

The journey to the ruler's house continued, and upon
arrival, Jesus saw the musicians who had been hired to play
the dirges, as was customary when a death occurred. He told
them, however, "Give place: for the maid is not dead, but
sleepeth" (Mt 9:24). They responded by laughing with unbelief. Jesus, having put the people out of the house, took the
maid by the hand, and she was immediately restored. Because Jesus used a word for sleeping (Gr. *katheudo*) not
customarily used in Scripture for death, some expositors believe that she was not actually dead, but merely in a stupor.³
Most commentators, however, believe that Christ was merely
declaring to them that she was sleeping, in the sense that she
would soon rise. Actually, her parents were correct that she
was dead. The report of the miracle was given widespread
notice and added to the fame of Christ, which would have
involved a degree of deception if she were not actually dead.

HEALING OF TWO BLIND MEN, 9:27-31

This account, found only in Matthew, records Christ's encounter with two blind men who followed Him, saying, "Son of David, have mercy on us" (9:27). Apparently, because Jesus did not heal them immediately, the blind men followed Him into the house. Having thus tested them, Jesus asked if they believed He was able to heal. When they replied in the affirmative, He touched their eyes saying, "According to your faith be it unto you," and they were healed. Although He told them not to tell anyone, they nevertheless spread abroad His fame. The prohibition of revealing that they had been healed was probably due to the fact that Jesus did not want to excite followers who would come to Him simply to be healed.

ANOTHER DEMONIAC HEALED, 9:32-35

As the blind men were leaving with their newfound sight, a man was brought in, possessed of a demon and unable to talk. This account also is found only in Matthew. Christ, according to the record, immediately healed him so that he was able to speak, and as the multitudes watched, they marveled, saying that such miracles had never happened before in Israel. The Pharisees, however, continued to be unbelieving, accusing Him of casting out demons by Satan, the prince of demons. The account of this miracle is followed by a statement summarizing Christ's ministry of teaching and preaching, accompanied by healing all who came to Him.

COMPASSION OF JESUS FOR THE MULTITUDES, 9:36-38

Although the miracles of Christ had attracted hundreds of followers, Jesus was all too aware of their spiritual needs. Their faith was superficial, and they were like sheep without a shepherd. His compassion for them moved Him to say to His disciples that they should pray for laborers, for the harvest was great and the laborers few. The great miracles He had performed, recorded in Matthew 8-9, were not accepted

by many of the Jews, and growing evidence of unbelief is
found in the chapters which follow. As Kelly observes, "The
Lord is utterly rejected in chapter 11. And then chapter
12 gives the final pronouncing of the judgment on that
generation. . . . The consequence is that the Lord turns
from the unbelieving race and introduces the kingdom of
heaven, in connection with which He gives the parables in
chapter 13."[4]

In what sense did Jesus introduce the kingdom of heaven
at this point? Obviously, He had been talking about kingdom principles all through the gospel of Matthew. The
change here relates to the kingdom in its mystery form, the
kingdom as it will exist between the first and second com-
ings of Christ, in contrast to the millennial kingdom, predicted in the Old Testament and to be fulfilled after His
second advent.

PART FIVE

THE REJECTION OF THE KING AND THE KINGDOM

10

The Twelve Apostles Commissioned

TWELVE APOSTLES NAMED AND GIVEN AUTHORITY, 10:1-6

IN CONNECTION with Christ's commissioning the twelve disciples to preach, accompanied by power to cast out unclean spirits and to heal disease, Matthew names the twelve apostles in pairs (cf. Mk 3:16-19; Lk 6:13-16; Ac 1:13), unlike the other gospels, possibly indicating that they were sent forth in pairs[1] (cf. Mk 6:7). There are small variations in order and in the names given to the disciples in each of the gospels. Only Matthew describes himself as a tax collector, and there are variations in the name of Lebbaeus, surnamed Thaddaeus, whom Luke calls Judas, the brother of James, to distinguish him from Judas Iscariot. Those named as apostles are commissioned and sent forth to perform a ministry on behalf of God.

APOSTLES SENT ONLY TO ISRAEL, 10:6-23

The discourse in which Christ commissions the twelve has been considered by some interpretaters as a collection of sayings spoken by Christ on many different occasions. As presented by Matthew, however, it is represented as a single discourse, and there is no valid reason for questioning this presentation. Obviously, Christ repeated many of His instructions at different times and in different places, and that there should be similarity to some statements here is not surprising.

The instruction given by Christ to the twelve was to go "to the lost sheep of the house of Israel," and not go to the Gentiles or the Samaritans (cf. Mk 6:7-13; Lk 9:1-6). His first and primary obligation was to deliver the message of the kingdom to Israel, and neither time nor personnel would permit reaching the others. Later, the gospel was to go to every creature. The apostles were given authority to perform miracles, even to raising the dead. While they seem to have been successful in casting out demons and curing all diseases, there is no record that any dead were raised at this time.

Luke records a sending out of seventy disciples, apparently subsequent to the sending of the twelve, or in addition to them (Lk 10:1). The seventy also report success in casting out demons (v. 17). Matthew does not refer to the seventy, but their instructions were similar to those given to the twelve.

In sending them forth, Jesus instructed them not to take provisions of money or clothing and to depend upon the cities in which they preached to provide for them. If they were not welcomed in a particular place, they were to shake off the dust of their feet against it and to pronounce a solemn judgment that it would be more tolerable for the land of Sodom and Gomorrah in the day of judgment than for that city.

The disciples' task was to be a difficult one, as they would be as sheep in the midst of wolves, but their demeanor should be that of being wise as serpents and harmless as doves. They were to beware of men who might deliver them to the Sanhedrin, but if they were brought before governors and kings, they were not to be filled with care but to rely on God to enable them to speak in that hour. Jesus predicted that ultimately there would be persecution, with brother delivering brother to death, father the child, and children their parents, and they would be hated of all men. It is apparent that these prophecies go beyond their immediate experience and were to be fulfilled after Pentecost. Jesus declared they would not be able to fulfill their tasks of reaching all the cities of Israel until the Son of man had come. This seems to anticipate the second coming of Christ, and views the entire present church age as a parenthesis not taken into consideration in this prophecy.

COST AND REWARD OF DISCIPLESHIP, 10:24-42

Continuing His instructions to the twelve, beginning in Matthew 10:24, Jesus discussed the whole matter of discipleship and its reward, including material that extended far beyond the disciples' immediate situation. Having introduced the thought that discipleship extends until the Son of man returns, He gave instructions covering the whole period. Jesus reminded them that if He, their Master, was called Beelzebub, it is understandable that men would similarly abuse His followers. Beelzebub was the name of a god of the Philistines (2 Ki 1:2), also known as Baal, which the Jews equated with the devil, or Satan.

Jesus instructed His disciples not to fear name-calling. The time would come when truth would be fully revealed and darkness and unbelief condemned. They were not to fear those who could kill the body but not kill the soul, but rather fear the one able to destroy both soul and body in hell. Although God alone has the power of death, the reference here is to Satan, whose activities ultimately result in the destruction of both soul and body.

The disciples were assured of the care of the Father. If two sparrows were worth a farthing, or one-fourth of a cent (equal to about twenty-five cents today), and a sparrow could not fall to the ground without the Father's permission, they could be assured that they were more valuable than many sparrows and that the very hairs of their head were numbered. Jesus promised them that if they confess Him before men, He will confess them before God the Father; but if they deny Him, they will be denied before God the Father.

Jesus told them bluntly, however, that His purpose was not to bring peace on earth, but rather a sword. A son would be set against his father, a daughter against her mother, and the daughter-in-law against her mother-in-law. A man's foes would be those of his own household.

In stating that He had not come to bring peace among men, Jesus was referring to His first coming and the result of the proclamation of the gospel of the kingdom. He would be a divider of men. Ultimately, however, He was to bring peace and good will among men, as the angels announced at His birth (Lk 2:14). The Scriptures define many kinds of peace, such as peace with God (Ro 5:1), possessed by every Christian; the peace of God (Phil 4:7), which is a fruit of the Spirit (Gal 5:22); and the promise of peace on earth to be realized in the future millennial reign of Christ, as in Isaiah 11. The Scriptures make plain that there is no peace for the wicked (Is 57:21). Peace is only possible for those who are the recipients of the grace of God by faith.

Disciples accordingly must choose between love of Christ and of the family. Although normally, children should love their father and mother, they are not to love them more than they love Jesus. While parents should love their children, they should not love them more than they love Christ. A true disciple must take up his cross and follow after Jesus. In losing his life for Christ's sake, he shall find it. Not only disciples, but those who receive a disciple in Christ's name will receive their reward. Even a cup of cold water given in the name of a disciple will be rewarded in God's time. The words of Jesus, applicable to the twelve as they went forth, have echoed down through the centuries since, and have encouraged brave men and women to be true even unto death.

11

The Growing Opposition
to Jesus

DISCOURSE ON JOHN THE BAPTIST, 11:1-15

HAVING SENT FORTH the twelve with instructions to preach
the kingdom of heaven and having given them authority to
perform miracles (Mt 10:7-8), Jesus departed alone to teach
and preach in the cities of Galilee. During His tour, John
the Baptist, earlier announced as being in prison (Mt 4:12),
sent two of his disciples to Jesus with the question, "Art
thou he that should come, or do we look for another?"
(11:3). Lenski points out that the expression, "he that
should come," "signifies the Messiah and is used in that
specific sense especially also by the Baptist, 3:11; Mark 1:7;
Luke 3:16; John 1:27. This designation was derived from
Ps. 118:26 and Ps. 40:7."[1]

John had been imprisoned in the fortress of Machaerus,
the royal house of Herod, facing the Dead Sea, because of
his fearless attack upon the immorality of Herod, who was
living in adultery with Herodias, his brother Philip's wife
(Mt 14:3-4). Significantly, the Jewish leaders had been silent
concerning this public scandal.

The question that the disciples of John communicated to
Jesus has been interpreted by some as indicating a wavering
faith in Christ on the part of John the Baptist, and others,
who have come to John's defense, regard John as asking
a natural question. Undoubtedly, John had anticipated that
Jesus would not only be "the Lamb of God, [who] taketh
away the sin of the world" (Jn 1:29), but would be one
who also would judge sin. John had declared, according to
Matthew 3:10, "The axe is laid unto the root of the trees:
therefore every tree which bringeth not forth good fruit

is hewn down, and cast into the fire." He had also predicted
that Christ would baptize with fire (v. 11) and that He
would "gather his wheat into the garner," but would "burn
up the chaff with unquenchable fire" (v. 12). John, languish-
ing in prison, did not sense any divine deliverance from a
wicked world. Instead of God triumphing, it seemed that
Herod, in spite of his wickedness, was still in power.

Accordingly, John needed reassurance and clarification. In
the background was the Jewish interpretation of the Old
Testament prophecies, which offered the puzzle of a suffering Messiah who would also be a glorious ruler (cf. 1 Pe
1:10-12). While John should not be represented as questioning the validity of the revelation that came to him, that
Jesus was indeed the Messiah who would save Israel from
their sins, the question had been raised in his mind whether
he should look for still another to bring the judgment of
God upon a wicked world, and fulfill the predictions of
the glorious reign of the Messiah.

The same questions of the ultimate triumph of God undoubtedly face everyone in suffering for Christ's sake. If
our God is omnipotent, why does He permit the righteous
to suffer? The answer, of course, is that the time of God's
judgment has not yet come but that the final triumph is certain. The genuineness of John's perplexity should not be
questioned, as he attempted to reconcile his concept of a
triumphing Messiah with his own situation in prison and
the reports that came to him of the works of Christ, which
were acts of mercy rather than acts of divine judgment.
Understandably, John needed reassurance and further information.

In answer, Jesus told the disciples of John to tell him
what they heard and saw. As stated in Matthew 11:5, His
works were many: "The blind receive their sight, and the
lame walk, the lepers are cleansed, and the deaf hear, the
dead are raised up, and the poor have the gospel preached
to them." It is most significant that Jesus did not attempt
to answer the real question of John, of why judgment on
the wicked was not being inflicted and why the people of
Israel had not yet been delivered. Instead, Jesus pronounced

a blessing on those who would not be offended by the apparent delay in fulfilling predictions of divine judgment. Interestingly, later in this chapter He delivered a message of judgment on the cities of Galilee, but first Jesus called attention to the unique role of John as the prophesied messenger which would come before the Messiah.

Lest there should be any inference from His remarks that John was weak or vacillating, He appealed to the fearless witness of John which had led to his imprisonment. Those who had gone out in the wilderness to hear John had not gone because he was a weak reed, shaken by every wind. Instead, they found a man who thundered demands for repentance. They did not find a man clothed in soft raiment. John, in prison in Herod's house, was undoubtedly still clad in the rough garments of the wilderness. Was John a prophet? Jesus answered yes. John was not only a prophet but the prophesied messenger of the Messiah. In verse 10, Jesus quoted Malachi 3:1, "Behold, I will send my messenger, and he shall prepare the way before me." The quotation in Matthew, similar to the quotation in Luke 7:27, changes the phrase "before me" in Malachi to "before thee," and therefore interprets the Malachi prophecy as referring, first, to John the Baptist as the messenger, and second, to the Lord as "messenger of the covenant." There is allusion also to Isaiah 40:3, a specific reference to John the Baptist, "The voice of him that crieth in the wilderness, Prepare ye the way of the LORD, make straight in the desert a highway for our God." Mark combines the two Old Testament references in describing the ministry of John (Mk 1:2-3). Among the prophets before Jesus, there were none greater than John the Baptist, but Jesus declared that in the future kingdom of heaven on earth, the least of God's servants would have even a greater privilege.

How can we explain this contrast? The key may be found in that John is described as one "born of women," probably referring to the sinful descent of men from Eve (cf. Job 14:1; 15:14; 25:4; Ps 51:5). Because of his great mission in preparing the way for Christ, John is declared to be greater than the prophets who had predicted Christ.

The privilege of God's servants who will live in the presence
of Christ in the millennial kingdom, however, is even greater,
as this will be the complete fulfillment of Messianic prophecy.

The question of John why God permits the wicked to
triumph in their violence was recognized by Jesus when He
stated, "And from the days of John the Baptist until now
the kingdom of heaven suffereth violence, and the violent
take it by force" (Mt 11:12) pointed out that Jesus, until
now, the prophets prophesied the future triumph but did
not realize it (v. 13). Both John the Baptist and Jesus were
to suffer at the hands of wicked men and die; this is the
main import of what Jesus said. The interpretation that He
called here for resolute courage on the part of the disciples
is not the main point. In closing His comment on John the
Baptist, Jesus added, "And if [you] will receive it, this is
Elias, which was for to come" (v. 14). This must be interpreted in the light of Matthew 17:10-13, where John the
Baptist is again related to fulfilling the prophecy of Malachi
4:5-6, that Elijah the prophet would come before the day
of the Lord. Some expositors find complete fulfillment of
the prophecy about the coming of Elijah in John the Baptist.
Others identify one of the two witnesses in Revelation 22
as Elijah sent back to earth. In the light of Christ's explanation in Matthew 17:10-13, it is questionable whether any
future appearance of Elijah is necessary. Jesus closed His
commendation of John the Baptist with the exhortation, "He
that hath ears to hear, let him hear" (11:15). The test
of faith that comes as we await God's future triumph is
common to all believers.

UNREASONABLENESS OF UNBELIEF, 11:16-19

In contrast to His commendation of John for his resolute
faith and courage, Jesus commented on the Jews' vacillating
and unreasonable attitude of unbelief. Morgan points out
that there are four classes of unbelief in this chapter: (1)
John's perplexity (11:1-15); (2) the unreasonable unbelief
of Christ's generation (11:16-19); (3) the impenitent unbelief of the cities of Galilee (11:20-24); (4) the unbelief

of the wise as compared to the faith of babes (11:25-30).[2]

Jesus likened the generation who heard His message to children playing in the marketplace, acting out a make-believe wedding. When they were unable to attract other children to join them, they changed to a make-believe funeral with no better result. They then complained, "We have piped unto you, and ye have not danced; we have mourned unto you, and ye have not lamented" (v. 17). In like manner, Jesus said, John came as a prophet of the judgment of God, neither feasting with them nor drinking. The reaction of the multitude was, "He hath a devil" (v. 18). By contrast Jesus came and freely ate with them at their dinners, and they objected to this, saying, "Behold a man gluttonous, and a winebibber, a friend of publicans and sinners" (v. 19). Unbelief can always find excuses and can justify criticism of servants of God.

JUDGMENT ON THE UNREPENTANT CITIES
OF GALILEE, 11:20-24

In anticipation of God's ultimate judgment upon wicked unbelief, Jesus declared a solemn judgment on the cities of Galilee in which He had done so many mighty works. He pronounced a woe on Chorazin and Bethsaida, cities which eventually went into ruin. He declared that if the mighty miracles done in Galilee had been performed in Tyre and Sidon, they would have been brought to repentance in sackcloth and ashes. Accordingly, although Tyre and Sidon would be judged by God in the day of judgment, the judgment on the cities of Galilee would be more severe.

His most biting words were for Capernaum, which He described as "exalted unto heaven," but which "shalt be brought down to hell" (v. 23). He declared, in connection with Capernaum, that if the miracles He had performed there had been done in Sodom, it would have been brought to repentance and would have been preserved instead of destroyed. Anyone who visits the ruins of Capernaum today and sees the pitiful remains of what was once a beautiful city, can realize the literalness with which this prophecy has been fulfilled. Significantly, Tiberias, not far away, was not condemned and is not in ruins.

INVITATION TO PERSONAL DISCIPLESHIP, 11:25-30

In commenting on the unreasonableness of unbelief, Jesus thanked God that those who come in childlike faith are also recipients of divine revelation concerning the Son. This is not to support the concept that the Christian faith is unreasonable, but rather that unbelief is not intelligent in the light of revelation concerning God and His Son.

It is a profound truth that God has revealed His divine wisdom to those who have trusted Him and has hidden His divine wisdom from those who are wise in the knowledge of this world. It is part of God's gracious provision for those willing to trust Him and receive His Son as Saviour.

This great truth, however, is eclipsed by the profound statement of verse 27, sometimes referred to as a great Christological passage. Here, Christ declared that all things had been committed unto Him by God the Father. In keeping with this truth and the infinity of divine wisdom, no one really knows the Son as does the Father, and no one knows the Father in the way that the Son knows Him. But to some extent, this can be revealed by the Son to man in spite of his limitations. The infinity of the knowledge of God and the infinity of the authority of Christ over all things, whether in heaven or hell, whether angels, devils, or men, time, or eternity, is a comprehensive statement of the deity of Christ and the background of His gracious invitation that follows in verse 28.

In the verses which follow, Jesus, having turned from the general unbelief which characterized the cities of Galilee, extended a personal invitation to the individuals among them who would find in Christ rest of heart and soul. In verse 28, He invited all who labor and are heavy laden to come to Him, and to those who do, He promised to give rest. Whether their load is the burden of guilt of sin or the sorrows that are natural to life but which are too great for human strength to bear, Jesus urged needy souls to come to Himself.

Jesus extended the invitation, "Take my yoke upon you, and learn of me; for I am meek and lowly in heart: and ye shall find rest unto your souls. For my yoke is easy, and my burden is light" (vv. 29-30). In exhorting them to take His "yoke," Jesus was inviting them to discipleship. A pupil enrolling for instruction under a teacher is considered as coming under a "yoke." Instead of exchanging one burden for another, however, it is exchanging one which is onerous and crushing for one which is light and rewarding. There is an inner satisfaction and rest of soul in being a disciple of Christ which is unknown by the child of the world, who attempts to bear his own burden.

> I heard the voice of Jesus say,
> "Come unto me and rest;
> Lay down, thou weary one, lay down
> Thy head upon my breast."
> I came to Jesus as I was,
> Weary and worn and sad;
> I found in Him a resting place,
> And He has made me glad.
>   HORATIUS BONAR

12

Jesus Rejected by the Pharisees

DISCIPLES ACCUSED OF VIOLATING THE SABBATH, 12:1-8

THE GROWING REJECTION of the Pharisees, who earlier had been friendly to Jesus, becomes apparent in this chapter. First, there are three incidents relating to the Sabbath, in which Jesus is accused of breaking the Mosaic law (Mt 12:1-21); second, Jesus' power is attributed to the devil (vv. 22-37); third, the Pharisees demand a sign other than miracles (vv. 38-50).

The opening incident tells how the disciples, walking through the green fields on the Sabbath, began to pluck ears of grain and eat them because they were hungry. Mark 2:23-28 and Luke 6:1-5 also record the story. The Pharisees, on the alert for any ground of accusation of Jesus and His disciples, immediately accused them of doing that which is not lawful to do on the Sabbath. As Morgan points out, the hostility of the Pharisees began when Christ forgave sin (Mt 9:1-8), was increased by Jesus' associating with publicans and sinners (vv. 9-13), and now is inflamed by Christ's ignoring their petty rules about the Sabbath.[1]

The Pharisees did not accuse the disciples of stealing, as plucking a few ears of grain was permitted by Deuteronomy 23:25, but the law forbade any work on the Sabbath (Ex 20:10). The Jewish traditions made this very specific and equated plucking ears with reaping grain, which was forbidden on the Sabbath. Lenski notes that the penalty could be death for such an infraction, if the act was deliberate.[2]

Although Jesus Himself had not participated in the act, He immediately defended His disciples, presenting three arguments. First, He called attention to David's experience,

86

recorded in 1 Samuel 21:1-6, when David was hungry while fleeing from Saul. The priest gave him bread taken off the table of shewbread when it was replaced with fresh bread, even though normally, such bread was reserved as holy, for the priests alone. Technically, this was breaking the law, but David was not condemned because of it, illustrating that satisfying hunger was more important than observing a technicality.

A second argument was derived from the fact that the priests in the temple broke the law by many of their duties in their work in maintaining the sacrifices and the other rituals. Jesus called attention to the fact that they were blameless.

His third argument was His own person, as one who is greater than the temple. If Jesus could not condemn them, why should the Pharisees be critical? As He stated in Matthew 12:8, "For the Son of man is Lord even of the sabbath day."

Jesus further analyzed the basic problem of the Pharisees, however, which was that they put technical observance of the law, such as sacrificing, as more important than showing mercy. He stated that if they knew the meaning of the statement, "I will have mercy and not sacrifice" (Ho 6:6; cf. Mic 6:6-8), they would not have condemned the disciples whom the Lord pronounced "guiltless." Jesus had referred to the same thought in answering the Pharisees in Matthew 9:13. The problem was not what the disciples had done but the merciless hearts of the Pharisees.

JESUS ACCUSED OF VIOLATING THE SABBATH BY HEALING, 12:9-14

On the same Sabbath, Jesus entered the synagogue and was confronted by a man with a paralyzed hand. The Pharisees saw this as another opportunity to accuse Jesus if He would heal the man on the Sabbath, and they raised the question, "Is it lawful to heal on the sabbath days?" (12:10).

According to the parallel accounts in Mark 3:1-5 and Luke 6:6-11, Jesus asked the man with the paralyzed hand to stand before the whole assembly. In Mark and Luke,

He only raised the question as to whether it was lawful
to heal on the Sabbath, but in Matthew He used an illustration. If a sheep would fall into a pit on the Sabbath day,
would the owner not lift it out? Was a man not better than
a sheep? Jesus concluded, "Wherefore it is lawful to do
well on the sabbath days" (Mt 12:12). With this introduction, He asked the man to stretch forth his hand, and it
was made immediately well. The action infuriated the Pharisees, who had neither Scripture nor logic to refute this
miraculous work of God. In their frustration, the Pharisees
are recorded in verse 14 to have held a council as to how
they might destroy Jesus.

OTHERS HEALED ON THE SAME SABBATH, 12:15-21

Not wishing to incite the Pharisees further, Jesus then
withdrew, but multitudes followed Him, and the Scriptures
record simply, "He healed them all," at the same time instructing them not to publish the healings. This is interpreted by Matthew as fulfilling Isaiah 42:1-3, which Matthew
quotes. In Matthew 12:21, Matthew summarizes the meaning, "And in his name shall the Gentiles trust," which is
an interpretive conclusion of the entire passage.

PHARISEES ACCUSE JESUS OF HEALING BY DEMONIC POWER, 12:22-37

Following the many miracles already recorded, an outstanding case of need was presented to the crowd in one
who was demon possessed and both blind and dumb. Such
a pitiful person should have aroused the sympathy even
of the Pharisees. When Jesus, with amazing power, healed
him so that he could both speak and see, and by inference
cast out the demon, it brought amazement to the people,
and they said, "Is not this the son of David?" (v. 23).

The Pharisees countered by accusing Him of casting out
demons by Beelzebub, the prince of demons. Beelzebub was
actually a heathen deity, referred to earlier by Jesus in
Matthew 10:25, and one supposedly in authority over the
demons.

Jesus answered the Pharisees by showing the illogic of their statement. He pointed out that this would be a kingdom divided against itself. It would be Satan casting out Satan. If the casting out of demons is by Beelzebub, then by whom did the Pharisees who were exorcists cast out demons? The point was that only the power of God or someone under the power of God could accomplish this.

Jesus then drove home His point. If demons have been actually cast out, then it must have been by the Spirit of God, and then, in the person of Christ, the kingdom of God had come unto them. One could not enter the demonic realm victoriously unless he first had bound the strong man (v. 29). The Pharisees had to make a choice. They were either with Jesus or against Him. But if they were against Him, they were guilty of blasphemy against the Holy Spirit, a sin which by its nature is not forgiven (vv. 31-32).

There has been much misunderstanding about blasphemy against the Holy Spirit. Here it is properly defined as attributing to Satan what is accomplished by the power of God. Such a sin is not unpardonable in itself, but rather because it rejects the person and work of the Holy Spirit, without whom repentance and restoration are impossible. As far as it applies today, it is not the thought that one seeking pardon will not find it, but rather that one who rejects the Holy Spirit will not seek pardon. It is the ultimate in unbelief. In verse 33, He points out that a good tree brings forth good fruit and a bad tree brings forth bad fruit. They must judge Him on the basis of His works.

The unbelief of the Pharisees calls forth the strongest language. Christ addressed them, "generation of vipers," or poisonous snakes. He declared that they were evil and therefore could not speak good and warned them that as unbelievers, every idle word they speak will be called to account on the day of judgment. He concluded in Matthew 12:37, "For by thy words thou shalt be justified, and by thy words thou shalt be condemned." This was addressed to the unsaved Pharisees, not to Christians who were justified by faith and whose sins had been forgiven.

UNBELIEVING PHARISEES SEEK A SIGN, 12:38-45

Having thus been challenged to face the evidence that Jesus was indeed what He claimed to be, the Pharisees, in their unbelief, asked for a spectacular sign. Jesus answered them in an unsparing indictment. He declared "An evil and adulterous generation seeketh after a sign; and there shall no sign be given to it, but the sign of the prophet Jonas" (v. 39). He then recited the facts of the experience of Jonah, how he was three days and three nights in the great fish, and He described this as a prophetic incident, anticipating that the Son of Man will be three days and three nights in the heart of the earth. In other words, He was predicting His death and resurrection as the supreme sign for those seeking evidence of His claims. In the incident of Jonah, the men of Nineveh repented, even though they were unbelieving Gentiles. Here Jesus, who was far greater than Jonah, was before His own people, and they would not believe.

Jesus cited another illustration of the queen of the south who heard and believed in the wisdom of Solomon (1 Ki 10:1-13). Now a greater than Solomon was here, and the Jews would not believe. Again the illustration is of belief among the Gentiles which would emphasize the point He was making to the Pharisees.

In concluding His talk with the Pharisees, Jesus pointed out the emptiness of religion without the supernatural power of God. In Matthew 12:43-45, He described the case of a man who, delivered of an unclean spirit or demon, proceeded to set his life in order religiously. His house, however, although swept and garnished, was empty. By this it is meant that the demons had left him and permitted some improvement in his religious life, but that he was far short of being born again and renewed by the Spirit of God. The reference to the evil spirit walking through "dry places" is based on the idea that the desert is the haunt of demons.[3] The evil spirit, upon returning, brought seven other spirits and dwelt in the man, so that his last state was worse than his first. Jesus stated that, in like manner, the wicked generation of the Pharisees will experience the emptiness of their religion, which will lead to greater spiritual bondage.

CENTRAL PLACE OF TRUE DISCIPLESHIP, 12:46-50

As Jesus was concluding His controversy with the Pharisees, word came to Him that His mother and brothers were outside and desired to speak to Him. Jesus used the occasion to emphasize the need of discipleship above all earthly relationships. He dramatically asked, "Who is my mother? and who are my brethren?" Then, according to verse 49, "He stretched forth his hand toward his disciples, and said, behold my mother and my brethren!" He went on, in the concluding verse of the chapter, to define a disciple as one who does the will of His Father in heaven. "The same," Jesus declared, "is my brother, and sister, and mother." Coming at the conclusion of this chapter, it emphasizes the futility of mere religion or family relationships. Rather, the important issue was to be a disciple and to do the will of God. Although Jesus was at all times courteous to His mother, He never attributed to her any special qualities (cf. Jn 2:4). There is nothing in the Scripture to justify the exaltation of Mary to the role of a mediator between God and man.

PART SIX

THE PERIOD BETWEEN
THE TWO ADVENTS

13

The Mysteries of
the Kingdom

INTRODUCTION

THE THIRTEENTH CHAPTER of Matthew marks a new division in the gospel, in which Jesus addresses Himself to the problem of what will occur when He goes back to heaven as the rejected King. The gospel of Matthew began with the proofs that Jesus was indeed the promised Son who would reign on the throne of David (chap. 1), supported by the visit of the wise men and the early ministry of John the Baptist (chaps. 2-3). After His temptation, Jesus presented the principles of His coming kingdom in the Sermon on the Mount (chaps. 5-7), emphasizing spiritual and moral principles that govern the kingdom of God, but especially as these applied to the prophesied kingdom on earth, which the Messiah-King was to bring when He came. The Sermon on the Mount accordingly contained timeless truths always applicable, some truths that were immediately applicable to Christ's day on earth, and some truths that were to have their fulfillment in the millennial kingdom.

Following the presentation of the principles of the kingdom, in Matthew 8-10, the miracles which served as the prophesied credentials of the King were itemized. It becomes apparent, however, that increasingly, the Jews were rejecting these evidences that Jesus was indeed their Messiah and prophesied King.

Accordingly, in chapter 11, His rejection and the postponement of the kingdom were anticipated. In most severe language, Jesus itemized their sinful rejection with severe indictment upon the cities where His mighty works were done. Chapter 11 closed with an invitation to individual believers to come unto Him for rest. The further rejection of Jesus is recorded in chapter 12, climaxing in the charge of the Pharisees that He performed His miracles in the power of the devil. Jesus likened the state of His wicked generation to a man possessed of eight evil spirits (12:45).

With this as a background, chapter 13 faces the question, What will happen when the rejected king goes back to heaven and the kingdom promised is postponed until His second coming? The concept of a kingdom postponed must be understood as a postponement from the human side and not from the divine, as obviously God's plans do not change. It may be compared to the situation at Kadesh-Barnea, when the children of Israel, bound for the promised land, because of unbelief, had their entrance postponed for forty years. If they had believed God, they might have entered the land immediately.

What is contingent from the human standpoint, however, is always planned from the divine standpoint. The rejection of Christ by His own people and His subsequent death and resurrection were absolutely essential to God's program. Humanly speaking, the kingdom, instead of being brought in immediately, was postponed. From the divine viewpoint, the plan always included what actually happened. The human responsibility remains, however, and the rejection of the kingdom from this standpoint caused the postponement of the promised kingdom on earth.

This chapter, accordingly, does not only introduce a new subject and a new approach but also involves a new method of teaching, namely that of parables. While many of the illustrations which Christ used were designed to make plain the truth, parables were intended to reveal the truth only to believers and required explanation in order to understand them. In a sense, they were riddles which required a key, but supplied with the key, the truth became prophetically eloquent.

As Tasker expresses it, "Jesus deliberately adopted the parabolic method of teaching at a particular stage in His ministry for the purpose of withholding further truth about Himself and the kingdom of heaven from the crowds, who had proved themselves to be deaf to His claims and irresponsive to His demands . . . From now onwards, when addressing the unbelieving multitude, He speaks only in parables (34), which He interprets to His disciples in private."[1]

In this chapter are presented in the seven parables the mysteries of the kingdom. Only Matthew records seven parables. The parables of the sower and mustard seed are found in Mark 4:1-9, 13-20, 30-32, and in Luke 8:5-15. The parable of the leaven is found in Luke 13:20-21. The other four parables are only in Matthew. The parables are designed to reveal the mysteries of the kingdom, that is, the present age.

Mysteries, a word used of secret rites of various religious cults, refers to truth that was not revealed in the Old Testament but is revealed in the New Testament. More than a dozen such truths are revealed in the New Testament, all following the basic definition of Colossians 1:26, which defines a mystery as that "which hath been hid from ages and from generations, but now is made manifest to his saints." A mystery truth, accordingly, has two elements. First, it has to be hidden in the Old Testament and not revealed there. Second, it has to be revealed in the New Testament. It is not necessarily a reference to a truth difficult to understand, but rather to truths that can be understood only on the basis of divine revelation.

The Old Testament reveals, in clear terms, the earthly reign of Christ when He comes as King to reign on the throne of David (which truths are not mysteries). Matthew 13 introduces a different form of the kingdom, namely the present spiritual reign of the King during the period He is physically absent from the earth, prior to His second coming. The mysteries of the kingdom, accordingly, deal with the period between the first and second advent of Christ and not the millennial kingdom which will follow the second coming.

PARABLE OF THE SOWER, 13:1-23

The scene of this prophetic sermon of Jesus was the Sea

of Galilee. Because of the great multitudes thronging the
shores, Jesus went into a small boat a short distance from
the shore, and by this means, was able to command a view
of the entire multitude. While they stood, He sat in the
boat in the role of a religious teacher.

The first paragraph does not have the precise formula
of the later paragraphs, "The kingdom of heaven is likened
unto," but is, rather, an introductory parable, serving as a
basis for all that follows. In the parable, a sower went forth
to sow, sowing his seed upon four kinds of earth. Although
sometimes the ground was prepared by plowing, in other
cases, seed would be sown with no preparation whatever,
which seems to be the case in this parable. Some of the
seed fell on the wayside (i.e., the hard-beaten path), where
there was no receptivity, and fowls came and devoured it.
Some seed fell on the second type of soil defined as "stony
places" (v. 5). This refers to stony ground with sufficient
soil to allow the seed to sprout but with insufficient depth
to allow adequate roots. Beginning to grow, the new plants
withered in the heat of the sun.

Some seed fell among thorns, that is, soil that was good
enough but full of weeds. Here, the competition of the
thorns was too much, and the young plants were choked
out. The fourth soil receiving the seed was described as
"good ground" (v. 8), bringing forth seed up to one hundredfold. In each case, the seed is the same, but the difference is in the receptivity of the soil.

In the conclusion of His presentation of the parable of
the sower, Jesus made the challenge, "Who hath ears to
hear, let him hear" (v. 9). Later, after Christ had sent the
multitude away (v. 36), the disciples came to Him to ask
why He spoke unto them in parables. His explanation was
that it was proper for them, His disciples, to know the mysteries of the kingdom of heaven, but to the people who were
largely unbelieving, it was not. Christ declared the principle,
"For whosoever hath, to him shall be given, and he shall
have more abundance: but whosoever hath not, from him
shall be taken away even that he hath" (v. 12). Accordingly, Christ stated that He spoke in parables that the un-

believers might not understand and would thereby fulfill the prophecy of Isaiah 6:9-10, that the people would not hear the message. His disciples, however, were to be blessed by this new revelation which was not revealed to the prophets and the righteous men of old but was now being revealed to them (Mt 13:17). This confirms the previous definition of a mystery as a truth not revealed in the Old Testament but now revealed in the New Testament.

Some have found it difficult to harmonize the concept that truth is revealed in such a way that unbelievers cannot understand it. The point is that there is a long background of unbelief and disregard of previous revelation. Accordingly, when additional revelation is given to believers, it is couched in terms that only they will understand. In a sense, unbelievers have sinned away their day of opportunity. It is in keeping with the principle that darkness follows light rejected.

In Matthew 13:18-23, the parable of the sower is explained. The birds that devoured the seed by the wayside represented satanic influence, which supports the hardness of the heart that rejects the message. The seed on shallow ground pictured superficial reception of the Word, where the Word does not bear fruit. The seed among thorns depicted "the care of this world, and the deceitfulness of riches" which choke the Word and make it unfruitful (v. 22). The seed on the good ground, which brings forth fruit up to an hundredfold, represented the one who not only hears the Word but understands it and lets it bring forth its fruit abundantly.

As this parable makes plain, there is no anticipating in the present age that there will be universal reception of the truth, as postmillenarians teach. Most of those who hear the message of the kingdom will reject it. Some, however, will receive the message, cherish it in their heart, and believe in the truth of the kingdom. This first parable establishes the basic character of the present age, awaiting the return of the rejected King. The age will include some who believe, many who will not believe.

PARABLE OF THE TARES, 13:24-30; 36-43

In the second parable, Jesus likewise used the figure of a sower, but this time, dealt with the character of the seed rather than its reception. In this parable, the sower sowed the good seed, described as wheat, and the enemy sowed tares, referring to rye grass, the darnel which often grows up with the wheat. One side effect of the darnel seed is that it is subject to a parasite fungus, which infects seed and is poisonous to both men and beasts.[2]

In the parable, when the servants asked whether they should uproot the tares, the instruction was to let both go to the harvest time, because uprooting the tares would also uproot the wheat. Accordingly, Jesus stated, "Let both grow together until the harvest" (v. 30). As Spurgeon comments, "Magistrates and churches may remove the openly wicked from their society; the outwardly good who are unworldly worthless they must leave; for the judging of hearts is beyond their sphere."[3] At the harvest, the tares are gathered first, then the wheat is gathered into the barn.

In the interpretation in Matthew 13:36-43, when the disciples later privately asked Jesus concerning the meaning of this parable, He identified the field as the world, the sower as the Son of man who sowed the good seed, the enemy as the devil who sowed the tares. The good seeds represented the children of the kingdom, and the tares the children of the wicked one, that is, the devil. The reapers were identified as the angels; the time of the harvest was "the end of this world," or more properly translated, "the consummation of this age." The judgment was described as a work of the angels gathering out of the kingdom of the Son of man any that would offend, and casting them into a furnace of fire. The judgment is parallel to that described in Matthew 25:31-46, where the sheep are separated from the goats.

Posttribulationists have made much of the order of the judgment described in 13:30, that is, that the tares are gathered first and that later the wheat is gathered into the barn. This is used as an argument for posttribulationism, or the teaching that the rapture occurs in connection with the establishment of the kingdom. This argument, however, is invalid.

Matthew 13 is not dealing specifically with the church age, the period between Pentecost and the rapture, but with the entire period of the kingdom in its mystery form, that is, the period between the first and second advents, during which the King is absent and which includes the period between the rapture and the second coming. The rapture is not in view at all. As far as the order of events is concerned, in the seventh parable, where the good and bad fish are separated, the order is reversed with the good gathered first.

A reasonable conclusion is that the order of events is indeed the destruction of the wicked and the ushering of the righteous to the millennial kingdom. However, both are simultaneous events in fulfillment, although actually the tares are destroyed before the kingdom is brought in fully.

The second parable, as a whole, makes clear the dual line of development within the sphere of profession, with the true believer not clearly identified until the time of judgment. This parable is not a picture of the universal triumph of the gospel, as the postmillennialists teach; neither is it a fulfillment of an earthly reign where Christ is supreme on earth. Rather it is the period before the return of the King, who was rejected in His first coming.

PARABLE OF THE MUSTARD SEED, 13:31-32

In this parable, the kingdom of heaven was compared to the small mustard seed which became such a large plant that birds were able to lodge in its branches. This mustard plant is a species different than the common one used as a condiment. Although left without interpretation, it anticipated that Christendom as a sphere of profession will grow rapidly from a small beginning to an organization with great power and wealth. While the plant included both true believers and those who professed to believe, the mustard plant was distinguished from the birds lodging in its branches which were unbelievers (cf. Dan 4:20-22).

Some have noted that the mustard seed described as "the

least of all seeds" is not actually the smallest seed, and that this is an error in the Scriptures. The answer is twofold. The Greek word translated "smallest" (*mikroteron*) is actually a comparative and should be translated "smaller," as it is in the *New English Bible* and in the *New American Standard Bible*. The thought is that it is "very small." Second, as Lenski points out, "Jesus is speaking of the seeds that were ordinarily planted in ancient gardens, hence the remark that botanists know about many seeds that are still smaller is pointless."[4]

The parable of the mustard seed is also found in Mark 4, where it is related to the kingdom of God. This has supported the view of many that the kingdom of God and the kingdom of heaven are identical, as they are occasionally found in parallel passages. There is some indication in Scripture, however, that the kingdom of heaven emphasizes the professing character of the kingdom as including unbelievers who look like believers, as illustrated in the tares, in contrast to the kingdom of God, containing only true believers. It is significant that the kingdom of God is not compared to the second parable, that of the wheat and the tares, as those in the kingdom of God are genuine believers. Putting Matthew and Mark together, the conclusion can be reached that both the number of true believers (the kingdom of God) as well as the sphere of profession in the present age (the kingdom of heaven) will grow rapidly. This is in contrast to the future millennial kingdom, which Christ will bring at His second coming, which will begin abruptly as a worldwide kingdom, rather than as a product of gradual growth.

PARABLE OF THE LEAVEN, 13:33-35

In this parable, the kingdom of heaven is likened unto leaven hidden in meal (cf. Lk 13:20-21). In biblical times, it was customary to retain a small portion of leavened dough from each batch to mix in with the next batch of dough, thereby leavening the new dough. In modern times, yeast is usually used. What does the leaven represent? Postmillenarians and amillenarians, like Lenski, usually assume dogmatically that leaven cannot represent evil in this parable, although it is universally used to represent evil in both the Old and New Testaments. Lenski states, for instance, "It is impossible to use leaven in this sense when picturing the kingdom."[5] If the kingdom was all good, this would be true, but the other parables make clear that there are tares among the wheat, bad fish as well as good fish in the net. The kingdom includes both good and evil. To make the leaven synonymous with the gospel as a permeating and ameliorating principle in the world may coincide with postmillenialism but does not coincide with this chapter in its presentation of the present age. It is more evident than ever in the last third of the twentieth century that the gospel has not permeated the whole world and that evil tends to permeate the entire professing church, which is exactly what Matthew 13 teaches.

In the Old Testament, leaven is used consistently to represent evil. In sacrifices, which represent Jesus Christ, such as the unleavened bread on the table of shewbread, no leaven was permitted. In cases where leaven was permitted, they inevitably represented human situations, as the peace offering of Leviticus 7:11-13, and the two loaves anticipating typically the professing church, mentioned in Leviticus 23:15-18. In the New Testament, leaven was used by Christ of the externalism of the Pharisees, of the unbelief of the Sadducees, and of the worldliness of the Herodians, and in general of evil doctrine (Mt 16:6-12; Mk 8:14-21). In Paul's letters, likewise, leaven represents evil, as in I Corinthians 5:6-8 and Galatians 5:7-10.

In the parable, the meal represented that which is good, as it was made from wheat and not from tares. The professing church, however, is permeated by evil doctrine, externalism, unbelief, and worldliness, which tend to inflate the church and make it larger in appearance, even as the leaven inflates the dough but actually adds nothing of real worth. The history of the church has all too accurately fulfilled this anticipation, and the professing church in the world, large and powerful though it may be, is permeated by the leaven of evil which will be judged in the oven of divine judgment at the end of the age. The parable applying to the kingdom of heaven in its mystery form applies to the professing church which will continue in the world after the true church, the body of Christ, is caught up at the time of the rapture. To some extent, evil will extend even to the kingdom of God, which includes the body of true believers in the church as well as those who come to Christ after the rapture. As Luke 13:20-21 brings out, even true believers fall far short of perfection and can embrace to some extent worldliness, externalism, and bad doctrine.

Parable of the Treasure, 13:44

The parable of the treasure is linked with the sixth parable, the parable of the pearl, and the final parable of the good and bad fish, as three parables reflecting the divine point of view rather than the historic human point of view, which was presented in the first four parables. Like the third and fourth parable, no explanation is given, and expositors have tended to find support for their overall view of the chapter. A common interpretation, such as is advanced in Trench's work on parables, is that the man who finds the treasure is the believer who finds Christ, with the same interpretation carried over to the merchant who finds the pearl.[6] Everyone agrees that Christ is a treasure whom all the world has not discovered, but upon close examination, the interpretation is shallow and unsatisfactory.

In the parable, the man was represented as hiding the treasure and selling all he had to buy it. The facts are, of course, that a believer in Christ has nothing to offer and the treasure is not for sale. The believer does not buy a field, representing the world, in order to gain Christ. Further, upon discovery of the treasure, a believer shares it with others rather than hides it.

The key to the parable is to determine what the treasure was that was held in the field. Although the interpretation should not be dogmatically held, there is scriptural evidence that what was referred to here was none other than the nation Israel. Although Israel is an obvious factor in the world, apart from scriptural revelation, no one would recognize Israel as a treasure, and especially a treasure for which anyone would sell all that he has to buy.

Scriptural support is given for interpreting the treasure as Israel. According to Exodus 19:5, God declared to Israel, "If ye will obey my voice indeed, and keep my covenant, then ye shall be a peculiar treasure unto me above all people: for all the earth is mine." According to Psalms 135:4, "The Lord hath chosen Jacob unto himself, and Israel for his peculiar treasure."

The fact that Israel is a treasure not recognized by the world and therefore hidden is all too evident today. Even among evangelical Christians, there are those who question whether Israel is an important biblical nation today with a prophetic future. Yet as we trace the gospel narratives, it is clear that Jesus came with a special purpose of redeeming Israel, although at the same time He reconciled the world unto Himself. It was Jesus, therefore, who sold all that He had in order to buy the treasure, Israel, and to purchase it with His own blood (Phil 2:7-8; 1 Pe 1:18-19). During the present age, Israel is a hidden entity in the world, only to emerge at the end of the age as a major factor in the prophetic fulfillment leading up to the second coming of Christ.

Parable of the Pearl of Great Price, 13:45-46

In this parable, the same thought was presented as in the preceding one; only here, the pearl seemed to represent the church rather than Israel. In the world of gems, the pearl is uniquely formed organically. Its formation occurs because of an irritation in the tender side of an oyster. There is a sense in which the church was formed out of the wounds of Christ and has been made possible by His death and sacrifice.

The parable emphasized that the church has been made possible by the merchant who sold all that He had to secure the great pearl. So Christ, leaving the glory of heaven, made the supreme sacrifice of dying on the cross in order to make possible the formation of the church. The concept of the church as a living organism, composed of living stones which are added each time a believer is saved, was an apt portrayal of the formation of the true church in the present age, and made clear that this is one of the major purposes of God in the interadvent period. In the treasure and the pearl are the two major purposes of God for Israel and the church from a spiritual point of view, and His purposes for both are realized, even though there is the dual line of development of good and evil culminating in the second coming of Christ.

PARABLE OF THE DRAGNET, 13:47-50

The seventh parable, similar in many ways to the parable of the wheat and the tares, summarized the main ideas of the entire chapter. Like the first two parables, it was interpreted immediately. The kingdom of heaven was compared to a large net, described by Lenski as "the largest kind of net, weighed below with corks on top, sweeping perhaps a half mile of water."[7] Because of its large character, the net collects a multitude of different kinds of fish, described in the text as "every kind." Nets of this size were too large to empty into a boat and had to be drawn to shore. Here the fish were sorted. Those that were bad, or for any reason unusable, were cast back into the sea. The good fish were gathered into the vessel.

This familiar operation on the shores of the Sea of Galilee was compared to the judgment at the end of the age. Angels were described as separating those who are wicked from among the righteous, the wicked being described as wailing and gnashing their teeth as they were cast into the furnace of fire (Mt 13:50). The situation is parallel to the judgment of the nations in 25:31-46. The righteous who remain after the wicked are gathered out are able to enter into the kingdom. The general situation is the same as the separation of the wheat and the tares and their judgment, described in 13:41-43.

The fulfillment of the prophetic truth in this parable will occur at the second coming of Jesus Christ, when the world is judged and the kingdom instituted. It is clear from this parable, as those preceding, that the present age does not end in a postmillennial triumph, with the entire world being Christianized; neither does it fulfill the kingdom promises of the Old Testament nor does it describe the period when all nations will serve the Lord. Rather, as in preceding parables, it describes the dual line of good and evil, continuing until the time of the end when both the good and evil are judged according to their true character.

It is significant that the net representing the kingdom of heaven as a sphere of profession included all kinds, both wicked and righteous, and that the separation did not come until the end. This passage serves to distinguish the kingdom of heaven from the kingdom of God which includes only the righteous. Neither the parable of the wheat and the tares nor the parable of the good and bad fish, as related to the kingdom of God, is mentioned in the other gospels.

CONCLUDING STATEMENT ABOUT THE PARABLES, 13:51-52

At the conclusion of the parables, Jesus asked the disciples, "Have you understood all these things?" Amazingly, they replied, "Yea, Lord." It is rather obvious that they did not understand the parables, except in their general teachings. It would have required much more perspective, the clear revelation of the present age, and, to some extent, perspective of history, for them to have really understood these parables. At this time, they did not understand that there would be an age between the two advents. Christ did not challenge their assurance, however, but rather told them that if they were truly instructed in these truths, they would be able to bring out of their treasure house of truth things both new and old.

CHRIST'S FINAL VISIT TO NAZARETH, 13:53-58

After concluding His discourse at the Sea of Galilee, Christ went back to Nazareth. In His earlier visit, recorded in Luke 4:16-29, although some commended His gracious words (v. 22), others challenged His claim to be a prophet, and, when rebuked by Christ, attempted to throw Him over a cliff (vv. 23-29). In this second and last visit to Nazareth, the same rejection occurred, though this time, less violently. They recalled that He was Joseph's son and that His brothers and sisters lived among them.[8] Again, as in the earlier visit,

Christ stated, "A prophet is not without honour, save in his own country, and in his own house" (Mt 13:57). Their unbelief barred mighty works such as had occurred elsewhere. This final touch, emphasizing His rejection by His own city and His own people, was part of the larger rejection summarized in John 1:11, "He came unto his own, and his own received him not."

PART SEVEN

THE CONTINUED MINISTRY OF THE REJECTED KING

14

The Compassion of the Rejected King

EXECUTION OF JOHN THE BAPTIST, 14:1-12

THE GROWING REJECTION of Christ and His ministry, anticipated in the preceding chapter, now had its toll in the execution of John the Baptist. John had been fearless in his denunciation of Herod Antipas who was living unlawfully with Herodias, his brother Philip's wife. Herodias, a New Testament Jezebel, had plotted against Herod's first wife, the daughter of Aretas, king of Arabia, who had to flee for her life. Herodias, although a niece of Herod Antipas, began to live with him in an unlawful union.[1]

John had said plainly, "It is not lawful for thee to have her" (Mt. 14:4). For this affront to Herod and Herodias, John had been placed in prison, but Herod was restrained from doing more because he feared the reaction of the Jews who counted John as a prophet.

This did not deter Herodias, however, but she bided her time. When Herod was having a drunken feast in honor of his birthday, she had her daughter, Salome, dance before those celebrating the birthday. This pleased Herod to the point that he promised Salome anything she would ask, to half the kingdom. She, having been instructed by her mother, asked for the head of John the Baptist on a large platter, such as was used for food. Herod, although reluctant to give the order, nevertheless, under the pressure of the circumstances, commanded that it should be done. John, summoned out of his dark cell where he had had gloomy thoughts about his own future and the future of the kingdom, ended his lifework abruptly at the executioner's block, and the head was delivered to the damsel on a platter as she requested.

111

His sorrowful disciples came, claimed the body which had been thrown out as refuse, and gave it a decent burial.

For John, it meant leaving the damp castle of Machaerus, built on the cliffs east of the Dead Sea, for a sudden entrance into glory. Like many great prophets before him, he had sealed his testimony with his own blood. When the disciples came to tell Jesus, it was another evidence of the growing rejection of Jesus and His message and a stark reminder of the awfulness of sin and unbelief. Parallel references are found in Mark 6:14-29 and Luke 9:7-9.

FEEDING OF THE FIVE THOUSAND, 14:13-21

Upon hearing the tidings of John's execution, Jesus withdrew into an unpopulated place. He wanted to be alone with His disciples and desired to confer with them privately, according to Mark 6:30-31. Although Jesus was rejected by those in authority, the people were still enthusiastic followers of Jesus, and they followed Him out of many cities until they found Him. As Jesus viewed the great multitude, His heart was moved with compassion toward them both for their physical ills and their spiritual needs. All four gospels record this important incident in the life of Jesus (Mk 6:30-44; Lk 9:10-17; Jn 6:1-14). Although Matthew does not mention that He taught them, Mark 6:34 declares, "He began to teach them many things."

After a long day of teaching and healing, the disciples counseled Jesus to urge the multitude to go away that they might find food in the villages nearby. As far as the disciples were concerned, this was an easy way out. As in the case of the Samaritan woman in John 4, and in the case of the little children who were brought to Jesus in Mark 10, so here they wanted to avoid involvement in the need. But Jesus replied, "They need not depart; give ye them to eat" (Mt 14:16). The disciples, forgetting the power of Jesus to do miraculous things, protested that they had only five loaves and two fishes—enough for one person but not for five thousand.

Jesus did not argue with them, but commanded them to bring the five loaves and two fishes to Him. He then ordered the multitude to sit down in an orderly fashion on the grass, and, having the food in His hand, He broke it and gave it to the disciples to distribute. The miracle of multiplication took place, and verse 20 records, "They did all eat, and were filled." The fragments gathered in twelve baskets were far more than the boy's lunch that had been placed into the hands of Jesus at the beginning. The multitude, described as five thousand besides the women and children, had been miraculously fed.

This illuminating incident of the miraculous power of Jesus to take what little was placed in His hand and to bless it until it was sufficient for the multitude has encouraged all believing hearts. They have realized their own impotence and lack of resources, but have been encouraged by the miraculous power of God to take little and make much of it.

Matthew does not mention what is recorded in John 6:14-15, that the multitudes, impressed with this tremendous miracle, not only recognized Christ as the predicted Prophet but wanted to take Him by force and make Him a king. The multitude reasoned that with such a miraculous king who could heal the sick, raise the dead, and multiply food, they had one who had sufficient power to give them victory over the oppression of Rome. Like Moses, who gave manna from heaven and Elisha who miraculously fed a hundred men (2 Ki 4:42-44), Jesus seemed to be a great leader. This was not the way, however, in which the kingdom was to come, and their faith was a superficial confidence that came from having full stomachs. All too soon, some of them would be part of the mob crying, "Crucify him."

JESUS SAVES THE DISCIPLES IN THE STORM, 14:22-33

The disciples were undoubtedly thrilled at the enthusiasm of the multitude to make Jesus King, and it served to renew their hopes, in spite of the growing rejection, that Jesus would be victorious and that they would reign with Him in the kingdom on earth. Jesus had to impel them to get into a boat and go to the other side, somewhat against their will. Meanwhile, Jesus Himself sent the multitude away, and, in the gathering darkness, went alone to the nearby mountain to pray.

Meanwhile, the disciples, crossing the Sea of Galilee, perhaps at its northern tip, were caught in one of the sudden storms that were so characteristic of the sea, located as it was between high hills which surrounded it.[2] According to Matthew 14:24, they were tossed with waves and the wind was against them. Early in the fourth watch, probably between three and six A.M., Jesus joined them, walking across the sea to their boat. In the darkness, this was a terrifying spectacle to the disciples, who cried out with fear because they thought they were seeing a ghost.

To alleviate their fears, Jesus spoke to them, "Be of good cheer; it is I; be not afraid" (v. 27). Peter, wanting reassurance, said, "Lord, if it be thou, bid me come unto thee on the water" (v. 28). Jesus invited him to come, and Peter began to walk on the water to see Jesus. Seeing the sea lashed by the wind, he became afraid and began to sink. When he cried, "Lord, save me" (v. 30), Jesus extended His hand and, rebuking Peter, said, "O thou of little faith, wherefore didst thou doubt?" (v. 31). When they both arrived in the boat, suddenly the wind ceased. The disciples worshiped Him, bowing down before Him and exclaiming, "Of a truth thou art the Son of God" (v. 33). There is no reason to reject this outstanding miracle, except on the unsupportable assumption that miracles are impossible.

HEALING IN GENNESARET, 14:34-36

Upon landing on the other side, they came to Gennesaret, the area between Capernaum and Tiberias, northwest of the Sea of Galilee. According to John 6:24, Jesus probably landed first near Capernaum and then later, leaving Capernaum, went into the larger area of Gennesaret. His privacy was short-lived, for as soon as the people learned of His presence, they streamed out of cities from as far away as Tiberias, according to verse 23, in order to be healed. Matthew summarizes their confidence in Jesus in these words: they "besought him that they might only touch the hem of his garment: and as many as touched were made perfectly whole" (Mt 14:36). Although rejected by the leaders of Israel, Jesus still had compassion on those who put their trust in Him. In a world so wicked that it would behead a prophet like John the Baptist, and so unspiritual that it wanted to make Jesus a king by force, the compassion of Christ was yet extended to all who had genuine need. What was true of a wicked and unbelieving world in the first century is still true in the twentieth.

15

The Rejected King's
Continued Ministry of Mercy

CONTROVERSY WITH THE SCRIBES AND PHARISEES, 15:1-9

Chapter 15 runs parallel to Mark 7:1—8:9, with some variation in the details and order of the discourse. It is clear that both Matthew and Mark are summaries of incidents that were actually much longer and more detailed.

The Pharisees and scribes were incensed at the disciples because they did not follow the tradition of washing of hands when they ate bread. They drew the implication that this disregard of tradition was taught by Jesus as a matter of principle rather than as a single act of transgression of ceremonial law.[1] Mark gives a longer explanation, that what was involved was not simply the washing of hands but the washing of cups, pots, brass vessels, and tables (Mk 7:4). The traditions referred to were the *haggada* and the *halacha* which were teachings derived only in part from Scripture. The Pharisees paid more attention to these ceremonial washings than they did to the Scriptures themselves.

Jesus answered their question by another question, "Why do ye also transgress the commandment of God by your tradition?" (Mt 15:3). He then cited the fifth commandment (Ex 20:12) and Leviticus 20:9, which imposed the death penalty on one who cursed his father or his mother. He pointed out that they controverted the Scriptures in their honor of father and mother by their allowance that a child could declare something a gift or dedicated to God, and, by this means, free himself of the obligation to care for his parents. Jesus summarized this, "Thus have ye made the commandment of God of none effect by your tradition" (Mt 15:16). Jesus did not accuse the Pharisees of cursing their fathers and mothers, but He did point out that the deep-seated principle of honoring the father and mother is violated by their tradition.

After having denounced their doctrine, Jesus then turned to their own spiritual need. Addressing them as hypocrites, He quoted from Isaiah 29:13 that Israel would draw nigh to God with their lips but not their hearts. Such worship, Christ said, is empty because it teaches the commandments of man in place of the doctrines of God. The real need of the Pharisees was a changed heart, not more religious traditions.

TEACHING ON THE WICKED HEART OF MAN, 15:10-20

After having used the objection of the Pharisees as an occasion for exposing the spiritual need of man, He pointed out that the spiritual law is the opposite of the natural law, namely, that not what goes into the mouth defiles a man as the Pharisees held; rather it was that which came out of the mouth that defiled him. Matthew records that the disciples warned Jesus that He had offended the Pharisees. In answering this, Jesus pointed out that the Pharisees were blind leaders of the blind and, eventually, because of their blindness, would fall into the ditch. They were plants not planted by God the Father and would ultimately be rooted up. In the parallel account in Mark 7, these comments are omitted.

When Jesus went into the house to get away from the people, as explained in Mark 7:17, the disciples and Peter in particular (Mt 15:15) wanted Him to explain what He had said. Jesus had said, in effect, that food did not cause spiritual problems for men; it was rather what had come out of one's heart in the form of words and actions. Jesus itemized such things as "evil thoughts, murders, adulteries, fornications, thefts, false witness, blasphemies" (v. 19).

These things do not necessarily proceed from the mouth but do proceed from the heart. And these things, Jesus said, are the real problem and the real defilement of a man, not when he eats with hands which have not been ceremoniously washed. The occupation with the outward religious ceremony, instead of inner transformation of the heart, has all too often

attended all forms of religion and has plagued the church as
well as it has Judaism. How many Christians, in the history
of the church, have been executed for difference of opinion
on the meaning of the elements of the Lord's Supper or the
mode of baptism or for failure to bow to church authority?
The heart of man, which is so incurably religious, is also
incurably evil, apart from the grace of God.

WITHDRAWAL TO TYRE AND SIDON, 15:21-28

Having previously attempted to withdraw into the desert
(Mt 14:13), Jesus again departed from the multitudes which
thronged Him, going probably the longest distance away
from Jerusalem. Proceeding to the far northwest of the coast,
where Tyre and Sidon were located, He encountered a woman
of Canaan who pleaded with Him to heal her daughter who
was demon possessed. In the parallel account in Mark
7:24-30, the woman is declared to be a Greek, a Syropheni-
cian, meaning that she was a Gentile, using the more contemporary name for her nationality.

Although she addressed Jesus as "Son of David," He did
not answer her. Her repeated cries irritated the disciples,
who suggested that Jesus send her away. In an explanation
of why He had not replied, Jesus told the disciples, "I am
not sent but unto the lost sheep of the house of Israel"
(Mt 15:24). The woman, however, was not to be easily
discouraged, and bowing and worshiping before Him, she
said simply, "Lord, help me" (v. 25).

Jesus, attempting to explain to the woman His commission
to preach to the house of Israel, said, "It is not meet to take
the children's bread and to cast it to dogs" (v. 26). The
woman, in reply, pleaded that even dogs were allowed to eat
crumbs which fell from the table. In response to this faith,
Jesus said, "O woman, great is thy faith: be it unto thee
even as thou wilt" (v. 28). Matthew comments that her
daughter was healed immediately, implying that they had a
later report as to what the outcome of it was.

According to Mark, Jesus also told the woman, "The devil
is gone out of thy daughter" (Mk 7:29). Mark also goes on

to say that when the woman returned home, she found her daughter laid upon a bed and that the demon had departed (v. 30). The story well illustrates the power of prevailing prayer, when coupled with implicit faith. How much has been accomplished by prayer, and how many times children of God have not because they ask not. This incident is the only recorded miracle on this trip of Jesus, many miles away from His familiar area of ministry. Could it not be that, though she was a Gentile and even though dispensationally it was not the time for blessing among the Gentiles, Christ had come expressly to meet the need and faith of this woman? The lesson of this miracle should be to encourage Christians to fulfill the command of God to pray in the name of Christ, claiming the promise, "Whatsoever ye shall ask the Father in my name, he will give it [to] you" (Jn 16:23).

Return to Galilee, 15:29-31

Upon His return to Galilee from His short visit to the coast, the multitudes again found Jesus in the mountains. In His customary role as a Teacher, He sat down, healing the lame, the blind, the dumb, the maimed, and many others, with the people glorifying the God of Israel because of this unusual visitation. Mark 7:31-37 singles out one outstanding case of a man deaf with an impediment in speech whom Jesus healed.

Feeding of the Four Thousand, 15:32-39

The period of miracles following His return to Galilee apparently extended over three days, or at least parts of three days, and lack of food might cause people to faint on their way home.

This incident should be contrasted to the feeding of the five thousand. As Edwin W. Rice has pointed out, "Here the crowds are chiefly of Gentile or semi-Gentile origin; the five thousand were mainly Galilean Jews. Here four thousand are fed; before five thousand. Here they sat on the ground, for the summer sun had burned up the grass; before, they were on grass as it was early spring."[2] Other details also differ.

As in the feeding of the five thousand, the earlier incident, Jesus asked what the disciples had available. This time, He found that they had seven small loaves and a few fishes, about enough for one person, in contrast to five loaves and two fishes in the earlier incident. This time the disciples apparently anticipated a miracle. Again, following the preceding order of the feeding of the five thousand, the multitude was asked to sit down. Jesus gave thanks for the food and, breaking it, gave to the disciples to distribute. This time there were seven large baskets of food left over, in contrast to twelve small baskets in the feeding of the five thousand. The place was Decapolis, the opposite side of the lake from the feeding of the five thousand. Sending the multitude away with full hearts and full stomachs, Jesus went by boat to Magdala, or Magadan, an area just north of Tiberias on the west shore of the Sea of Galilee.

16

Teaching in Anticipation of Rejection

PHARISEES AND SADDUCEES SEEK A SIGN, 16:1-4

THE PHARISEES, who had questioned the disciples' disregard of their traditions, now joined by the Sadducees, sought to trap Jesus into giving them a sign from heaven. This was the first time the Pharisees and Sadducees, usually in disagreement, joined hands to trap Jesus.[1] Earlier (Mt 12:38), they had asked for a sign and were given the sign of the prophet Jonah, with its prediction of the death and resurrection of Christ. Their asking for a sign indicated that they were unimpressed by the miracles and teaching of Christ, the very credentials predicted in the Old Testament.

Jesus, in His reply, alluded to their spiritual stupidity. He pointed out that when it came to seeing signs relating to weather, they could understand; but when it came to the signs of the times, they were unable to relate intelligently to them.

In closing His comments, Christ said that a wicked and adulterous generation will not be given a sign, except the sign He had given them earlier when they had asked the same question, the sign of the prophet Jonah. Although the Pharisees were not accused of being adulterers, spiritually, they were in the same state as those who had no morality and no religion. If He had given them some miraculous sign from heaven, they would have returned to the same accusation recorded in Matthew 12:24, that it was a miracle accomplished only by the power of Satan. Faith is not given to those who are seeking support for unbelief.

121

LEAVEN OF THE PHARISEES AND SADDUCEES, 16:5-12

According to Mark 8-10, the Pharisees had questioned Him while in Dalmanutha, located on the west shore of Galilee. Upon conclusion of His exchange with the Pharisees, Jesus and His disciples again proceeded by boat to the eastern shore. When they arrived, the disciples found that they had forgotten to take bread (Mt 16:5). This would not have been so serious near Capernaum, but the eastern shore was relatively unpopulated.

Using this as an occasion for driving home a spiritual point, Jesus warned them against the leaven of the Pharisees and Sadducees. The disciples thought He was referring to the fact that they had taken no bread. Jesus rebuked them for their concern, reminding them of the feeding of the five thousand and the feeding of the four thousand. He went on to state that He was warning them of the leaven of the Pharisees and the Sadducees. Leaven here, as elsewhere in the Scripture, is a symbol of permeating evil. They were not to be influenced by the infection of unbelief derived from these religious leaders.

PREDICTION OF THE CHURCH, 16:13-20

Proceeding north and east from the Sea of Galilee, Christ came to the borders of Caesarea Philippi. There He questioned His disciples about their faith in Him, as also recorded in Mark 8:27-30 and Luke 9:18-21. He drew out of them first what others had said about Him. The response had been varied. Some people had considered Him John the Baptist raised from the dead, others Elijah the prophet, others Jeremiah or one of the other prophets. Only Matthew mentions Jeremiah.

Having prepared the way, Jesus then asked the important question, "But whom say ye that I am?" In reply, Simon Peter, frequently the spokesman for the twelve, declared, "Thou art the Christ, the Son of the living God" (Mt 16:16). Only Matthew adds the expression, "of the living God."

Pronouncing a blessing on Peter as the one who had received this revelation from God the Father, Jesus made the important announcement about the church, which was not recorded in the narratives of the other gospels. He said, "And I say also unto thee, That thou art Peter, and upon this rock I will build my church; and the gates of hell shall not prevail against it."

As *The Anchor Bible* states, there is a "play on words" in the Greek of Matthew which is not clear in the English translation.[2] Peter *(Petros)* means a loose stone. The "rock" is *petra,* a large or massive rock, like a cliff. The passage has often been cited to indicate the primacy of Peter as the first pope and the justification for the whole system built upon this concept. It is clear from other Scripture, however, that the rock upon which Christ intended to build is Himself, the solid rock, not Peter, one stone in the church composed of many living stones (1 Pe 2:5). What Jesus said, then, was, "Thou art a little rock, *and upon* this massive rock [pointing to Himself] I will build my church."

It was not Peter upon which the church would be built but upon the person to whom Peter had witnessed in his confession of faith, Christ, the Son of the living God. As Lenski puts it,

> The church does not rest on a quality found in Peter and in others like him. . . . The church is not built on the confession her members make, which would change the effect into the cause. By her confession the church shows on what she is built. She rests on the reality which Peter confessed, namely, "the Christ, the Son of the living God."[3]

Some Protestants, however, continue to interpret this as referring to Peter, not as a pope, but as a believer of the first generation, a stone upon which others can build.[4] In any case, the evidence in support of Peter as a bishop of Rome is lacking.

The dynamic words, "I will build my church," significantly are found in the gospel of Matthew, which more than the other gospels is given to the explanation of why the promised kingdom of the Old Testament was not brought in at the first coming of Christ. Here Matthew is introducing very simply the concept which is developed in the upper room discourse, John 13-17, and in the Acts and epistles, that God has a present purpose to be fulfilled in calling out His church, before the ultimate kingdom purpose is fulfilled.

The fact that Christ stated it as a future purpose indicates that His present ministry was not building the church, and, accordingly, even the mystery form of the kingdom was not precisely the same as the church.

As H. A. Ironside expresses it, "The building of this spiritual temple did not begin until after He had ascended to heaven, and the Spirit of God came as the promised Comforter."[5]

The word *build* is also significant because it implies the gradual erection of the church under the symbolism of living stones being built upon Christ, the foundation stone, as indicated in 1 Peter 2:4-8. This was to be the purpose of God *before* the second coming, in contrast to the millennial kingdom, which would follow the second coming. Against this program of God, the gates of hell (hades) will not be able to hold out. Amillenarians tend to ignore this momentous declaration. Tasker, for instance, leaves it without a comment.[6]

After this great pronouncement, Christ added, "I will give unto thee the keys of the kingdom of heaven: and whatsoever thou shalt bind on earth shall be bound in heaven: and whatsoever thou shalt loose on earth shall be loosed in heaven" (Mt 16:19). In this declaration, Christ was making clear the authority and important place of Peter as having the message which unlocks the entrance into the kingdom of heaven.

This, however, is no justification for attributing to Peter authority which was not shared with the other disciples. Although the singular is used here in the word *thee,* in 18:18, a similar pronouncement is made using *ye,* applying to all the disciples. In a sense, every believer who has the gospel has the right to declare that those who believe the gospel are loosed on earth as well as in heaven, and to declare that those who reject the gospel are bound in earth as well as in heaven.

Jesus concluded His discourse on this important theme by charging His disciples not to tell anyone that He was Jesus the Christ. This strange command for silence is probably best understood as meaning that it was not propitious at this point to spread further the claim that He was indeed the Messiah. The time would come when they would proclaim it fearlessly, even though it would lead most of them ultimately to a martyr's death.

JESUS AGAIN FORETELLS HIS DEATH AND RESURRECTION, 16:21-23

In anticipation of His ultimate rejection, Jesus repeated here earlier warnings concerning His death and coming resurrection. Mark 8:31-33 and Luke 9:22 refer to the same incident. Peter, having risen to great heights of faith in the preceding context, then demonstrated his lack of understanding by rebuking Jesus. In contrast to Christ's commendation of Peter, in Matthew 16:17-18, Jesus here rebuked Peter, "Get thee behind me, Satan: thou art an offence unto me: for thou savourest not the things that be of God, but those that be of men." The problem here was lack of spiritual discernment so common to man but not in keeping with Peter's place of leadership among the disciples. Like many modern readers of the Bible, Peter did not want to accept what did not agree with his hopes and ambitions. The disciples who had been led to faith in the person of Christ were not yet prepared to accept His work on the cross.

Earlier, Jesus had spoken of this in veiled language, as when He predicted that if the Jews destroyed the temple, He would raise it again in three days (Jn 2:18-22). This had occurred two years before. To Nicodemus, who came with his questions, in John 3, Jesus had said that He had to be lifted up, even as the serpent in the wilderness, in order to save those who believed in Him (vv. 14-18). In His interchange with the Pharisees, in Matthew 12:38-41, He had indicated that He would spend three days and nights in the heart of the earth. The same thought had been repeated in

Matthew 16:4. Now, however, the time had come to speak plainly. Their faith in Him would have to be more than confidence that He was the Messiah of Israel. They would also have to believe that He was the Lamb of God, who had come to take away this sin of the world.

COST AND REWARD OF DISCIPLESHIP, 16:24-28

After introducing the fact of His death, Jesus proceeded to teach His disciples the basic principles of discipleship. Parallel accounts are found in Mark 8:34-38 and Luke 9:23-26. He had taught them earlier on the same subject (Mt 10:21-42). Discipleship would not immediately fulfill glorious expectations of reigning with Christ in His kingdom or being in places of power and influence. The road to glory is a road of suffering, He taught them. It is only by losing one's life that one is able to save it. The principles of spiritual triumph differ from the principles of worldly triumph. Negatively, one must deny himself; positively, he must take up his cross and follow Jesus.

As the road to triumph differs for a disciple, so also does the reward. For the world, there is immediate gain but ultimate loss: for the disciple, there is immediate loss but ultimate gain. As Jesus pointed out, ultimately the man who loses his own soul in the process of gaining the whole world is exchanging his future glory for a temporary reward.

Reaching forward prophetically to the time of His second coming, Jesus declared, "Then he shall reward every man according to his works" (16:27). This applies both to the lost soul and to the one who is saved. Having prophetically reached out to the consummation, He then made the present application in the closing verse of chapter 16, "There be some standing here, which shall not taste of death, till they see the Son of man coming in his kingdom." Jesus was not saying, as some have construed it, that the second coming would occur before those of His generation tasted death. He was introducing, rather, the transfiguration of chapter 17, which anticipated, in vision, the glory of the Son of man coming in His kingdom.

Taken as a whole, chapter 16 is symbolic of the broad Christian point of view of life, with its suffering and rejection by the world, the opposition of unbelief, the testing of being a disciple now, and the promise of future glory and blessing. After the cross would come the glory of the resurrection and the coming kingdom. While there are many present blessings in being a believer, the best is yet ahead.

17

The Coming Kingdom After His Suffering and Death

TRANSFIGURATION, 17:1-9

SIX DAYS after Peter's notable confession, recorded in chapter 16, Jesus took Peter, James, and John, the inner circle, to a high mountain, apart from the other disciples (cf. Mk 9:2-13; Lk 9:28-36). Many believe this to be Mt. Hermon,[1] north of Caesarea Philippi, but Matthew does not give the name of the mountain, nor does Mark or Luke.

Matthew gives the most complete detailed account of the transfiguration, showing that he is not as dependent upon Mark's gospel as some have taught. Luke relates that the event occurred "about eight days" after Peter's confession (Lk 9:28), meaning a week. There is no contradiction between the accounts. Luke also mentions that Jesus was praying and the disciples were sleeping when the transfiguration took place, and suddenly, the face of Christ shone as the sun, and His raiment also took on a supernatural light. Mark states that His raiment was "exceeding white as snow" (Mk 9:3), and Luke mentions especially that "the fashion of his countenance was altered" (Lk 9:29). In determining the nature of the transfiguration, it is sufficient to conclude that it was a real and supernatural revelation of the glory of God, not just an appearance or a theophany.

As Jesus was transfigured before His disciples, they were abruptly awakened and, wide-awake, saw Moses and Elijah talking with Jesus. Luke says that they were discussing the coming death of Jesus, which would be accomplished at Jerusalem (Lk 9:31). Attempting to do something about this, Peter, responding to the situation although he had not been addressed, said to Jesus, "Lord it is good for us to be here: if thou wilt, let us make here three tabernacles [tents]; one for thee, and one for Moses, and one for Elias" (Mt 17:4). Both Mark and Luke comment that Peter did not know what he was saying, as it was not a sensible proposition.

The answer to his suggestion, however, was a bright cloud which overshadowed all of them, and out of the cloud came a voice of God the Father, "This is my beloved Son, in whom I am well pleased; hear ye him" (17:5). Matthew alone records that, in response to this heavenly vision and command, they fell on their faces and were very much afraid. Jesus commanded them, however, to arise and stop being afraid, and with this assurance, when they lifted up their eyes, Moses and Elijah as well as the cloud had disappeared, and Jesus was restored to normal appearance.

As they were coming down the mountain to rejoin the other disciples, Jesus instructed them to tell no one of the vision until after His resurrection. Obviously, to tell of this vision would have only aggravated the problem of the people who wanted to make Jesus King by force.

What is the meaning of the transfiguration? The Scriptures do not provide an immediate commentary on the purpose of the transfiguration. W. A. Criswell suggests that the purpose was to encourage Jesus in view of His coming death, as well as the disciples in the trials which they would face.[2] Probably the disciples needed far more than Jesus' spoken assurances to offset the frequent references to His death, which they could not fit into their concept of the Lord's future program. That it left an indelible effect upon the disciples is clear from 2 Peter 1:16-18, where Peter refers to it, and in John 1:14, where John mentions it. It was a dramatic and reassuring experience that no matter what happened, the glory of the kingdom was still ahead.

Numerous questions can be raised about the incident. Why were Moses and Elias, or Elijah, selected? Probably the best answer, as Lenski suggests, is that Moses was the greatest lawgiver of the Old Testament and Elijah was the first of the great prophets.[3] It is also true that Moses represents those who, through death and resurrection, will be in glory, and Elijah represents those who will be in glory without dying. The fact that they both have bodies gives some support to the idea of an intermediate body in heaven, prior to the day of resurrection or translation, although Lenski brushes this aside as not being taught in the passage.[4]

The selection of Peter, James, and John, rather than all the disciples, was appropriate, following the example of Moses, who, when he went up into the holy mountain, took with him Aaron, Nadab, and Abihu (Ex 24:1). The transfiguration of Christ, however, far exceeded the glory which Moses experienced. While the companions of Moses, including the seventy elders, apparently saw the glory of God, none of them were permitted to accompany Moses when he went up into the mountain to receive the law. The disciples, in the transfiguration of Jesus, were witnesses of the entire transaction.

Taken as a whole, the transfiguration was the fulfillment of Matthew 16:28, where they had been promised that they would see the Son of man coming in His kingdom. The transfiguration was the prophetic view of the glorious Christ.

QUESTION ABOUT ELIJAH, 17:10-13

The appearance of Elijah on the mount reminded the disciples of a problem they had with the prediction of the coming of Elijah before the day of the Lord (Mal 4:5-6). They now raised this question, "Why then say the scribes that Elias must first come?" (Mt 17:10). As Lenski observes, "It was the popular expectation that Elijah would first teach the Jews, settle all their disputed questions, again give them the pot of manna and Aaron's rod that blossomed, etc."[5]

In His answer, Jesus acknowledged that the scribes had correctly understood that Elijah was related to the restoration of Israel. Jesus solved the problem by affirming that Elijah had already come and that the scribes had not recognized him. The disciples understood this to be a reference to John the Baptist (cf. Mal 3:1; Mt 11:14; Lk 1:17). Scholars differ as to whether John the Baptist completely fulfilled the prophecy of Elijah, or whether a future appearance of Elijah is necessary. The theory of a yet future appearance of Elijah is connected with the view that he is one of the two witnesses in Revelation 11.[6] The evidence that John the Baptist at least in part fulfilled the prophecy of Elijah is clear, but a future appearance of Elijah is debatable.

HEALING OF THE DEMON-POSSESSED CHILD, 17:14-21

As also recorded in Mark 9:14-29 and Luke 9:37-43, upon the return to the valley, Jesus encountered the other nine disciples in trouble. A child had been brought, severely afflicted with epilepsy caused by demon possession. The expression that he was a "lunatick" is often understood as indicating that he was epileptic on the basis of the symptoms, although he may have also had mental unbalance, as Morgan believes.[7] The case was presented to Jesus by his father, who, kneeling before Jesus, pleaded mercy for his son, whom the disciples could not cure. The incident, no doubt, had been embarrassing to the nine disciples and may have provoked ridicule of the crowd.

The failure of the disciples moved Jesus to say, "O faithless and perverse generation, how long shall I be with you? how long shall I suffer you? bring him hither to me" (Mt 17:17). Although addressed generally to the generation, it obviously was a rebuke to the nine disciples.

When the child was brought to Jesus, the devil was cast out and the child was cured immediately. Mark 9:20-26 indicates that there was an exchange of conversation between Jesus and the father, in which it was brought out that the child had had this difficulty ever since he was small, and sometimes it caused him to fall into fire or into the water. Jesus, addressing the father, said, "If thou canst believe, all things are possible to him that believeth" (Mk 9:23). The father, in response, cried out, "Lord, I believe; help thou mine unbelief" (v. 24). Even as Jesus was talking, the child "fell on the ground, and wallowed foaming" (v. 20). The situation was attracting a crowd, and Jesus immediately cast out the spirit, according to verse 25. It left the child as one dead, and Jesus took him by the hand and lifted him up (vv. 26-27).

Later, as Mark 9:28 indicates, when they had returned to the house, the disciples asked why they could not cast out the demon. Jesus, in reply, made clear to them that their problem was not the demon or the child but their own unbelief. To the disciples, He said, "If ye have faith as a grain of mustard seed, ye shall say unto this mountain, remove hence to yonder place; and it shall remove; and nothing shall be impossible unto you" (Mt 17:20). Jesus added, however, "Howbeit this kind goeth not out but by prayer and fasting" (v. 21). What Jesus could accomplish in a word, the disciples needed to accomplish through prayer and fasting.

The lessons of this incident are obvious. It is not the greatness of the problem that is the difficulty; it is the lack of faith on the part of believers. How quickly Jesus responded to the simple and sincere cry of the father of the child, "Lord, I believe; help thou mine unbelief" (Mk 9:24).

ANNOUNCEMENT OF CHRIST'S DEATH AND RESURRECTION REPEATED, 17:22-23

With the approaching feast, which would be the time that Jesus would be crucified, He again reaffirmed not only that He would die and be raised, but that He would be betrayed by His friends into the hands of His enemies (cf. Mk 9:30-32; Lk 9:43-45). This time, the disciples did not raise objections, but the Scriptures record, "And they were exceeding sorry" (Mt 17:23). Morgan observes that their sorrow arose not from sympathy but from their lack of understanding of both His death and resurrection.[8] Tasker thinks the sorrow is because of the assertion that Jesus would be "betrayed."[9] The lengthening shadow of the cross is beginning to stretch over the incidents that were to lead Jesus to Jerusalem.

PROBLEM OF TRIBUTE, 17:24-27

Following these incidents, they came to Capernaum for what would be the last visit there before He went to Jerusalem to die. The tax collectors, who were collecting the temple tax, approached Peter because neither he nor Jesus had paid the tax. Matthew alone records this incident. The custom was based on the law which required every Israelite, above twenty years of age, to pay a half shekel in the support of the temple (cf. Ex 30:13-14; 2 Ki 12:4; 2 Ch 24:6; Neh 10:32). It was normal to have this tax collected just before the Passover. Peter had assured the tax collector that his Master would pay the tribute.

Before Peter could talk to Jesus about it, Jesus anticipated the question and asked him, "What thinketh thou, Simon? of whom do the kings of the earth take custom or tribute? of their own children, or of strangers?" (Mt 17:25). Peter replied that taxes were collected of strangers not of children.

Jesus, having made His point that Jesus and His disciples should not have to pay tax, nevertheless, instructed Peter to cast a hook into the sea, pick up the first fish that came, and open its mouth. He would find a piece of money which he could take to pay the tribute tax (v. 27). Although many have tried to explain away this incident because Matthew does not go on to complete the story, it seems clear that Peter caught the fish with the money in its mouth and paid the tax. According to Mark 12:13-17, the Pharisees were especially desirous to catch Jesus in breaking the law of the tribute. Jesus, at this point as He was facing Jerusalem, did not want to make a small issue important.

18

Teachings Concerning Greatness and Forgiveness

Sermon on the Little Child, 18:1-14

THE DISCIPLES HAD GATHERED in the home which Jesus had established in Capernaum (Mt 17:24; Mk 9:33). The incident that followed is recorded also in Mark 9:33-50 and Luke 9:46-50. As the disciples gathered, the question was raised, "Who is the greatest in the kingdom of heaven?" (Mt 18:1). According to Mark 9:33, Jesus had raised the question, "What was it that ye disputed among yourselves by the way?" Apparently, they did not answer immediately, for Mark 9:34 states, "But they held their peace: for by the way they had disputed among themselves, who should be the greatest." Breaking the awkward silence, apparently one of the disciples asked the question recorded in Matthew 18:1. As Ironside says, "It is a question that no truly noble soul would ever ask."[1]

In answer to their question, Jesus called a little child to Him, possibly a neighborhood child whom He knew well. When the disciples observed the little child standing in their midst, Jesus then took the child in His arms (Mk 9:36) and said to the disciples, "Verily I say unto you, Except ye be converted, and become as little children, ye shall not enter into the kingdom of heaven. Whosoever therefore shall humble himself as this little child, the same is greatest in the kingdom of heaven" (Mt 18:3-4).

Undoubtedly, the disciples had been unduly concerned about their status in the coming kingdom. It is clear that they were still anticipating an earthly kingdom, in which Jesus would be the King and they would be His privileged servants. In asking the question concerning who would be the greatest, they did not mean that one of their number should have charge over the others, but rather that probably several of them should take precedence. Jesus had previously singled out Peter, James, and John, as in Matthew 17:1, for special honor. What would the role of each of the disciples be?

Jesus, in effect, was saying that they were asking the wrong question. They should have been asking, How can I best serve the King? rather than, How can I best serve myself? The child in the arms of Jesus was a graphic illustration of loving trust, immediate obedience in coming to the arms of Christ, and in seeking only the position of being loved. True greatness involved taking an attitude of unpretentious humility instead of seeking a position of power. These were great lessons for the disciples to learn.

Jesus used the occasion, however, to speak of the importance of human personality, as illustrated in the child who has no position or wealth and no power. Instead of seeking greatness in the kingdom, the disciples should be seeking how they can serve ordinary human beings, such as this child. Jesus stated that if they received a child in His name, it signified that they were in a proper relationship of faith in Christ Himself.

These teachings of Jesus were in sharp contrast to that which was popular in the heathen world, where children were often used as human sacrifices and often suffered cruelty and neglect. The disciples, accordingly, were warned not to offend a child. It would be better to be drowned in the deep sea with a millstone around one's neck than to offend a little one. It would be better to have a hand or foot cut off or an eye plucked out than to offend one of these, especially in spiritual things.

Jesus concluded His exhortation in 18:10, "Take heed that ye despise not one of these little ones; for I say unto you, That in heaven their angels do always behold the face of my Father which is in heaven." The Scriptures do not teach that each child has a particular angel, but apparently, angels are assigned the care of children in general. These angels have immediate access to God the Father. Some have suggested the possibility that *angels* refers to the spirits of children who have died.[2] In either case, however, the importance that God gives to the welfare of children is clearly taught. As Criswell expresses it, "God sees in the lowliest believer such value that He will take infinite pains to save him."[3]

The passage continues in verse 11, "For the Son of man is come to save that which was lost." Most manuscripts omit verse 11, and many regard it as inserted from Luke 19:10. Whether or not it was in Matthew's original text, it is, of course, true.

To illustrate the importance of one child, Jesus used a shepherd who has a hundred sheep. If one goes astray, he does not argue that one out of a hundred is unimportant, but rather leaves the ninety and nine and seeks the lost sheep. When he finds the sheep, he rejoices over it more than over the continued safety of the ninety and nine. If a shepherd has such regard for one sheep, how much more regard does God the Father have for one little one? The statement of Matthew 18:14 summarizes the teaching, "Even so it is not the will of your Father which is in heaven, that one of these little ones should perish."

Commentators, such as Lenski, sometimes interpret this as justifying infant baptism, or the thought that all little ones who die before reaching the age of accountability are saved.[4] The term, "the will of your Father," must be taken in the sense of desire, not the sovereign will of God (cf. 2 Pe 3:9). The fact is that some little ones grow up and perish. There is justification, however, on the basis of other Scripture for the doctrine that all children who die before reaching a responsible age go to heaven (2 Sa 12:21-23). The thought here is the loving concern of the Father, not the doctrine of election or the question of infant baptism. A disciple who is seeking the true interest of the kingdom of God would have concern for the child rather than for his own position of authority in the kingdom.

Sermon Concerning Forgiveness, 18:15-35

Having related the disciples to children in the preceding

context, Jesus then related the disciples to children of God who may be adults physically, even though they are immature spiritually. He introduced first the case of a brother or child of God who has injured one of the disciples in some way (cf. Lk 17:3-4). What should a disciple do in such an instance?

Jesus instructed him first to go alone to the brother, tell him his fault, and seek an adjustment. The implication is that this may bring the matter to proper solution. If, however, the brother would not heed such an admonition, the disciple was instructed to take two or three witnesses with him and attempt to get the matter resolved by this means. This was in keeping with the law as stated in Deuteronomy 19:15, to which allusion is made in the New Testament also (Jn 8:17; 2 Co 13:1; 1 Ti 5:19).

If this form of entreaty failed, then he should tell it to the "church" or "assembly." Obviously, church organization, as seen in the New Testament, had not yet been established, and it is more probable that He was referring here to a Jewish assembly, with which the disciples were familiar. If the offender refused to correct the matter in front of the whole assembly, he was then to be considered an outsider and was no longer worthy to be considered a brother. It is significant that there was no recognition of church authority, such as a bishop or elder, or even the authority of the disciples themselves.

However, Jesus went on immediately to discuss the authority of the disciples. In Matthew 18:18, He declared, "Verily I say unto you, Whatsoever ye shall bind on earth shall be bound in heaven: and whatsoever ye shall loose on earth shall be loosed in heaven." It should be noted, first of all, that *ye* is plural. This authority was not given to Peter individually as a pope, but rather it belonged to all of the disciples, and they shared it, according to the preceding verse, with the assembly. The idea was that collectively they had a right to apply the spiritual principles of divine judgment to those who ignore such truth. In applying them correctly, they were recognizing a situation which God had established, whether this referred to binding or loosing, and they were serving as God's representatives. It should be obvious that their binding or loosing was true only as God confirmed it.

Proceeding from the matter of judging a brother, the importance of two or three agreeing was then applied to prayer. Here, instead of the necessity of an entire assembly agreeing, even two or three who agree may be assured that God would answer. There is no instance in Scripture in which two or three of the disciples of Jesus agreed in prayer and the answer was not forthcoming. Only when they prayed singly, as in the case of Paul seeking removal of this thorn in the flesh, was there divine disapproval. This rule must not be applied in extreme literalness, as obviously, two or three may sometimes be wrong; and in the church today, the general principle of 1 John 5:14-15, that our prayers must always be subject to the will of God, is operative. When spiritual-minded Christians, however, agree as to an objective to be realized through prayer, there is greater assurance of the answer than if they come to God singly.

Peter returned to the question of forgiveness and asked the Lord in Matthew 18:21, "Lord, how oft shall my brother sin against me, and I forgive him? till seven times?" Lenski observes, "The old Jewish teaching was that three times was enough," based on Amos 1:3 and 2:6.[5] Peter was attempting to be generous in doubling the usual limit of forgiveness.

Jesus replied, however, "I say not unto thee, Until seven times: but, Until seventy times seven (Mt 18:22). There is some discussion in commentaries on this figure because of a mistranslation of Genesis 4:24, which Lamach is to be avenged seventy and sevenfold, that is, seventy-seven times.[6] The Septuagint translates it "seventy times seven," omitting the Hebrew *and*. There is no clear evidence that Christ was referring to the Septuagint rendering of Genesis 4:24, but it is evident in Matthew that Jesus meant seventy times seven, or four hundred and ninety. This meant that Peter should go on forgiving without counting the number of times, following the example of God himself, who does not impute sin to those who have trusted in Him.

To illustrate the necessity of forgiveness on the human

plane in light of the grace of God in forgiving sinners, Jesus used the illustration of a king who called his servants to account. This would be a normal instance for a monarch in Christ's day. The first servant owed the king ten thousand talents. The value of a talent could be as little as three hundred seventy-five dollars for a small, silver, Attic talent, or as much as thirty thousand dollars for a gold talent. Lenski believes that what was in view here was the Attic talent, worth twelve hundred dollars.[7] If this figure is used, ten thousand talents would be equivalent to at least twelve million dollars. If a Hebrew silver talent was in view, it could amount to as much as twenty million dollars. A gold talent would have been worth much more. In any case, a large sum is intended.

Because of the enormity of the debt, the king commanded the man to be sold as a slave along with his wife and children. This was common practice. Faced with this summary judgment, the servant, falling down, worshipped his lord and pleaded, "Lord, have patience with me, and I will pay thee all" (Mt 18:26). On the basis of his urgent plea, the king was moved to compassion, released him, and forgave his debt.

Continuing the account, however, our Lord described how this same servant, forgiven by the king, found another servant of the king, who owed him a hundred pence, or one hundred denarii, each worth about sixteen cents and amounting to about one day's wages for a laborer. Taking the servant by the throat, he demanded payment. When his fellow servant fell down at his feet and pleaded for patience, he was remanded to prison until he paid the debt. The amount owed was too small to justify selling him into slavery, and being cast into prison was a normal procedure.

Other servants of the king who had witnessed both incidents reported the matter. The king, outraged, summoned the servant before him and reminded him how he had been forgiven and how this should have given him like compassion on his fellow servant. In the light of the circumstances, the king then delivered him to tormentors until he should pay what was due. Such action was not uncommon in the ancient world, and the punishment involved included imprisonment, heavy labor, meager food, and even torture.

It is clear that this is a story which has only partial fulfillment in God's dealings with His disciples. There is no justification here for the doctrine of purgatory or the concept that a believer can lose justification once bestowed. The penalties refer to this life rather than the life to come in both instances, and chastisement can be experienced even by those who are the objects of God's grace, if they do not judge their own life in the light of God's forgiveness (cf. 1 Co 11:27-32; Heb 12:5-10). The illustration, however, enforces the exhortation of Jesus to Peter not to stop forgiving a brother, a truth which is supported by many scripture references (Ps 18:25; Mt 5:7; Lk 6:37; Eph 4:32; Col 3:13; Ja 5:9).

Translated into terms of Christian profession today, it is clear that a believer in Christ should be occupied with how graciously God has forgiven his wrongs rather than with how the world or the church recognizes his rights. Emotionally, we should be occupied with the love of God and should be seeking to express our love for Him in obedient service, however lowly and however unrecognized we remain by the church or the world.

19

Jesus Ministers in Perea

DISCOURSE ON DIVORCE, 19:1-12

LEAVING CAPERNAUM for the last time, Jesus began His journey which was to end in Jerusalem and the cross. The expression "into the coasts of Judaea beyond the Jordan" means the region beyond Judea to the east of the Jordan. By taking this route, Christ avoided Samaria, where He had ministered before, and passed through territory that was new to His public ministry. As He went, crowds following Him from Galilee were joined by others.

Morgan points out that the crowds had four classes: those who came with need, bringing their sick; those who came to trap Him; those who came in admiration; and at least one with a sincere question.[1] A parallel account to Matthew 19 is found in Mark 10:1-31. Only Matthew records, however, that His ministry included healing the sick.

Both Mark and Matthew, however, record the question of the Pharisees regarding divorce, recorded in Matthew 19:3, "Is it lawful for a man to put away his wife for every cause?" Matthew observes that the Pharisees did this in order to tempt Jesus, as the law of Moses clearly provided for divorce, but they wanted to raise the tricky question as to what just causes for divorce were. Perhaps some in the crowd had heard the Sermon on the Mount, in which Jesus had said that divorce should be limited to cases where there was fornication (5:31-32), which was more strict than the law of Moses.

Jesus, in answering them, appealed to the law of creation, that God had made both male and female, and had ordained that marriage should make them "one flesh." Jesus, therefore, referred to the basic law of creation and concluded,

141

"What therefore God hath joined together, let not man put asunder" (19:6).

The Pharisees then brought up the fact that the law of Moses was more lenient. Jesus replied by indicating that this was a concession to the hardness of their hearts, but this was not God's intention in marriage. Accordingly, He repeated the principle laid down in Matthew 5, that unless fornication breaks the marriage, divorce and remarriage constitutes adultery.

As Lenski observes, behind the Pharisees' question was a controversy in different schools of thought among the Jews, in which the school of Shammai was strict, and the school of Hillel, which permitted divorce for almost any cause, was more lax and had been followed by many of the Jews.[2] The debate hinges on Deuteronomy 24:1, where divorce was permitted if the husband "found some uncleanness in her," which could be interpreted as almost any sort of disfavor. Jesus avoided the trap of the Pharisees by appealing to the original purpose in marriage. While arguing from Deuteronomy 24:1, they were neglecting Genesis 1:27. Mark records additional conversation between the Pharisees and Jesus.

The answer of Jesus also perplexed the disciples, and later, according to Mark 10:10, when they were "in the house," they asked Him further about it. The disciples said to Jesus, "If the case of the man be so with his wife, it is not good to marry" (Mt 19:10). Creatures of their generation, even though they were disciples of Christ, they regarded the difficulty of divorce, which could be granted only on the ground of the unfaithfulness of the wife, as making the whole marriage relation an undesirable union. Actually, what they were saying was that they preferred the easier way, which had become traditional among the Jews, that of securing a divorce simply because the wife is no longer attractive to the husband.

The use of this passage to support celibacy by the Roman church is without justification. It is clear that Jesus did not view marriage as undesirable, except in special cases, as in His own state of celibacy. Replying to the disciples, He pointed out that marriage is not for everyone. Some are born eunuchs, that is, without normal sexual desire. Others, especially slaves, have been castrated. Still others "have made themselves eunuchs for the kingdom of heaven's sake" (v. 12). By this, He did not mean self-imposed castration, as was once advocated by the early church and practiced, for instance, by Origen, through incorrect understanding of this passage.

In a word, not all are obligated to be married and some obviously, to fulfill their calling, cannot be. This, however, does not obviate the normal law of marriage, nor does it change or limit the strict limitations placed upon divorce. On the other hand, the tendency to rule out divorce for any cause whatever seems unjustified on the basis of Christ's teaching and also on the basis of the Old Testament prohibition of the remarriage of divorced couples who have married another, which recognizes the fact of the divorce. The complete teaching of the New Testament on divorce includes Paul's exhortation in Romans 7:1-3 and in 1 Corinthians 7:10-16. These passages permit divorce, but remarriage is allowed only in cases where divorce is caused by fornication or after the death of one party to the marriage.

JESUS BLESSES THE CHILDREN, 19:13-15

Although there is no definite connection between the discourse on divorce and the incident regarding children, it is obvious that one of the evils of divorce is the effect on the children. As Jesus was teaching, ambitious parents brought their small children to have Jesus put His hands on them and pray for them (cf. Mk 10:13-16; Lk 18:15-17). The scene was probably the same as "in the house," mentioned in Mark 10:10. The disciples felt that this was an unwarranted intrusion into the privacy of Jesus, and attempted to restrict the children, but Jesus rebuked the disciples instead saying, "Suffer little children, and forbid them not, to come unto me; for of such is the kingdom of heaven" (Mt 19:14). While there is no mention that He actually prayed for them, Mark's gospel adds that He took the children up in His arms and blessed them (Mk 10:13-16). It is of interest that children instinctively recognized in Jesus one who loved them and cared for them, and they came to Him freely. The one who was the Friend of publicans and sinners was also the Friend of children.

RICH YOUNG RULER, 19:16-22

Later, departing from the house, Jesus was approached by a young man who raised the question, "Good Master, what good thing shall I do, that I may have eternal life?" Parallel accounts are found in Mark 10:17-27 and Luke 18:18-27. Mark 10:17 records that he came running and kneeled before asking his question. A similar question had been asked by the lawyer in Luke 10:25-29 on another occasion.

In reply, Jesus first called attention to the fact that he had called Him "good," which properly refers only to God. As Glover notes, *"Good Master* is compliment, not adoration. He has *no sense of sin,* which shows that his standard was poor and conscience dull."[3] But Jesus did not wait for the young man's reply. He instructed him that if he really wanted to enter into life, he should keep the commandments. When the young man replied, asking which commandments, Jesus quoted some of the Ten Commandments concerning murder, adultery, stealing, bearing false witness, and honoring one's father and mother. Significantly, Jesus did not quote the tenth commandment, forbidding covetousness, but added the commandment not found in the Ten Commandments, "Thou shalt love thy neighbour, as thyself" (Lev 19:18).

The young man replied that he had kept all these commandments from his youth. Obviously, he had a fine, moral character, but he sensed that something was lacking, and he asked, "What lack I yet?" Possibly he was troubled by the tenth commandment. Mark 10:21 adds at this point, "Jesus beholding him loved him."

But one thing was still lacking, and Jesus said to him, "If thou wilt be perfect," that is, reach the ultimate goal, "go and sell that thou hast, and give to the poor, and thou shalt have treasure in heaven: and come and follow me" (Mt 19:21). The reply of Christ seems to have left the young man

speechless, as he coveted riches, and he went quietly away
in deep disappointment, for he had great possessions.

The question is naturally raised by this incident whether
it is necessary for a rich man to give up all his possessions in
order to receive eternal life. Is not salvation by faith and by
grace and not by works?

The answer seems to be that in this instance, the questioning of Jesus brought out the shallowness of the young man's
faith. When it came right down to it, he trusted his riches
and his position more than he trusted in Jesus Christ. His
real problem was lack of faith in Christ, whom he considered a good Teacher but who apparently was not to be regarded as one who had the right to demand that he give up
all in order to follow Him. Faith is ultimately a choice, and
the young man chose riches rather than Jesus.

RELATION OF DISCIPLESHIP TO RICHES, 19:23-30

After the young ruler had left, Jesus observed to His disciples, "Verily I say unto you, That a rich man shall hardly
enter into the kingdom of heaven" (19:23). In contrast to
the prevailing opinion of the Jews, who, through their riches,
thought they were gaining favor with God, Jesus pointed
out that often riches are a stumbling block rather than a
stepping-stone for those entering the kingdom. He further
commented, "It is easier for a camel to go through the eye
of a needle, than for a rich man to enter into the kingdom
of God" (v. 24). The disciples replied in their amazement,
"Who then can be saved?"

Various explanations have been given for Christ's illustration of a camel going through a needle's eye. As Lenski
points out, the Talmud used an elephant in the same illustration and the Koran used the same illustration as Jesus did.[4]
Thus construed, He was saying, in effect, that it is impossible.

Some have taken the needle's eye to be a reference to a
small, low gate into a walled city requiring one entering to
take off his load and crawl through the hole on his knees,[5]
but there is no evidence that this is the intended meaning.
Like the reference to the blind guides, as in Matthew 23:24,

who strain at a gnat and swallow a camel, He was illustrating that which is impossible to do naturally. Jesus was not saying simply that it is difficult for rich men to be saved. What He was saying was that it takes a miracle, a supernatural work of God. This is clear in the comment of Jesus in answering the disciples' question, "Who then can be saved?" He stated, "With men this is impossible; but with God all things are possible" (19:26). The new birth, as an act of creation, is not something that comes naturally or easily.

Note should be taken that in verse 24, Jesus used the expression "the kingdom of God" in contrast to the usual expression "kingdom of heaven." If there is a distinction, the kingdom of God refers to the sphere of salvation, not merely the sphere of profession. A rich man could profess to follow Christ, but apart from supernatural grace, he could not enter into salvation.

The discourse of Christ on the place of riches on earth in contrast to "treasure in heaven" (v. 21) led to Peter's next question, "Behold, we have forsaken all, and followed thee; what shall we have therefore?" (v. 27).

To this practical question, Christ gave a specific answer. He stated that in the "regeneration," or restoration of the kingdom, "When the Son of man shall sit in the throne of his glory," the disciples also "shall sit upon twelve thrones, judging the twelve tribes of Israel" (v. 28). This is clearly a picture of the millennial earth, not heaven. Late in Christ's ministry, He supports the concept that the kingdom, while postponed as far as human expectation is concerned, is nevertheless certain of fulfillment following His second coming.

In addition to the promise that they shall sit on thrones acting as judges, Jesus gave the promise to all His disciples who, for Christ's sake, have forsaken houses, brethren, sister, father, mother, wife, children, or lands, that they shall receive an hundredfold reward in addition to having eternal life. There is no uncertainty about the riches of heaven, which will endure long after the treasures of the rich young ruler have been dissipated.

One final word of caution was given by Jesus, "But many that are first shall be last; and the last shall be first" (v. 30).

By this, Jesus meant that God's estimation of worthiness for reward may be entirely different than man's estimation. Those prominent in this life may not necessarily be first in reward in the life to come. The widow who gave her two mites but had nothing else to give may be ahead of those who have given much. Those who labor merely for reward may miss it. His discussion of this point is illustrated in the next chapter.

20

The Journey to Jerusalem

<small>PARABLE OF THE HOUSEHOLDER AND THE LABORERS,
20:1-16</small>

IN AMPLIFICATION of His answers to Peter's question in
19:27, "What shall we have, therefore?" Christ used an
illustration, found only in Matthew, of a wealthy man who
owned a vineyard. There does not seem to be any significance
to selection of the vineyard, except that it was a common
feature of life in Israel. In seeking laborers to work in his
vineyard, the owner promised them the usual daily wage of
a "penny," the Greek denarius, worth about sixteen cents
and the normal daily pay for a laborer or a Roman soldier.
Later in the day, seeing others idle in the marketplace, he
invited them to join his laborers. Apparently, no specific
agreement was made as to how much they would receive, except that he would do "whatever is right." Later he found
others in the sixth and ninth hour, referring at noon and 3:00
P.M. Finally, at the eleventh hour, or 5:00 P.M., he found
still others whom he invited to enter the vineyard to work.

At nightfall, the laborers came for their hire, and to each
he gave the same wage. This caused complaint on the part
of those who had labored all day, and they said "These last
have wrought but one hour, and thou hast made them equal
unto us, which have borne the burden and heat of the day."
But the owner of the vineyard replied, "Friend, I do thee
no wrong: didst not thou agree with me for a penny? Take
that thine is, and go thy way; I will give unto this last, even
as unto thee. Is it not lawful for me to do what I will with
mine own? Is thine eye evil, because I am good?" (vv.
13-15).

Complicated explanations of the spiritual meaning of this
illustration are not wanting. Melanchthon, for instance, made

the denarius represent temporal blessings and what is called "good" (v. 15) refer to life eternal, or eternal blessings.[1]

A simple explanation is better. By this illustration, Christ makes clear that God is sovereign. He may not reward according to length of toil or even according to the work performed, but according to "whatever is right" (vv. 4, 7). He chooses those for reward according to His own judgment. Some of the rewards are temporal, but the implication is that the full reward awaits the end of the day, reward in heaven.

JESUS' DEATH AND RESURRECTION AGAIN PREDICTED, 20:17-19

All of Jesus' ministry in Perea was relentlessly taking Him closer to the cross. Soon now they would be crossing the Jordan, passing through Jericho, below sea level, and then up the steep winding road to Jerusalem, about 2,550 feet above sea level. As they were walking the hot desert road to Jericho, Christ took occasion to separate His twelve disciples from the multitude and remind them that at the end of the road, there was a cross (cf. Mk 10:32-34; Lk 18:31-34). How cheap was the goal of reward symbolized by the denarius in comparison to what Jesus Himself was going to experience.

This was not the first time that Jesus had mentioned His death and resurrection to the disciples (cf. Mt 12:38-42; 16:21-28; 17:22-23). It, of course, had been announced as early as Genesis 3:15 that Satan would "bruise his heel." The shadow of the cross hung over Christ from the time He was born. He had clearly announced this to the disciples in Matthew 16:21-23, when Peter had attempted to rebuke Him. He had mentioned it again in Matthew 17:22-23, following the transfiguration. Now as they were moving closer and closer to Jerusalem, He said to His disciples, "Behold, we go up to Jerusalem; and the Son of man shall be betrayed unto the chief priests and unto the scribes, and they shall condemn him to death, And shall deliver him to the Gentiles to mock, and to scourge, and to crucify him: and the third day he shall rise again." As Morgan points out, Jesus gave accurately the details of His coming death and resurrection, and there is no question about His certainty of it.[2] Morgan states, "There is utmost accuracy in the details, and a calm, quiet knowledge of the actual things before Him."[3]

Interestingly—although in Matthew 16 Peter rebuked Jesus, and in 17:23 it states, "They were exceeding sorry"— here, as far as Matthew's record is concerned, they were silent. Mark 10:32-34 indicates that before He gave them this prediction, the disciples were "amazed" and "afraid." According to Luke 18:34, the disciples "understood none of these things: and this saying was hid from them, neither knew they the things which were spoken." Putting these passages together, it seems that the disciples had a fore-boding that the trip to Jerusalem was dangerous, but they could not bring themselves to believe literally what Jesus was saying.

REQUEST OF THE MOTHER OF JAMES AND JOHN, 20:20-24

The unwillingness of the disciples to face the reality of Christ's suffering and death is illustrated in the next incident, in which the mother of James and John, the wife of Zebedee, came to Jesus seeking favors for her sons (cf. Mk 10:35-41). When she bowed before Him, Christ asked her, "What wilt thou?" Her request was abrupt and to the point, "Grant that these my two sons may sit, the one on thy right hand, and the other on the left, in thy kingdom" (Mt 20:21). Her ambition was the same as that of the disciples, recorded in Matthew 18:1-14, and the question of Peter in 19:27. Here, their desire for power and position emerges again in the petition of this ambitious mother. Perhaps she can be ex-cused partially in desiring her sons to have a prominent place in serving the Lord, but it was a request relating to ambitions of earth rather than to the glory of God.

Jesus dealt with her gently. He replied, "Ye know not what ye ask. Are ye able to drink of the cup that I shall drink of, and to be baptized with the baptism that I am baptized with?" Here, as also recorded in the parallel account in Mark 10:35-41, James and John broke in and answered, "We are able." How little they knew what they were saying. Jesus replied sorrowfully to them, "Ye shall drink indeed of my cup, and be baptized with the baptism that I am baptized with" (Mt 20:23). Early in the ministry of the church, James was to lay down his life as a martyr. Although the evidence is not complete, John may also have died a martyr's death as did some of the other disciples. Although they were to die in one sense as Jesus died, even this did not justify granting their mother's petition. Jesus completed the answer, "But to sit on my right hand, and on my left, is not mine to give, but it shall be given to them for whom it is prepared of my Father."

The other disciples were furious at this attempt to secure preference for these two. They apparently concluded that James and John had influenced their mother to make this request. As Criswell points out, "The fact that the other disciples were angered at James and John shows that they were in heart and spirit no better than the two brothers. . . . They all wanted the first place."[4] Both James and John as well as the other ten disciples were far from giving up their attempts to gain the place of power in the kingdom, and their scheming continued, even to the time of the Last Supper in the upper room. How frail and faulty are the human instruments that God must use to accomplish His purposes!

Jesus Comments on Their Ambitions, 20:25-28

Using this incident as an occasion for further discussion of the disciples' ambition to be great, Jesus pointed out some obvious lessons. He acknowledged that in worldly kingdoms, places of power with great authority are sought. But He declared that in the kingdom of heaven, it shall be different, "But it shall not be so among you: but whosoever will be great among you, let him be your minister: And whosoever will be chief among you, let him be your servant" (Mt 20:26-27). The goal in the kingdom is not to rule but to serve. Jesus used His own ministry as an illustration, "Even as the Son of man came not to be to ministered unto, but to minister, to give his life a ransom for many" (v. 28). The road to privileged authority is often paved with lowly service.

HEALING OF TWO BLIND MEN, 20:30-34

In the journey to Jerusalem, a great multitude had followed them from Jericho. As the company moved along, they encountered two blind men sitting beside the road. When they heard that it was Jesus who passed by, mindful of the stories that they had heard of His healing power, they cried out, "Have mercy on us, O Lord, thou son of David" (20:31). Rebuked by the multitude, they only cried the more, repeating their request.

Hearing their petition, Jesus stood still, and calling them to Him, He asked, "What will ye that I shall do unto you?" It was a most dramatic situation, as the crowd thronged about, wondering what would happen. The blind man answered simply, "Lord, that our eyes may be opened." Jesus, having compassion on them, touched their eyes; they immediately received their sight and followed Christ. The incident, as recorded in Matthew with parallel accounts in Mark 10:46-52 and Luke 18:35-43, is significant as emphasizing the title "Son of David," which was to be prominent in His triumphal entry into Jerusalem.

The account of Mark 10 differs from Matthew's account, in that it mentions only one blind man who is named, "blind Bartimaeus, the son of Timaeus," and adds considerable detail to the conversation between them. That Mark omits reference to the second blind man is no serious problem. Luke's gospel represents it as being "nigh" or "near" Jericho, as if they were about to enter Jericho. The variations in these accounts have given rise to the allegation that the Scriptures are in error in some of the details.

Most of the problems dissolve when it is realized that there were two Jerichos: the Old Testament Jericho and the new city, which Herod the Great had built. It may be that Jesus was between the two cities when the miracle took place.

Lenski offers another solution. The order of events, according to Lenski, includes Jesus' having passed through the city (Lk 19:1) without finding lodging. After meeting Zacchaeus, Jesus and His disciples then went back into Jericho and spent the night in his house. On this return to Jericho, the blind men were healed. This permits all the accounts to harmonize.[5]

The problem is not in the details that are given but the details which are omitted. If the full story were told, all of the gospel accounts would undoubtedly be found accurate. As it is, each account adds something to the others. Most significant is the fact that those who sought Jesus earnestly received the demonstration of His miraculous power.

21

Jesus' Arrival in Jerusalem

THE FINAL HOURS of Jesus' life on earth drew near, and, in Matthew 21, the cross was less than a week away. In sharp contrast to the shame of the cross is the triumphant entry into Jerusalem, described by all four gospels (cf. Mk 11:1-10; Lk 19:29-38; Jn 12:12-19). As Tasker expresses it, "Jesus entered Jerusalem for the last time in a manner which showed that He was none other than the Messiah, the Son of David, who was coming to Sion to claim the city as His own.[1]

The four accounts of the triumphal entry differ in some respects but are not in contradiction. John's gospel, written sixty years after the event, gives some of the most interesting details, including the fact that the night before the triumphal entry, Jesus had an intimate supper in the home of Lazarus, Martha, and Mary, as recorded in John 12:1-11.

Matthew mentions Bethphage, a village no longer in existence, which apparently was close to Bethany on the eastern side of the Mount of Olives, just a few miles from Jerusalem. Anticipating His entry into Jerusalem, Jesus sent two of the disciples, not named in any of the gospel accounts, into the village of Bethphage, to secure an ass and her colt to serve as His transportation as He entered Jerusalem. He told them they would find both animals tied; they were to untie them and bring them to Him. If anyone asked why they were doing this, they were to reply, "The Lord hath need of them" (21: 3). Mark 11:5 and Luke 19:31 indicate that the question was asked, but the disciples were not stopped from borrowing the beasts. Matthew does not record the question, but only Matthew records that there were two animals and that Jesus sat on the colt.

Matthew calls attention to the precise fulfillment of Old Testament prophecy which he quotes. Without following the exact words of the Old Testament, Matthew quotes Zechariah 9:9, prefaced by the phrase from Isaiah 62:11, "Tell ye the daughter of Zion." He omits from Zechariah 9:9 the phrase, "O daughter of Jerusalem." The reference to Zion is a specific reference to a hill in Jerusalem, the exact location of which is disputed today, but Zion is often used as a title for Jerusalem itself. There is no need to spiritualize Zion and make it represent the church, as it is a geographic designation especially related to the King and the kingdom.

The main point is contained in the quotation from Zechariah 9:9, which prophesies that the Messiah King of Israel, unlike earthly kings, would come in a lowly or meek manner sitting upon an ass and a colt, the foal of an ass. No king had ever come to Israel in this manner, as kings usually came on horses (cf. Rev 6:2; 19:11).

Matthew, intent on establishing the triumphal entry as a fulfillment of prophecy of the coming of Jesus as King to Jerusalem, ignores some of the details and simply records that the disciples brought the ass and the colt and put their garments on both of them. Jesus probably sat only on the colt, as mentioned in the other gospels, which had never been ridden before (Mk 11:2; Lk 19:30). To form a saddle, they threw their outer garments on both beasts, even though Jesus used only the colt.

As they proceeded to Jerusalem, they were accompanied by a crowd familiar with Christ's miracle of raising Lazarus (Jn 12:17-18), and were met by another multitude coming out of the city of Jerusalem, which went before Him (Mt 21:9). Both groups outdid themselves in honoring Jesus, laying their garments on the ground for the beasts to travel over and cutting down branches from trees and spreading them in a festive way along the road. John alone mentions that the branches were from palm trees. Although they were treating Jesus as their King, in keeping with the meaning of the triumphal entry, it seems clear that they did so with only partial understanding. John comments, "These things understood not his disciples at the first: but when Jesus was glori-

fied, then remembered they that these things were written
of him, and that they had done these things unto him" (Jn
12:16).

In greeting Him, however, the multitudes fulfilled the prophecies of just such an entry into Jerusalem (Zec 9:9) and
addressed Jesus with the words, "Hosanna to the son of
David: Blessed is he that cometh in the name of the Lord;
Hosanna in the highest" (Mt 21:9). *Hosanna* is a translitera-
tion of a Hebrew expression meaning, "grant salvation," but
is used here more as a greeting or ascription of praise. Most
significant is the reference to Christ as the Son of David. They
recognized that He was in the kingly line, although they do
not seem to have entered fully into the concept that He was
coming into Jerusalem as its King.

As they came into Jerusalem, both the multitude which
accompanied Him and the multitude which met Him were
confronted by still others who asked, "Who is this?" The
entire city, according to Matthew, was excited by the arrival
of Christ. The multitude answered the question by saying,
"This is Jesus, the prophet of Nazareth of Galilee." It is
possible that some of the multitude were pilgrims from Galilee, in Jerusalem at this time for the feast of Passover, and
that therefore, they were claiming Jesus proudly. The form
of the verb *said* in 21:11 indicates that they repeated the
information again and again.

Matthew does not record the details which followed that
day. It was probably Sunday afternoon when Christ came
into Jerusalem. Mark 11:11 records that He looked into the
temple and then went out to Bethany with the twelve for
the night.[2] The events which follow, in Matthew 21:12-17,
probably occurred on Monday.

Jesus' Second Cleansing of the Temple, 21:12-17

Early on Monday morning, Jesus returned to Jerusalem,
and, entering into the temple, which Matthew significantly
refers to as "the temple of God," He began to cast out those
who sold and bought in the temple and overthrew the tables
of the money changers and the seats of those who sold

the doves for the sacrifice (cf. Mk 11:15-18; Lk 19:45-47). There is no excuse for trying to harmonize this with a much earlier incident, recorded in John 2:13-16, which was at a previous Passover. There is obvious resemblance between the two cleansings, but the point, of course, is that the first cleansing was ineffective in bringing about any permanent cure.

Jesus rebuked them with the words, "It is written, My house shall be called the house of prayer; but ye have made it a den of thieves" (Mt 21:13). The custom was to require the people to exchange Roman money for temple money at an arbitrary rate and also to force them to buy the animals or doves for sacrifice at a high price exacted in the temple. As Lenski expresses it, they had "a grand lucrative monopoly. If one bought his animals here, had his money exchanged here, these would be accepted; otherwise he might have trouble on that score."[3] In doing this, the temple authorities were robbing the people and making a farce out of the whole sacrificial system. The area where the animals were kept and sold was in the great court of the temple, which never was intended to serve as a stockyard.

It is significant that on this occasion, as in the first cleansing of the temple, there was no resistance offered. There was something about the bearing of Jesus that silenced these money-loving merchants, and undoubtedly the people approved. Jesus had no illusions that His act would result in any permanent good, but it was part of His solemn judgment pronounced upon Jerusalem and His generation. Luke records that prior to going into the temple, He wept over the city (Lk 19:41-44). Matthew records a similar lamenting over Jerusalem prior to the Olivet discourse (Mt 23:37-39).

After the cleansing of the temple, Matthew alone of the four gospels records, "And the blind and the lame came to him in the temple; and he healed them" (21:14). The result of His cleansing of the temple and the miraculous healings which took place inspired the crowd once again to repeat their acclamation of the preceding day, "Hosanna to the son of David."

The chief priests and the scribes, who apparently were silent at the indictment of Jesus on the corruption of the temple, now spoke up and expressed their displeasure that Jesus was greeted as the Son of David, recognizing as they did that this was connecting Jesus with the promise of the kingly line of David. They said to Jesus, "Hearest thou what these say?" (v. 16). However, they were helpless and were at a loss to know what to do with the enthusiasm of the crowd. The Jewish leaders were especially concerned because the young people, referred to as "the children" (v. 15), had joined in the ascription of praise to Christ. These were boys, who like Jesus, had come to the temple for the first time at the age twelve.

In answer to their question, however, Jesus replied by quoting from Psalm 8:2, "Yea; have ye never read, Out of the mouth of babes and sucklings thou has perfected praise?" In effect, He was saying, "The youths are right, and you are wrong." If babes who barely can speak can praise the Lord, how much more these youths now twelve years of age and older? In claiming Psalm 8:2, Jesus, in effect, was also claiming to be God and, thus, worthy of praise. He left the scribes and the Pharisees stunned with no more to say.

That night, once again, Jesus probably went out to Bethany and lodged. By thus leaving Jerusalem, He placed Himself outside the area where the scribes and Pharisees could order His arrest after the crowd had left the temple.

CURSING OF THE FIG TREE, 21:18-22

The incident recorded here in Matthew in regard to the fig tree is presented as another significant incident in Jesus' last days. Mark 11:12-14, the only other account, makes it clear that it actually occurred on Monday morning, prior to the incident of the cleansing of the temple. It is now brought in by Matthew because of the significant comment of Jesus on the next day, which was Tuesday morning.

Matthew records that Jesus, coming into the city on Monday morning of His last week, was hungry. No explanation is given, but the assumption is that Jesus had not eaten before He left Bethany. Morgan believes Jesus spent the night "in some long lone vigil on the hillside, in a quiet and secluded place."[4] Seeing a fig tree with leaves on it, He came to pick its fruit. Normally, fruit grows on a fig tree before the leaves come out in spring, but it is not clear whether the figs would be left over from the previous year or whether the tree, because of being more sheltered from winter than others, had started its spring growth early. According to the parallel passage in Mark 11:13, "The time of figs was not yet." Finding the tree with only leaves and no fruit, He said, "Let no fruit grow on thee [henceforth] forever" (Mt 21:19). This, however, was not observed immediately, and refers to the experience of the disciples on Tuesday morning, approximately twenty-four hours later. Perceiving that the fig tree had withered, the disciples were amazed that this had occurred so quickly.

Many questions have been raised about this incident, including the problem that Jesus as God should have known that there was no fruit on the tree. Here, Matthew is apparently speaking from the viewpoint of human intelligence only, but the whole incident was planned as a means of conveying truth to the disciples.

In answer to their wondering, Jesus gave them a sermon on faith. Jesus informed His disciples that if they had real faith in God, they would not only be able to curse the fig tree effectively as He had done, but, He told them, "If ye shall say unto this mountain, Be thou removed, and be thou cast into the sea; it shall be done" (v. 21). He added the great promise, "And all things, whatsoever ye shall ask in prayer, believing, ye shall receive" (v. 22). In other words, they should not marvel, but believe and pray.

Many expositors see in the fig tree a type of Israel, fruitless and yet showing leaves, typical of outer religion.[5] This is frequently tied to Matthew 24:32, referring to "a parable of the fig tree." There is no scriptural support for this interpretation contextually. There is no ground today to support Lenski in his statement made in 1943, "Judaism stands blasted from the roots to this day."[6] Israel, instead, is marvelously revived today. Jesus made no application to Israel as a nation here; nor does the context of the fig tree in Matthew 24 refer to Israel. While Jeremiah 24:1-8 uses good and bad figs to represent the captives in Israel as contrasted to those remaining in the land, actually, there is no case in the Bible where a fig tree is used as a type of Israel. In view of the silence of Scripture on this point, it is preferable to leave the illustration as it is, a lesson on faith and the miraculous rather than a lesson on fruitlessness.

AUTHORITY OF JESUS CHALLENGED, 21:23-27

Upon the return of Jesus to the temple, probably on Tuesday morning of the last week, as He was teaching, the chief priests and the elders brought up the question which they were unprepared to raise the preceding day, "By what authority doest thou these things? and who gave thee this authority?" (Mt 21:23).

Once again, the Jewish leaders were trying to trap Jesus in utterances which they could label blasphemy (cf. Mk 11:27-33; Lk 20:1-8). They made no attempt, however, to arrest Him or to expel Him from the temple, as they feared the people. They were no match for Jesus, however, in an interchange of questions, and Jesus replied that He would answer their question if they would answer His first: "The baptism of John, whence was it? from heaven, or of men?" (Mt 21:25).

The Pharisees were caught in a dilemma. As Allen expresses it, "If the authorities had given credence to John, they would have had no need to ask by what authority Jesus acted."[7] If the Pharisees said the baptism of John was only of men, they would be opposed by the people who believed John was a prophet. If they said it was from heaven, then they would be obliged to believe his message affirming the deity of Jesus. Accordingly, they answered Jesus, "We cannot tell" (v. 27). Jesus replied that if they could not identify the authority of John, then He did not need to tell them by what authority He cleansed the temple. The point, of course, is that they were not seeking a real answer, as they knew that Jesus claimed the authority of God.

PARABLE OF THE TWO SONS, 21:28-32

To expose the unbelief of the chief priests and the scribes, Jesus introduced three parables, the parable of the two sons (21:28-32), the parable of the householder (21:33-46), and the parable of the marriage feast (22:1-14). To start with, Jesus used a simple story of a father who asked his two sons to work in his vineyard, a parable found only in Matthew.

The first son, when instructed to work in the vineyard, replied, "I will not," but later on, thought better of it and began to work. The second son replied quickly, "I go, sir," literally, "I, sir," but he went not. Jesus then raised the question as to which one did the will of the father. They answered, "The first."

Then Jesus made the application. He said, "Verily I say unto you, That the publicans and the harlots go into the kingdom of God before you. For John came unto you in the way of righteousness, and ye believed him not: but the publicans and the harlots believed him: and ye, when ye had seen it, repented not afterward, that ye might believe him" (21:31-32). What had been subtly indicated before was now brought out in the open. They had rejected the ministry of John, whom even harlots and publicans had recognized as a prophet of God. They were like the son who said, "I go, sir," but who went not. By their confession, they stood condemned.

PARABLE OF THE HOUSEHOLDER AND HIS REJECTED SON, 21:33-46

To drive the point home still further, Jesus used another parable (cf. Mk 12:1-9; Lk 20:9-19). This time, He described a man who planted a vineyard, built a wine tower, and leased it to tenants. When the time of harvest came, he sent his servants to take the fruit of it, but the tenants treated the servants harshly, beating one, killing another, and stoning another. When he sent other servants, they were treated in like manner. Finally, he sent his son, thinking that they would have respect for him. But the tenants, recognizing him, said, "This is the heir; come, let us kill him, and let us seize on his inheritance (Mt 21:38). And so they caught the son and killed him.

Jesus then raised the question as to what the Lord of the vineyard would do under these circumstances. They replied, "He will miserably destroy those wicked men, and will let out his vineyard unto other husbandmen, which shall render him the fruits in their seasons" (v. 41).

Jesus then made the application. It is probably true, as Lenski points out, that no person would send his son into a situation where servants had previously killed his other representatives but would immediately call the authorities.[8] The contrast is between what men would do and what God had done. God did send His son, even though Israel had rejected His prophets earlier and killed them and had rejected John the Baptist.

Jesus made the application with tremendous force: "Did ye never read in the scriptures, The stone which the builders rejected, the same is become the head of the corner: this is the Lord's doing, and it is marvelous in our eyes?" (v. 42). Jesus was quoting from Psalm 118:22-23.

The figure of a stone is found often in Scripture, Jesus being referred to both as the foundation stone and the head of the corner (1 Co 3:11; Eph 2:20-22; 1 Pe 2:4-5). To Israel, Jesus was a stumbling stone and rock of offense (Is 8:14-15; Ro 9:32-33; 1 Co 1:23; 1 Pe 2:8). At the time of His second coming, He will be a smiting stone of destruction (Dan 2:34).

Jesus also made the further application, "Therefore say I unto you, The kingdom of God shall be taken from you, and given to a nation bringing forth the fruits thereof (Mt 21:43). Here, as Matthew does rarely, the expression "kingdom of God" is used, referring to the sphere of reality rather than a mere profession of faith. Jesus declared that the kingdom of God would be given to a nation which does bring forth proper fruit. This should not be construed as a turning away from Israel to the Gentiles but rather a turning to any people who would bring forth the fruits of real faith.

The word *nation* is without the article in the Greek and probably does not refer to the Gentiles specifically.

Carrying further the significance of Jesus as a stone, He stated, "And whosoever shall fall on this stone shall be broken: but on whomsoever it shall fall, it will grind him to powder" (v. 44). Here Jesus was referring to Himself as the Judge of all men. The rejected stone is also the smiting stone. As Criswell expresses it so forcibly, "These parables in the latter part of Matthew are somber, terrible, fearful. . . . They are parables of fire and fury and terrible rejection like a king taking account of unfaithful servants and visiting judgment with a drawn sword."[9]

The point of this parable was all too clear, and the chief priests and Pharisees realized that Jesus was talking about them. However, because of the presence of the people, they were helpless to do anything at this time. Their hatred of Jesus was only intensified by this exposure, and it gave impetus to the plot already formed to kill Jesus when they could. The shadow of the cross was lengthening over these closing events of the life of Jesus.

22

Jesus' Controversy with the Jewish Rulers

PARABLE OF THE MARRIAGE FEAST, 22:1-14

As JESUS DREW NEARER to the cross, His message became more and more directed to the representatives of the Jewish nation. In this chapter, He dealt with the three main groups: the Herodians, Sadducees, and Pharisees. The Herodians were political activists who supported the rule of Herod. The Pharisees were usually against them, ardently supporting Israel as against Rome. The Sadducees were the liberal theologians, questioning the miraculous, opposed to the Pharisees. The three parties hated each other, but they hated Jesus more. Jesus included them all in the parable of the wedding feast, the third in the series of parables (cf. Lk 14:16-24).

Jesus declared that the kingdom of heaven may be compared to the incident in which a king made a marriage feast for his son. His slaves were sent out to invite the guests, but the guests were not willing to come. The king sent them out a second time, reminding them that the feast was ready, but the guests were unconcerned and went about their business as if they had not received the invitation. Some of them actually treated the servants roughly and even killed some of them. When tidings of this reached the king, he sent forth his soldiers, destroyed the murderers, and burned their city.

The wedding, however, was still without guests, so he commanded his servants to invite anyone they could, and being invited, many came. As the wedding feast was progressing, however, the king saw one of the guests without a wedding garment. These garments were supplied by the host, and the guest not wearing the wedding garment was violating the normal custom. When confronted with his lack of a wedding garment, the guest was speechless. The king then gave orders to bind him hand and foot and cast him out. Jesus added the comment, "There shall be weeping and gnashing of teeth. For many are called, but few are chosen" (Mt 22:13-14).

G. Campbell Morgan observes that there were three distinct invitations. The first was the preaching ministry of Jesus, which constituted an invitation for the hearers to come. The second referred to a further invitation, which the nation would reject and which would result in the destruction of Jerusalem in A.D. 70. The third movement referred to the gospel age when all are bidden to come regardless of race or background.[1]

The lessons of the parable are clear. First, the king had issued a gracious invitation. The response was rejection of the invitation by those who would normally be considered his friends; second, their rejection would result in the king's taking severe action; third, their rejection would result in the invitation being extended to all who would come. The application to the scribes and Pharisees, who, as the representatives of Israel, would normally be invited, is clear. The rejection of Christ and His crucifixion is implied, and the extension of the gospel to Jew and Gentile alike is anticipated. While the invitation is broad, those actually chosen for blessing are few. The parable inspired the Jews to make another attempt to trap Christ into giving them a ground for His condemnation.

CONTROVERSY WITH THE HERODIANS, 22:15-22

The Pharisees, after taking counsel, decided they would send some of their number, accompanied by the Herodians, to attempt another encounter with Jesus (Mk 12:13-17; Lk 20:20-26). The Herodians, a political party who supported the dynasty of Herod, probably cut across the religious lines of both the Pharisees and the Sadducees. They came to Him with the subtle strategy, "Master, we know that thou art true, and teachest the way of God in truth, neither carest thou for any man: for thou regardest not the person of men"

(Mt 22:16). All of this, of course, was double-talk, as they did not really believe in Jesus.

The Herodians, having paved the way in a manner that they regarded as disarming Christ, then said, "Tell us therefore, What thinkest thou? Is it lawful to give tribute unto Caesar, or not?" (v. 17). As political experts, the Herodians thought that they had Jesus on the horns of a dilemma. If He said it was lawful to give tribute to Caesar, He could be accused of siding with the Romans as opposed to the Jews. If He denied that it was right to give tribute to Caesar, then He could be accused of rebellion against Roman law.

In this encounter, as in all others, Jesus easily handled the problem. The tax they were referring to was the poll tax, a small tax levied on women aged twelve to sixty-five and men aged fourteen to sixty-five. It was a relatively small tax, as the Romans also exacted a ten-percent tax on grain and a twenty-percent tax on wine and fruit, as well as other taxes for road and bridge improvements. The Pharisees had chosen the least of the taxes, but to pay it was to recognize Roman oppression, which was most unpopular with the Jews.

Jesus easily saw through their hypocrisy and said to them, "Why tempt ye me, ye hypocrites?" Jesus asked them to bring Him a piece of money suitable for tribute, and they brought Him a penny, or a Roman denarius, worth about sixteen cents. He then asked, "Whose is this image and superscription?" The answer was obvious, and they said, "Caesar's." Jesus then gave them an answer, "Render therefore unto Caesar the things which are Caesar's; and unto God the things that are God's." As they heard His answer, they marveled at the adroit way in which He had solved their problem, and they had nothing more to say. If they used Roman coins, then they were subject to Roman tax. The Herodians went away defeated in their intent to compromise Jesus on this issue. In His answer, Jesus also cut the knotty problem of the relation of church and state. As Criswell expresses it, "Our Lord said that there are obligations we have and duties we ought to perform in the sphere of both secular and sacred life, and our duties in one do not exclude our duties in the other. . . . A free church in a free state, and a free state with a free church, is to find the ideal of political and religious history as announced by the Lord Himself."[2]

CONTROVERSY WITH THE SADDUCEES, 22:23-33

Following His controversy with the Herodians, the Sadducees came with a similar intent to trap Jesus (cf. Mk 12:18-27; Lk 20:27-38). They were the liberals in the Jewish religion and opposed the Pharisees who were the conservatives. The Pharisees, however, were more liberal in their additions to tradition than the Sadducees; the Sadducees were more opposed to supernaturalism than the Pharisees. Accordingly they tried to trap Him theologically on the matter of resurrection.

Attempting to hide their true intent, the Sadducees began by quoting the law of Moses requiring a brother to marry the wife of a deceased brother and raise up children to him. They were referring to such passages as Deuteronomy 25:5-10, a regulation which entered into the marriage of Ruth and Boaz, recorded in Ruth 4:1-12. The Sadducees brought up the extreme case of a wife who successively married seven brethren all of whom preceded her in death. The question they raised was, "Therefore in the resurrection, whose wife shall she be of the seven? for they all had her" (Mt 22:28). The situation, to the Sadducees, illustrated the absurdity of the doctrine of resurrection.

Jesus gave them a direct answer. He stated that their problem was not in the doctrine of resurrection but in their ignorance of the Scriptures and of the power of God. He explained, "For in the resurrection they neither marry, nor are given in marriage, but are as the angels of God in heaven" (v. 30). In other words, their question was foolish because marriage is not a relationship realized in heaven.

Then proceeding to the real issue, the question of whether the dead are raised, Jesus said, "But as touching the resurrection of the dead, have ye not read that which was spoken unto you by God, saying, I am the God of Abraham, and the God of Isaac, and the God of Jacob? God is not the God of the dead, but of the living" (vv. 31-32). In His reply, Jesus not only affirmed resurrection but also the continuance of personal identity, in that Abraham would be Abraham, Isaac would be Isaac, and Jacob would be Jacob, an identity related to the resurrection of their bodies. The Sadducees could not attack this statement of Christ without being in the position of attacking Abraham, Isaac, or Jacob. They were neatly trapped in their own hypocrisy.

By this interchange with the Sadducees, Christ placed the Sadducees in direct conflict with the Scriptures, and again His questioners had nothing to say. The multitude listening was astonished at the ease with which His teaching disposed of these difficult questions. The defeat of both the Herodians and the Sadducees left the field only to the Pharisees to renew questions.

CONTROVERSY WITH THE PHARISEES, 22:34-46

When the word reached the Pharisees that Jesus had silenced those who had tried to question Him, they sent a lawyer who attempted to trap Christ in a question of theological law (cf. Mk 12:28-34). To Jesus he addressed the question, "Master, which is the great commandment in the law?" (Mt 22:36). As Morgan points out, there was controversy concerning which of the Ten Commandments was the greatest, some favoring the third.[3]

To this direct question, Jesus gave an immediate answer, quoting two commandments not in the ten. "Jesus said unto him, Thou shalt love the Lord thy God with all thy heart, with all thy soul, and with all thy mind. This is the first and great commandment. And the second is like unto it, Thou shalt love thy neighbour as thyself. On these two commandments hang all the law and the prophets" (vv. 37-40). Matthew does not report the rest of the interchange with the lawyer. In the parallel passage in Mark 12:28-34, record is made of the conversation, which Matthew omits, in which the lawyer, described as a scribe, recognized that Jesus had correctly answered the question. Mark 12:34 records Jesus' reply, "And when Jesus saw that he answered discreetly, he said unto him, Thou art not far from the kingdom of God. And no man after that durst ask him any question." Luke 10:25-28 mentions a similar incident, which had occurred earlier, where the same question and answer were given, which led to the parable of the good Samaritan to illustrate who is one's neighbor. It is not unnatural for the same question to have been raised more than once in the course of the three years of Christ's ministry.

Having silenced His questioners, Jesus then asked the Pharisees a question. In effect, as Tasker points out, Jesus asked "the all-important question 'What is *your* view of the Messiah?' "[4] When the Pharisees gathered before Him, Jesus posed the question, "What think ye of Christ? whose son is he?" They gave immediately the answer, "The son of David" (Mt 22:42). Then Jesus countered with a second question, "How then doth David in spirit call him Lord, saying, The LORD said unto my Lord, Sit thou on my right hand, till I make thine enemies thy footstool? If David then called him Lord, how is he his son?" (vv. 43-45). The theological problem of how the son of David could be greater than David was too much for their theological insights. They retired in confusion and gave up trying to trap Jesus with their questions. Their hypocrisy and unbelief led Jesus, in the next chapter, to denounce the scribes and Pharisees in unsparing language.

23

Jesus Condemns the Scribes and Pharisees

Hypocrisy of the Pharisees, 23:1-12

JESUS, AT THIS TIME, was thronged with pilgrims from all over Israel who had come to celebrate the Passover feast. Addressing Himself to them and to His own disciples, Jesus solemnly warned them concerning the scribes and Pharisees (cf. Mk 12:38-40; Lk 20:45-47). This discourse, as a whole, is found only in Matthew. Jesus began by acknowledging that they were seated in Moses' seat. While not saying it in so many words, He implied that they were usurpers who were not truly successors of Moses. But nevertheless, their position must be recognized. Accordingly, He told them, "All therefore whatsoever they bid you observe, that observe and do" (23:3).

By commanding them to observe and do what the Pharisees instructed them, Jesus certainly did not mean that they should follow the false teachings of the Pharisees but rather those teachings that naturally and correctly arose from the Law of Moses. In general, the Pharisees were upholders of the law and should be recognized for this.

Jesus went on immediately, however, to point out their hypocrisy and commanded the people, "But do not ye after their works: for they say, and do not" (v. 3). He then cited the hypocrisy of the Pharisees. They lay heavy burdens upon the people but would not do anything to make the load lighter. Their own works were done to be observed by men rather than God. They made broad their phylacteries, the Scriptures which they customarily bound to their forehead and to their left wrist, containing the Scriptures of Exodus 13:3-16; Deuteronomy 6:5-9 and 11:13-21. This they did, not only when they prayed in the morning, but throughout the day, for the purpose of being seen of men. They also enlarged the borders of their garments, the tassels referred to in Deuteronomy 22:12, which were tokens that they were holy men.

Jesus charged the Pharisees with loving the best places at the feasts and the chief seats in the synagogue. They loved to be called rabbi, which recognized that they were teachers and scholars. Jesus reminded them that their Messiah, "Christ," was their Master, and God was their Father. It is of interest that He referred to the Christ, or the Messiah, in Matthew 23:8, 10. What He was saying was that the Pharisees and scribes had forgotten the preeminence of God and of their Messiah.

This condemnation by Jesus of the pretentions of the scribes and Pharisees does not rule out reasonable recognition of authority in Israel or in the church, but obviously prohibits making this a goal in itself. He held before them instead the desirability of being a servant, or one who ministers, and He concluded, "And whosoever shall exalt himself shall be abased; and he that shall humble himself shall be exalted" (v. 12). His disciples were not to seek to be called rabbi and were forbidden to use the word *father* indiscriminately, even though Paul used *father* correctly in 1 Corinthians 4:15, and John addressed fathers in 1 John 2:13-14. The general teaching is clear. They were not to seek man-exalting titles such as rabbi, father, or minister to gain the recognition of men. Disciples of Christ should not exalt themselves but should seek to serve others and leave the exalting to God Himself.

JESUS PRONOUNCES SEVEN WOES UPON THE SCRIBES
AND PHARISEES, 23:13-36

In this section, climaxing the controversy of Christ with the scribes and Pharisees, seven solemn woes are pronounced upon them. Only Matthew records this scathing denunciation of these religious leaders of the Jews. These woes, in contrast to the Beatitudes, denounce false religion as utterly abhorrent to God and worthy of severe condemnation. No passage in the Bible is more biting, more pointed, or more severe than this pronouncement of Christ upon the Pharisees. It is significant that He singled them out, as opposed to the Sadducees, who were more liberal, and the Herodians, who were the politicians. The Pharisees, while attempting to honor the Word of God and manifesting an extreme form of religious observance, were actually the farthest from God.

His first condemnation, in 23:13, related to the fact that they did all they could to shut out others. False religion and pretense are always the worst enemies of the truth and are far more dangerous than immorality or indifference. As the religious leaders of the Jews, they were held guilty before God of blocking the way for others seeking to enter into the kingdom of God.

In verse 14, another woe is indicated, in which the scribes and Pharisees were charged with devouring widows' houses and making long prayers to impress others. The verse, however, is omitted in most manuscripts and probably should not be considered as rightly a portion of this Scripture. It may have been inserted from Mark 12:40 and Luke 20:47.[1] If it is included, it would bring the total woes to eight instead of seven.

In Matthew 23:15, the second woe is mentioned. In this one, the Pharisees were described as extremely energetic on both land and sea to make proselytes of the Jewish religion. But when they were successful, Jesus charged, "Ye make him twofold more the child of hell than yourselves." In referring to hell, Christ used the word *Geenna* or *Gehenna,* a reference to eternal damnation, rather than to Hades, the temporary abode of the wicked in the intermediate state. The Pharisees and their proselytes both would end up in eternal damnation.

A third woe is mentioned in verse 16, based on the trickery of the Pharisees, who held that swearing by the gold of the temple bound the oath. Jesus denounced them as both fools and blind, as obviously the gold was meaningless unless it was sanctified by the temple, and the gift on the altar was meaningless unless it was given significance by the altar. Repeating His accusation, He declared in verse 19, "Ye fools and blind: for whether is greater, the gift, or the altar that sanctifieth the gift?" Accordingly, Christ concluded that an oath based on the temple was binding, just as an oath based on heaven carried with it the significance of the throne of God and God who sits on the throne.

The fourth woe, mentioned in verse 23, has to do with hypocrisy in tithing. While they were so concerned in paying the tithe down to the smallest spice or seed, they omitted the really important matters: obeying the law and manifesting mercy and faith. He repeated His charge that they were blind, straining out a gnat or a small insect, but swallowing a camel. He was, of course, speaking figuratively of their dealing with minutiae but omitting the really important things.

The fifth woe is pronounced in verse 25, where He repeated the charge that they were hypocrites, merely actors acting a part. He charged them with cleaning the outside of the cup and the platter but being unconcerned about what was inside, where cleanliness really matters. He meant by this that they were concerned with ceremonial cleanliness, that which men observed, but not really concerned with holiness. While observing ceremonial rites of cleansing, they were not above extortion and excess.

In verse 27, Jesus mentioned the sixth woe. In this one, He described them as whited sepulchres, graves that had been made beautiful and white on the outside but within were full of dead men's bones. This illustrated that the Pharisees were outwardly righteous but inwardly full of hypocrisy and iniquity.

Jesus concluded with the seventh woe, in verse 29, in which He charged them with building tombs of the prophets and garnishing them with decorations and claiming that they would not be partakers with their fathers in martyring prophets. Jesus called their very witness to account, that they were the children of those who killed the prophets, and He told them, in verse 32, "Fill ye up then the measure of your fathers." In other words, do what your fathers did and even do worse. Jesus was, of course, referring to their intent to kill Him and to their later persecution of the church.

In the severest terms, in verse 33, Jesus addressed them, "Ye serpents, ye generation of vipers, how can ye escape the damnation of hell?" He described the scribes and Pharisees as poisonous snakes, destined for terrible judgment which would be theirs in hell, specifically Gehenna, the place of eternal punishment.

Jesus declared, in verse 34, that He would send to them prophets, wise men, and scribes who were also believers. Some of them they would persecute, some they would scourge and drive out of the synagogue, and others they would kill and crucify. Their works would justify bringing upon them the just condemnation coming from all the righteous blood shed upon the earth from the time of righteous Abel, killed by Cain (Gen 4:8), to the martyrdom of Zacharias, the son of Barachias (2 Ch 24:20-22). Zacharias, mentioned as the son of Jehoiada in 2 Chronicles 24:20, probably was the grandson of the priest and Barachias was his actual father. Richard Glover, in his outline of Matthew 23, summarizes the characteristics of hypocrisy in these words, "Hypocrisy is a hard taskmaster . . . lives only for the praise of men . . . concerns itself with the small things of religion . . . deals with externals chiefly . . . reveres only what is dead . . . finds a fearful judgment."[2]

The present sad chapter in the days of Israel's apostasy was the climax of the religious rulers' long rejection of the things of God. Jesus solemnly pronounced that all these acts of rejection of God and His prophets would cause judgment to come upon this generation, which they would bring to culmination by their rejection of God's only Son. This prophecy was tragically fulfilled in the destruction of Jerusalem and the scattering of the children of Israel over the face of the earth. Jerusalem, the city of God, and the magnificent temple, the center of their worship, were to lay in ashes as an eloquent reminder that divine judgment on hypocrisy and sin is inevitable.

LAMENT OVER JERUSALEM, 23:37-39

Probably no words of Jesus in His public ministry are more eloquent than the words recorded in Matthew of Christ's lament over Jerusalem (cf. His earlier lament over Jerusalem, Lk 19:41-44). Here is revealed the breaking heart of God over a people whom God loved, and yet a people who spurned that love and killed those whom God sent to them. The chapter that holds the most severe indictment of any of the discourses of Christ "ends in sobs and tears," as Criswell describes it.[3] Jesus declared, "O Jerusalem, Jerusalem, thou that killest the prophets, and stonest them which are sent unto thee, how often would I have gathered thy children together, even as a hen gathereth her chickens under her wings, and ye would not!" (Mt 23:37). The repetition of the address to Jerusalem signifies the deep emotion in which Jesus spoke, and can be compared to repetitions of similar character in Samuel 18:33, where Absalom is so addressed; Jesus' repeated address to Martha in Luke 10:41; and the call to Saul in Acts 9:4.

Jerusalem, which means "city of peace," was the scene where the blood of the prophets was spilled, and stones were cast at those who brought a message of love. Both the verbs for "killest" and "stonest" are present tense, speaking of habitual or characteristic action. Again and again, prophets had been killed and stoned, and the end was not yet. The figure of a hen, or any mother bird, connotes a brood of young gathering under protective wings, a familiar image in the Bible (Deu 32:11; Ps 17:8; 61:4).

How tragic the words, "Ye would not!" It was God's desire to save them, but it was their will to turn away. There was nothing left but to pronounce judgment, and Jesus did this in Matthew 23:38, "Behold, your house is left unto you desolate." By "house," undoubtedly He was referring to the city. It could, however, also relate to the nation itself, which was to suffer severely in dispersion over the world. The expression *left desolate* is contained in a simple verb meaning to be left alone. How alone is a city, a nation, or an individual from whom God has departed.

Even in the midst of this gloom and condemnation, however, a ray of light is given in verse 39, when Jesus said, "For I say unto you, Ye shall not see me henceforth, till ye shall say, Blessed is he that cometh in the name of the Lord." The generation to whom He was speaking was indeed to be left desolate, tragically alone, but there was hope for a future generation, a generation which would turn once again to the Lord. With these words, Jesus closed His last public discourse and left the temple for the last time (cf. Mt 24:1).

Moses had written long ago in Deuteronomy 30:1-3, "And it shall come to pass, when all these things are come upon thee, and thou shalt call them to mind among all the nations, whither the LORD thy God hath driven thee, and shalt return unto the LORD thy God, and shalt obey his voice according to all that I command thee this day, thou and thy children, with all thine heart, and with all thy soul; That then the LORD thy God will turn thy captivity, and have compassion upon thee, and will return and gather thee from all the nations, whither the LORD thy God hath scattered thee." Moses went on to predict their regathering and their possession of the land (Deu 30:4-5). In Deuteronomy 30:6, he stated "And the LORD thy God will circumcise thine heart, and the heart of thy seed, to love the LORD thy God with all thine heart, with all thy soul, that thou mayest live."

Other references to the same revival in the Old Testament are frequently found. The closing chapters of the prophecies of Isaiah mention again and again the coming revival of Israel, as, for instance, in Isaiah 65:18-25. Jeremiah, in like manner, prophesies Israel's future restoration in Jeremiah 30:1-11; 31:1-14, 27-37. Zechariah speaks of it in chapter 8, and 12:10; 13:1; 14:9-21. The New Testament picks up similar truth in Romans 11:25-36 and pictures Israel triumphant on Mount Zion in Revelation 14:1-5. While it is tragic that Israel did not know the day of her visitation at the time of the first coming of Christ, the godly remnant of Israel, that awaits His second coming to sit on the throne of David, will experience the blessing of the Lord and receive a new heart and a new spirit, of which Ezekiel spoke in Ezekiel 36:23-28.

The tragic note which ends Matthew 23 introduces the great prophecy of the end of the age, recorded in Matthew 24-25 and delivered privately to His disciples. This discourse details the prophecy of the coming kingdom and the time of reward and blessing for those who trust in the Lord.

PART EIGHT

THE OLIVET DISCOURSE
ON THE END OF THE AGE

24

The Signs of the End of the Age

INTRODUCTORY CONSIDERATIONS

THE DISCOURSE OF CHRIST on the Mount of Olives is one of the four major discourses of Christ and should be compared in its content to the Sermon on the Mount, dealing with the moral and ethical principles of the kingdom (Mt 5-7); the discourse on the present age; the kingdom in its mystery form while the King is absent (Mt 13); and the upper room discourse, dealing with the church as the body of Christ in the present age (Jn 13-17). By contrast, the discourse on the Mount of Olives contains Christ's teaching on the end of the age, the period leading up to the second coming of Christ to set up His kingdom on earth.

The Olivet discourse was delivered after Christ's scathing denunciation, in Matthew 23, of the hypocrisy and false religion which characterized the scribes and Pharisees, closing with His lament over Jerusalem, where the prophets of God through the centuries had been rejected and martyred.

PREDICTION OF DESTRUCTION OF THE TEMPLE, 24:1-2

After delivering the denunciation of the scribes and the Pharisees, Christ left the temple, according to Matthew 24:1-2; and as He left, His disciples pointed out the magnificence of the temple buildings. The temple had been under construction since 20 B.C., and, though not actually completed until A.D. 64, its main buildings apparently were largely finished. To the disciples, the temple seemed an impressive evidence of the solidarity of Israel's religious life and of God's blessing upon Jerusalem.

When the disciples pointed out the temple, according to verse 2, Jesus said, "See ye not all these things? verily I say unto you, There shall not be left here one stone upon another, that shall not be thrown down." The disciples apparently received these solemn words in silence, but their thoughts were sobering. The temple was made of huge stones, some of them many tons in size, carved out in the stone quarries underneath the city of Jerusalem. Such large stones could be dislodged only through deliberate force. The sad fulfillment was to come in A.D. 70, only six years after the temple was completed, when the Roman soldiers deliberately destroyed the temple, prying off stones one by one and casting them into the valley below. Recent excavations have uncovered some of these stones.

QUESTIONS OF THE DISCIPLES, 24:3

As they walked from the temple area through the Kidron Valley and up the slope of the Mount of Olives, the disciples, no doubt, were pondering these solemn words of Christ. Matthew 24:3 records that when Christ sat on the Mount of Olives, the disciples then came with their questions. According to Mark 13:3, questions were asked by Peter, James, John, and Andrew. Matthew 24:3 records, "And as he sat upon the mount of Olives, the disciples came unto him privately, saying, Tell us, when shall these things be? and what shall be the sign of thy coming, and of the end of the world?" The disciples had in mind, of course, that the destruction of Solomon's temple, in 586 B.C., preceded the time of captivity. How did the temple's future destruction relate to the promise of the coming kingdom and their hope that Christ would reign over the nation of Israel?

The discourse that follows depends for its interpretation on the question of whether these prophecies should be interpreted literally. Amillenarians, who do not interpret literally any prophecy concerning a future millennial reign of Christ, tend to take the prophecies in this discourse in a general rather than a particular way, and frequently try to find fulfillment in the first century in connection with the destruction of

Jerusalem. Postmillenarians, following the idea that the gospel will gradually triumph over the entire world, have to spiritualize it even more, because this discourse indicates a trend toward increasing evil, which Christ will judge at His second coming.

Liberal interpreters consider this discourse as only a summary of apocalyptic ideas current in the first century, presented here as if taught by Christ but probably not actually uttered by Christ. M'Neile, for instance, states,

> Some predictions of Jesus concerning the nearness of the End probably formed the basis upon which a Jewish-Christian writer compiled a series of sayings, many of them couched in the conventional language of Jewish eschatology. This theory of a Small Apocalypse is widely accepted in various forms by modern writings.[1]

After citing Moffat, B. Weiss, J. Weiss, Zahn, and others, M'Neile adds, "The compiler of it gave some doubtless genuine sayings of Jesus, and also some that reflect a later date when Christians had begun to realize that some delay must be expected before the Parousia."[2]

Those who take the Olivet discourse literally, of course, not only reject the liberal interpretation, but also the amillenarian view of this discourse. Premillenarians, accordingly, interpret the discourse as an accurate statement of end-time events, which will lead up to and climax in the second coming of Christ to set up His millennial kingdom on the earth.

Some variations, however, may also be observed in premillennial interpretation. Those who believe that the rapture, or translation of the church, occurs before the time of trouble at the end of the age usually do not believe that the rapture is in view at all in this discourse, as the rapture was first introduced in John 14:1-3, the night before Jesus was crucified, sometime after the Olivet discourse. Those accepting the posttribulational view, that the rapture of the church and the second coming of Christ occur at the same time, tend to ignore the details of this discourse in the same fashion as the amillenarians do. For instance, G. Campbell Morgan skips over Matthew 24:15-22, which is the most important portion

of Matthew 24.[3] If the details of this discourse are observed
and interpreted literally, it fits best with the view that the rapture is not revealed in this discourse at all, but is a later revelation, introduced by Christ in John 14 and revealed in more
detail in 1 Corinthians 15 and 1 Thessalonians 4. There, the
"blessed hope" that Christ will come for His church before
these end-time events overtake the world is revealed.

The period climaxing in the second coming of Christ to the
earth, according to many premillenarians, begins with the
rapture, or translation of the church, and is followed by the
rapid rise of a dictator in the Middle East who makes a
covenant with Israel. As a result of this covenant, Israel en-
joys protection and peace for three-and-a-half-years. Then the
covenant is broken, and the final three-and-a-half years leading up to the second coming of Christ is a period of great
tribulation and time of Israel's trouble.

The second coming of Christ begins His millennial reign
of one thousand years, which in turn is followed by the new
heaven and the new earth and the eternal state. The Olivet
discourse, accordingly, is in some sense a summary of the
same period described in Revelation 6-19.

In Matthew 24:3, the disciples had asked three questions:
(1) "Tell us, when shall these things be?"; (2) "What shall
be the sign of thy coming?"; and (3) What shall be the sign
"of the end of the world?" Matthew's gospel does not answer the first question, which relates to the destruction of
Jerusalem in A.D. 70. This is given more in detail in Luke,
while Matthew and Mark answer the second and third questions, which actually refer to Christ's coming and the end of
the age as one and the same event. Matthew's account of the
Olivet discourse records that portion of Christ's answer that
relates to His future kingdom and how it will be brought in,
which is one of the major purposes of the gospel.

COURSE OF THE PRESENT AGE, 24:4-14

Expositors have taken various approaches to the introductory remarks of Christ. G. Campbell Morgan, for instance,
regards the whole section of Matthew 24:4-22 as already ful-

filled in the destruction of Jerusalem. Morgan states, "Everything predicted from verse six to verse twenty-two was fulfilled to the letter in connection with the Fall of Jerusalem within a generation."[4] Alfred Plummer goes a step further and includes verse 28 as fulfilled in A.D. 70.[5]

Both Morgan and Plummer ignore the identification of the "great tribulation" in Matthew 24:15, 21 as a specific future period of time, and also ignore the details of the prophecy, not even attempting an exegesis of most of the verses. Accordingly, if the interpreter of this section wants to take the prophecies literally and find a reasonable explanation of the predictions, he must limit the introductory section to Matthew 24:4-14. While variations in interpretation occur, H. A. Ironside expresses a plausible view that verses 4-8 give general characteristics of the age, and that verses 9-14 emphasize the particular signs of the end of the age.[6]

Other premillennial interpreters, however, prefer to take Matthew 24:4-14 as a unit, describing the general characteristics of the age leading up to the end, while at the same time recognizing that the prediction of the difficulties, which will characterize the entire period between the first and second coming of Christ, are fulfilled in an intensified form as the age moves on to its conclusion. If Matthew 24:4-14 deals with general signs, then verses 15-26 may be considered as specific signs. The second coming of Christ is revealed in verses 27-31, which should be compared with the more detailed prophecy of Revelation 19:11-21.

In Matthew 24:4-14, at least nine major characteristics of this general period are described. These characteristics may be itemized as follows: (1) false Christs, 24:4-5; (2) wars and rumors of wars, 24:6-7; (3) famines, 24:7; (4) pestilence, 24:7; (5) earthquakes, 24:7; (6) many martyrs, 24:8-10; (7) false prophets, 24:11; (8) increasing evil and loss of fervent love, 24:12; and (9) worldwide preaching of the gospel of the kingdom, 24:13-14.

In general, these signs have been at least partially fulfilled in the present age and have characterized the period between the first and second coming of Christ. They should be understood as general signs rather than specific signs that the end is near. As stated in verse 8, these are the beginning rather than the end of the sorrows which characterize the close of the age.

Accordingly, through the centuries, there have been many false religious leaders or false Christs. War, famine, and pestilence are still with us. There is some evidence that there is an increase in earthquakes, and, of course, Scriptures record that the greatest earthquake of all time will occur just before the second coming of Christ (Rev 16:18-20). There have been many martyrs through the centuries and probably more in the twentieth century than even in the first century. False prophets and false teachings have plagued the church and the world. The increase in iniquity and loss of fervent love are all too evident in the world, and are detailed, for instance, in Christ's message to the churches of the first century in Revelation 2-3. Throughout the age also there is the announcement of the coming kingdom when Christ will reign on earth, which, of course, will be preached in intensified form as the end approaches. The age in general, climaxing with the second coming of Christ, has the promise that those that endure to the end (Mt 24:13), that is, survive the tribulation and are still alive, will be saved, or delivered, by Christ at His second coming. This is not a reference to salvation from sin, but rather the deliverance of survivors at the end of the age as stated, for instance, in Romans 11:26, where the Deliverer will save the nation Israel from its persecutors. Many, of course, will not endure to the end, in the sense that they will be martyred, even though they are saved by faith in Christ, and the multitude of martyrs is mentioned in Revelation 7:9-17.

Taken as a whole, the opening section, ending with Matthew 24:14, itemizes general signs, events, and situations which mark the progress of the age, and, with growing intensity, indicate that the end of the age is approaching. These signs, however, by their very characteristics and because they have occurred throughout the present age, do not constitute a direct answer to the question of "the sign" of the coming of the Lord.

Sign of the Great Tribulation, 24:15-25

This portion of the Olivet discourse is crucial to understanding what Christ reveals about the end of the age. The tendency to explain away this section or ignore it constitutes the major difficulty in the interpretation of the Olivet discourse. In the background is the tendency of liberals to discount prophecy and the practice of some conservatives of not interpreting prophecy literally. If this prediction means what it says, it is referring to a specific time of great trouble which immediately precedes the second coming of Christ. As such, the prediction of the great tribulation is "the sign" of the second coming, and those who see the sign will be living in the generation which will see the second coming itself. Accordingly, the interpretation of G. Campbell Morgan, which relates this to the fall of Jerusalem in A.D. 70, and the view of Alfred Plummer, which relates it to the second coming of Christ as if fulfilled in the first century, are unjustified interpretations, if the passage is taken seriously.[7]

The fact that the book of Revelation, which practically all expositors date after the destruction of Jerusalem, coincides so exactly with this presentation makes it clear that Christ was not talking here about fulfillment in the first century, but prophecy to be related to His actual second coming to the earth in the future. William Kelly states it concisely, "The conclusion is clear and certain: in verse 15 of Matthew 24, our Lord alludes to that part of Daniel which is yet future, not to what was history when He spoke this on the mount of Olives."[8]

The sign of the future tribulation is identified with what Christ calls the sign of "the abomination of desolation" (v. 15). Jesus said, "When ye therefore shall see the abomination of desolation, spoken of by Daniel the prophet, stand in the holy place, (whoso readeth, let him understand:) Then let them which be in Judaea flee into the mountains" (vv. 15-16). The event is so specific that it will be a signal to the Jews living in Judea at the time to flee to the mountains. What did Christ mean by the expression "the abomination of desolation"?

This term is found three times in the book of Daniel (Dan 9:27; 11:31; 12:11). Its definition is found in Daniel 11:31 in the prophecy written by Daniel concerning a Syrian ruler, Antiochus Epiphanes, who reigned over Syria 175-164 B.C., about four hundred years after Daniel.

In his prophecy, Daniel predicted, "They shall pollute the sanctuary of strength, and shall take away the daily sacrifice, and they shall place the abomination that maketh desolate" (11:31). As this was fulfilled in history, it is comparatively easy to understand what Daniel meant. Antiochus Epiphanes was a great persecutor of the people of Israel, as recorded in the apocryphal books of 1 and 2 Maccabees. In attempting to stamp out the Jewish religion, he murdered thousands of Jews, including women and children, and desecrated the temple of Israel, which precipitated the Maccabean revolt.

Antiochus, in attempting to stop the temple sacrifices, offered a sow, an unclean animal, on the altar, to render the Jewish temple abominable to the Jews (cf. 1 Mac 1:48). According to 1 Maccabees 1:57, the abomination of desolation was actually set up, and a statue of a Greek god was installed in the temple. For a time, the sacrifices of the Jews were stopped, and the temple was left desolate. The action of Antiochus in stopping the sacrifices, desecrating the temple, and setting up an idol in the temple is going to be repeated in the future as the signal of the beginning of the great tribulation.

This future abomination is described in Daniel 9:27: "He [the prince that shall come] shall confirm the covenant with many [Israel] for one week" (literally, "one seven," meaning seven years, as practically all commentators, even those who are liberal, agree). The prophecy continues, "And in the midst of the week he shall cause the sacrifice and the oblation to cease, and for the overspreading of abominations he shall make it desolate." The prediction is that a future prince will do just what Antiochus did in the second century B.C.

Further light is cast on this in Daniel 12:11, where it states, "And from the time that the daily sacrifice shall be taken away, and the abomination that maketh desolate set up, there shall be a thousand two hundred and ninety days," or approximately three-and-a-half-years preceding the second coming of Christ. H. A. Ironside summarizes it, "Our Lord tells us definitely here that His second advent is to follow at once upon the close of that time of trouble; so it is evident that this day of trial is yet in the future."[9]

The New Testament, in 2 Thessalonians 2:4, describes the same period, with the ruler setting himself up as God in the temple. Revelation 13:14-15 also records that an image of the ruler will be set up in the temple. These events did not take place in the first century in connection with the destruction of Jerusalem in A.D. 70, and are closely related to the future fulfillment on the second coming of Christ.

These predictions have raised questions concerning the meaning of Israel's present occupation of the city of Jerusalem. If sacrifices are going to be stopped in a Jewish temple in the future, it requires, first, that a Jewish temple be built, and second, that the sacrifices be reinstituted. This has led to the conclusion that the present possession of Israel of the temple site since 1967 may be a divinely ordered preparation, that in God's time, the temple will be rebuilt and the sacrifices begun again. Although this is difficult to understand in view of the fact that the shrine, the Dome of the Rock, is apparently on the site of the ancient temple and hinders any present erection of such a temple, many believe that, nevertheless, such a temple will be rebuilt and these prophecies literally fulfilled. If upon this revival of their sacrificial system such a future temple is suddenly desecrated, it would constitute a sign to the nation of Israel of the coming time of great trouble just preceding the second coming of Christ.

The sign is so specific that on the basis of it, Christ advised the children of Israel to flee to the mountain without hesitation when it occurs. His instructions were dramatic, as recorded in Matthew 24:16-20. They were to flee immediately to the mountains of Judea, not return to take clothes or other provisions, and pray that their flight will not be in the winter, when it would be most uncomfortable, or on the Sabbath, when their flight would be noticeable. Especially difficult would be the lot of those with small children. Christ summarizes these predictions in 24:21, "For then shall be great tribulation, such as was not since the beginning of the world to this time, no, nor ever shall be."

The great tribulation, accordingly, is a specific period of time beginning with the abomination of desolation and closing with the second coming of Christ, in the light of Daniel's prophecies and confirmed by reference to forty-two months. In Revelation 11:2 and 13:5, the great tribulation is a specific three-and-a-half-year period leading up to the second coming and should not be confused with a general time of trouble, such as was predicted earlier in Matthew 24:4-14.

Jesus also predicted that the period would be "shortened" (v. 22), literally, terminated or cut off (Gr. *ekolobothesan*). This does not mean that the period will be less than three-and-a-half years, but that it will be definitely terminated suddenly by the second coming of Christ.

That the period would be a time of unprecedented trouble is brought out clearly in Revelation 6-19. One of the various judgments, the fourth seal (6:7-8), predicts a fourth part of the earth perishing. In Revelation 9:13-21, the sixth trumpet refers to a third part of the world's population being killed. These are only part of the great catastrophies which fall one after another upon the world and which will climax in a great world war (16:12-16). The final judgment just before the second coming, described as the seventh bowl of the wrath of God (vv. 17-21), consists in a great earthquake, which apparently destroys cities of the world, and a hailstorm, with hailstones weighing a talent, or one hundred and ten pounds. Putting all these Scriptures together, it indicates that the great tribulation will mark the death of hundreds of millions of people in a comparatively short period of time.

Because the great tribulation is unprecedented in history and consists largely in judgments of God on an unbelieving world, many interpreters have come to the conclusion that the church will not have to go through this period. If the church must endure the great tribulation, the chances of survival are quite remote as it is obvious that many who do turn to Christ in that period perish as martyrs. They are described as "a great multitude, which no man could number, of all nations, and kindreds, and people, and tongues" (Rev 7:9), referring to both Jews and Gentiles who will die in the great tribulation. The possibility of rapture for the few that survive is not "the blessed hope" which is held before Christians in the New Testament.[10]

Our hope is not the horrors of the tribulation, but the blessed expectation of Christ's coming for His own (cf. 1 Th 4:13-18).

Having introduced the specific sign of the second coming, which is the great tribulation, Jesus then described other details of the period. Just as there have been false Christs throughout the age, so there will be an intensification of this at the end of the age. Jesus stated, "For there shall arise false Christs, and false prophets, and shall shew great signs and wonders; insomuch that, if it were possible, they shall deceive the very elect" (Mt 24:24). He went on, in verse 25, to state, "Behold, I have told you before." Here, He was referring to His frequent mention of false prophets (cf. Mt 7:15; 15:3-14; 16:6-12; 23:1-36; 24:11). While false Christs and false prophets have always been in evidence, they will be especially prominent at the end of the age in Satan's final attempt to turn people from faith in Christ.

SECOND COMING OF CHRIST, 24:26-31

One who believes the prophetic Scripture will have no difficulty identifying the second coming of Christ, because it will be a public event. Accordingly, Christ, in 24:26, stated, "Wherefore if they shall say unto you, Behold, he is in the desert; go not forth: behold, he is in the secret chambers; believe it not." Unlike the rapture of the church, which apparently the world will not see or hear, the second coming of Christ will be witnessed both by believers and unbelievers who are on the earth at that time. Christ described it in verse 27, "For as the lightning cometh out of the east, and shineth even unto the west; so shall also the coming of the Son of man be." Apparently, the heavens will be ablaze with the glory of God. According to Revelation 1:7, "Every eye shall see him, and they also which pierced him: and all kindreds of the earth shall wail because of him."

This declaration is supported by a cryptic statement in Matthew 24:28, "For wheresoever the carcase is, there will the eagles be gathered together." The meaning is that the glorious coming of Christ is the natural sequence to blasphemy and unbelief, which characterizes the preceding period. Just as when an animal dies, the vultures gather, so when there is moral corruption, there must be divine judgment.

This is further described in verses 29-30, "Immediately after the tribulation of those days shall the sun be darkened, and the moon shall not give her light, and the stars shall fall from heaven, and the powers of the heavens shall be shaken: And then shall appear the sign of the Son of man in heaven: and then shall all the tribes of the earth mourn, and they shall see the Son of man coming in the clouds of heaven with power and great glory." The frightening display of divine disruption of the heavens, which precedes the second coming described graphically in Revelation 6:12-14 and in many other of the judgments of God described in the book of Revelation, will be climaxed by the glorious appearing of Christ in heaven (cf. Rev 19:11-16). This will be a coming of the Lord to judge and subdue the earth and to bring in His earthly kingdom, and is in contrast to the rapture of the church, which is an entirely different event and with a different purpose.

His second coming to the earth is nevertheless a gathering of all "his elect" as stated in Matthew 24:31. Some believe this has a particular reference to the nation Israel as an elect nation. Probably the reference is to all those who are chosen, that is, the saints of all ages, whether in heaven or on earth, for all these will converge upon the millennial kingdom scene. While Matthew mentions only the elect of heaven, Mark 13:27 also mentions those on earth, referred to later in Matthew 25:32.

Taken as a whole, the second coming of Christ is a majestic event, not instantaneous like the rapture, but extending over many hours. This perhaps explains why everyone can see it, because in the course of a day, the earth will rotate and the entire world will be able to see the approach of Christ accompanied by the hosts of heaven, which will descend to the earth in the area of the Mount of Olives (Zec 14:4).

The entire passage from Matthew 24:15-31 is the specific answer to the disciples of the sign of His coming and of the end of the age, with the climactic sign being the second coming and the glory that attends it, and will fulfill the prophecy of Acts 1:11 that Christ will return as He went up into heaven, that is, His return will be physical, gradual, visible, and with clouds. Matthew 24:31 brings to a close the first doctrinal section of the Olivet discourse, and what follows is a series of applications and illustrations.

PARABLE OF THE FIG TREE, 24:32-33

In interpreting the illustrations which follow, while there may be secondary applications of the truth to the church awaiting the rapture, the laws of exegesis would dictate that the illustrations should relate to the doctrine of the second coming of Christ. Accordingly, while this passage may have a general application to saints in the present age, it will have a particular application to those who will await the second coming of Christ to the earth. Accordingly, in interpreting illustrations, the question should be raised, What does the context indicate?

This is especially appropriate in consideration of the fig tree. In 24:32-33, Christ stated, "Now learn a parable of the fig tree; When his branch is yet tender, and putteth forth leaves, ye know that summer is nigh: So likewise ye, when ye shall see all these things, know that it is near, even at the doors." A very popular interpretation of this passage considers the fig tree as a type, or illustration, of Israel. According to this view, the fact that Israel in the twentieth century is back in the land constitutes a budding of the fig tree, and may be taken as conclusive proof that the Lord's return is near.[11]

Commentaries which try to refer this entire passage to the destruction of Jerusalem in A.D. 70, of course, pass it over with no comment, as do G. Campbell Morgan and Willoughby C. Allen, or apply it to the destruction of Jerusalem, as does R. V. G. Tasker.[12]

Actually, while the fig tree could be an apt illustration of

Israel, it is not so used in the Bible. In Jeremiah 24:1-8, good and bad figs illustrate Israel in the captivity, and there is also mention of figs in 29:17. The reference to the fig tree in Judges 9:10-11 is obviously not Israel. Neither the reference in Matthew 21:18-20 nor that in Mark 11:12-14 with its interpretation in 11:20-26, gives any indication that it is referring to Israel, any more than the mountain referred to in the passage. Accordingly, while this interpretation is held by many, there is no clear scriptural warrant.

A better interpretation is that Christ was using a natural illustration. Because the fig tree brings forth new leaves late in the spring, the budding of the leaves is evidence that summer is near. In a similar way, when those living in the great tribulation see the signs predicted, they will know that the second coming of Christ is near. The signs in this passage, accordingly, are not the revival of Israel, but the great tribulation itself. Lenski, accordingly, is correct when he states that "all these things" mentioned in Matthew 24:33 refer to the preceding context.[13] That Israel's presence in the holy land is a dramatic evidence that the age is approaching its end may be supported by other passages, but this is not the point here.

Christ further commented in verses 34-36, "This generation shall not pass, till all these things be fulfilled. Heaven and earth shall pass away, but my words shall not pass away. But of that day and hour knoweth no man, no, not the angels of heaven, but my Father only."

What is the meaning of the expression *this generation?* Some have cited this as an illustration of an error on the part of Christ, for a generation is normally from thirty to one hundred years, and obviously, the prophecy of the second coming was not fulfilled in that period. Commentators offer a variety of opinions. Some refer "generation"' to the nation Israel.[14] The meaning, then, would be that Israel would continue as a nation until the second coming of Christ. Some take *generation* to refer to an indefinite period of time. Arndt and Gingrich, while offering the possibility that *generation* means nation or race, prefer age or period of time, and, accordingly, take it as instructing the disciples that the age leading up to the second coming will not end until the event of the second coming itself.[15] A third explanation is that the word *generation* means what it normally means, that is, a period of thirty to one hundred years, and refers to the particular generation that will see the specific signs, that is, the signs of the great tribulation. In other words, the same generation that will experience the great tribulation will also witness the second coming of Christ.

In any case, Christ points out that while prophecy is absolutely certain of fulfillment, the day of the second coming is not revealed, although the approximate time will be known by those living in the great tribulation.

To illustrate this approximate time of the second coming, He used the historic flood in the time of Noah. While those observing Noah building the ark could anticipate that a flood was impending, it was obvious that the flood could not come until the ark was completed. So also with the second coming. Unlike the rapture, which has no preceding signs and therefore could occur any time, the second coming of Christ to the earth to set up His kingdom cannot occur until the preceding signs have been fulfilled. When the ark was completed and Noah and his family and the animals were in it, those observing could anticipate that the predicted flood could occur any day. But even then, they could not predict the day nor the hour.

Like the days of Noah, the time of the second coming will be a period of judgment on the earth. Just as the flood came "and took them all away," referring to the judgment of unbelievers, so at the second coming, some will be taken away. According to Matthew 24:40-41, "Then shall two be in the field; the one shall be taken, and the other left. Two women shall be grinding at the mill; the one shall be taken, and the other left." Because at the rapture believers will be taken out of the world, some have confused this with the rapture of the church.

Here, however, the situation is the reverse. The one who is left, is left to enter the kingdom; the one who is taken, is taken in judgment. This is in keeping with the illustration of the time of Noah when the ones taken away are the unbelievers. The word for "shall be taken" in verses 40-41 uses the same word found in John 19:16, where Christ was taken away to the judgment of the cross. Accordingly, no one can know the day nor the hour, but they can know that when the second coming occurs, it will be a time of separation of the saved from the unsaved.

Emphasizing the necessity of watchfulness for the Lord's return, He used the illustration of the good man of the house who, anticipating the possibility that a thief would come, kept careful watch. Just as one cannot know when a thief may come, so the servants of God who live in the great tribulation should expect Christ to come (cf. 1 Th 5:2).

In addition to watchfulness, however, there should be careful service and preparation. This is illustrated in the parable of the servant, beginning in Matthew 24:45. Having been left in charge of his master's household in the absence of the master, the servant was challenged to do his duty well and not to live carelessly, thinking that the lord would not be coming soon. The careless servant will be severely judged as an unbeliever, in contrast to the good servant who will be rewarded by his Lord. An unfaithful slave could be put to death and punished severely. So will Christ judge a wicked world that does not look for His return.

While these illustrations, beginning in verse 32, have as their primary interpretation and exhortation the situation immediately preceding the second coming of Christ, there are parallels to those living today in expectation of the rapture. Believers today also need to be faithful, to be recognizing the signs of the times, and to be living in such a way that they are ready for the Lord's return. Even among those who differ in their basic interpretation of prophecy, there is this constant unifying note of being ready for the Lord's return. John Calvin, for instance, in commenting on 1 John 2:18, states, "It behooves us to comfort ourselves at this day, and to see by faith the near advent of Christ . . . nothing more now remained but that Christ should appear for the redemption of the world."[16]

Martin Luther likewise anticipated the early return of the Lord, stating "I think the last day is not far away."[17] He also adds, "The world runs and hastens so diligently to its end that it often occurs to me forcibly that the last day will break before we can completely turn the Holy Scriptures into German. For it is certain from the Holy Scriptures that we have no more temporal things to expect. All is done and fulfilled."[18] So today, even though we may not understand all the prophetic Word and may not interpret it alike, believers should be looking for the coming of the Lord. As stated in 1 John 3:3, "And every man that hath this hope in him purifieth himself, even as he is pure."

25

Judgments at the End
of the Age

THE FAMILIAR ILLUSTRATION of the ten virgins, as presented in Matthew 25, is a further effort by Christ to drive
home the necessity of watchfulness and preparation for His
second coming. An oriental wedding had three stages: first,
the legal marriage arranged by the parents of the bridegroom
and the bride; second, the traditional ceremony, when the
bridegroom, accompanied by his friends, would proceed from
his home to the home of the bride and claim her as his own;
third, the marriage feast held at the home of the bridegroom.

The illustration presumes that the legal marriage has already taken place and can reasonably be identified with the
marriage of Christ and the church already consummated at
the rapture. When Christ returns at His second coming, He
will bring His bride with Him. The five virgins who bring oil
in their vessels illustrate those that are ready for His return.
The five foolish maidens, although outwardly prepared, are
not really ready. When the time comes for the marriage feast,
they are not prepared to enter into the procession and join
the feast.

Although interpretation is not given in this passage, oil
may be taken here as representative of the Holy Spirit and
His work of salvation. When Christ comes to earth with His
bride, only those prepared by new birth will enter into the
wedding feast, which seems to be fulfilled in the millennium
or at least the first portion of the millennium. Some commentators desire to apply the ten virgins to the church in the
present age. The fact that the word *then* is used in 25:1
seems to refer to the second coming of Christ to the earth.

Although worthy expositors can be cited in support of this view,[1] it is preferable to interpret it strictly in the context of the second coming of Christ. Actually, the bride, the church, is not in view specifically. Although the Syriac and Vulgate versions of verse 1 read that they "went forth to meet the bridegroom and the bride,"[2] it is questionable whether this addition was in the original text, even though it is true that Christ will bring His bride with Him. The important point here, as in the preceding illustration, is that preparation should precede the second coming of Christ and that it will be too late when He comes.

What is true of the second coming is, of course, also true of the rapture, and believers today can derive a secondary application of this passage for their own need. In our modern world, where superficial religion is all too evident, this passage reminds us once again that apart from the work of the Holy Spirit, symbolized by the oil, no one is ready for the coming of the Lord.

PARABLE OF THE TALENTS, 25:14-30

The familiar parable of the talents in Matthew 25 is the sixth and final illustration Christ used in regard to preparedness for His second coming. Here, the emphasis is on serving rather than watching, as in the parable of the virgins.

As was customary in the ancient world, the master of the servants was pictured as turning over his property to his servants because he was going on a journey. He divided his property to his three servants according to their ability, giving five talents to one, two to another, and one talent to the third.

A talent was a large sum of money, varying greatly in value according to whether it was silver or gold, and could weigh from fifty-eight to eighty pounds.[3] A silver talent could be worth as much as $2,000, and a gold talent could be worth as much as $30,000. With the rise in price of these metals, today the value would even be higher. When taking into consideration that a man's wage in Christ's time was sixteen cents a day, the purchasing power of this amount of money was very large. At maximum, the five-talent man could have received as much as $150,000, a fortune, which would be worth millions today in purchasing power.

In the absence of his lord, the five-talent man doubled his money. In like manner, the two-talent man also doubled his money. The one who had received the single talent, however, buried his money in the earth and did nothing with it.

In the illustration, the lord of the servants, upon his return, called in his servants for their report. The five-talent man was able to report proudly that he had doubled his money. The two-talent man did likewise. It is significant that both the five-talent and the two-talent man were given precisely the same commendation, "Well done, thou good and faithful servant: thou hast been faithful over a few things, I will make thee ruler over many things: enter thou into the joy of thy lord" (25:21). The principle that rewards are given according to faithfulness is illustrated well in this parable.

The one-talent man, however, had to report that he had done nothing but bury his money. He offered the lame excuse, "Lord, I knew thee that thou art an hard man, reaping where thou hast not sown, and gathering where thou hast not strawed: And I was afraid, and went and hid thy talent in the earth: lo, there thou hast that is thine" (vv. 24-25). Whether or not the servant's accusation was true, it was only an excuse at best. If the servant had actually believed what he had said, it should have made him all the more diligent. His lord, accordingly, answered him abruptly and denounced him as a "wicked and slothful servant." He pointed out that the least he could have done was to put his money in the bank where it would have received interest.

An interesting question that is not directly answered in the text is why the one-talent man did not put it in the bank. Most expositors are rather vague in their explanation of this detail. The explanation seems to be that this wicked man had the same kind of cunning that Judas Iscariot used when he accepted the money for the betrayal of Christ. Judas had reasoned that if Jesus was indeed the Messiah, his betrayal would not matter, and he would be ahead thirty pieces of silver. If Jesus was not the Messiah, he at least would have the silver. So, the wicked one-talent man likewise reasoned:

If my lord returns, I will be able to give him back his talent and cannot be accused of being a thief, but if he does not return, there will be no record that the money belongs to him, such as would be true if I deposited it in the bank, and then I will be able to use the money myself. His basic problem, like the problem of Judas, was a lack of faith.

The one-talent man did not believe that it was sure his lord was coming back. It is therefore clear that his basic problem was that of being an unbeliever, not simply being unfaithful in service. Accordingly, the conclusion of the illustration, "For unto every one that hath shall be given, and he shall have abundance: but from him that hath not shall be taken away even that which he hath" (v. 29), refers to everyone who has faith or who is lacking faith.

Here, as elsewhere in Scripture, while works may be an evidence of salvation, they are never the ground of salvation. The one-talent man, while deficient in works, was condemned because of his lack of faith. Accordingly, the one-talent man is not an illustration of a backsliding Christian, as no Christian justified by faith and declared righteous by God could ever be cast into the outer darkness. A person who really believes in the first coming of Christ will also believe in His second coming and for the same reasons.

Taken as a whole, the illustrations, which interpret the doctrine of the second coming and make practical application of the truth, emphasize the two themes of watching and serving. What is true for those anticipating the second coming is also true for those who anticipate Christ's coming for His church.

JUDGMENT OF THE NATIONS, 25:31-46

The third section of the Olivet discourse begins with 25:31. The first section, 24:4-31, had answered the questions of the disciples concerning the signs of the end of the age and the coming of the Lord. The second section, 24:32—25:30, presented interpretations and applications of the truth of the second coming of Christ. Beginning in 25:31, Jesus went beyond the questions of the disciples to describe the period following the second coming.

Although conservative expositors agree that this is a judgment related to the second coming of Christ, there is extensive disagreement as to the nature of the judgment and its relation to the total prophetic plan. Amillenarians, who deny a future millennial reign of Christ, believe that this is a general judgment of all men that ushers in the eternal state. Lenski, for instance, states, "The whole human race will be assembled for the final judgment."[4] Other amillenarians, such as R.V.G. Tasker, likewise picture it as a judgment "of *all nations.*"[5] Postmillenarians likewise agree that it is a judgment of all men. Even Henry Alford, a premillenarian, states, "We now come to the great and universal judgment at the end of this period, also prophesied distinctly in order in Rev 20:11-15— in which *all the dead,* small and great shall stand before God."[6] Liberal writers, like A. H. M'Neile, agree.[7] These commentaries, however, correctly hold that this is not a parable, as the preceding illustrations of the virgins and the talents, but a literal prophecy.

A strict exegesis of this passage, however, does not support the conclusion that this is a general judgment. There is no mention of resurrection of either the righteous or the wicked, and "all nations" seems to exclude Israel. The conclusion that this is a final judgment is necessary to the amillenarians' point of view, but it is not taught in this passage. Accordingly, if the view that there is a kingdom of Christ on earth for a thousand years after His second advent is supported by other Scriptures, this passage fits naturally in such a prophetic framework, and, as such, constitutes the judgment of the living who are on earth at the time of the second coming of Christ in respect to their entrance into the millennial kingdom. This judgment therefore should be contrasted to the judgment of Israel (Eze 20:34-38) and the judgment of the wicked (Rev 20:11-15) which comes after the millennium has concluded. This passage, more precisely than any other, describes the judgment of the world at the beginning of Christ's millennial kingdom.

The time of the judgment is stated to be the period following the second coming of Christ, Matthew 25:31, "When the Son of man shall come in his glory, and all the holy angels with him, then shall he sit upon the throne of his glory." This judgment, therefore, should be distinguished from the judgment of the church in heaven, the judgment of the wicked at the end of the millennium, and the judgment of Israel.

At this judgment, "all nations," better translated "all Gentiles," are gathered before Him and are described as sheep and goats intermingled. In the judgment, the sheep are put on His right hand and the goats on His left. The sheep are invited to inherit His kingdom, and Christ will address them: "Come, ye blessed of my Father, inherit the kingdom prepared for you from the foundation of the world: For I was an hungred, and ye gave me meat: I was thirsty, and ye gave me drink: I was a stranger, and ye took me in: Naked, and ye clothed me: I was sick, and ye visited me: I was in prison, and ye came unto me" (vv. 34-36). When the sheep reply, in verses 37-39, asking when they did these deeds of kindness, the King will reply, "Verily I say unto you, Inasmuch as ye have done it unto one of the least of these my brethren, ye have done it unto me" (v. 40). In mentioning "my brethren," He is referring to a third class, neither sheep nor goats, which can only be identified as Israel, the only remaining people who are in contrast to all the Gentiles.

The King will then address the goats and dismiss them into everlasting fire, declaring that they have not done these deeds of kindness. When they protest, asking when they omitted these deeds, the King will reply, "Verily I say unto you, Inasmuch as ye did it not to one of the least of these, ye did it not to me" (v. 45). The passage concludes with the goats dismissed into everlasting punishment and the righteous entering into the blessings of eternal life.

This judgment fits naturally and easily into the prophetic program as usually outlined by premillenarians. The throne is an earthly throne, fulfilling the prediction of Jeremiah 23:5. Those who are judged are Gentiles (Gr. *ethne*), which, although sometimes used for Jews (Lk 7:5; 23:2; Jn 11:48, 51, 52; 18:35; Ac 10:22), is more characteristically used of Gentiles as distinguished from Jews, as for instance in Romans 11:13; 15:27; 16:4; Galatians 2:12; and is used in contrast to Jews in Romans 3:29 and 9:24.

If the evidence sustains the conclusion that this applies to Gentiles living on earth at the time of the second coming of Christ, a further problem is introduced by the nature of the judgment. How can deeds, such as giving the thirsty to drink, clothing the naked, and doing other deeds of kindness, form a basis for salvation? Ephesians 2:8-9 makes plain, "For by grace are ye saved through faith; and that not of yourselves: it is the gift of God: Not of works, that any man should boast." The Bible clearly teaches in many passages that salvation is by grace and by faith alone and is not based on works (Ro 3:10-12, 21, 28). The answer to this problem is that works are presented here, not as the ground of salvation, but as the evidence of it, in the sense of James 2:26, where it is declared, "Faith without works is dead"; that is, it is not real faith unless it produces works. While this solves the problem in part, the question still remains whether such deeds of kindness are sufficient to demonstrate salvation.

The answer to this problem is found in the context of this passage. Those described here are people who have lived through the great tribulation, a time of unparalleled anti-Semitism, when the majority of Jews in the land will be killed. Under these circumstances, if a Gentile befriends a Jew to the extent of feeding and clothing and visiting him, it could only mean that he is a believer in Jesus Christ and recognizes the Jews as the chosen people. Accordingly, in this context, such works become a distinctive evidence that the Gentiles described as the sheep are those who are children of God by faith in Jesus Christ.

This judgment, which results in the goats being cast into everlasting fire, is in keeping with the previous prediction of Christ in the parable of the wheat and tares and the parable of the dragnet (Mt 13:24-30, 31-43, 47-50), and is also clearly taught in Revelation 14:11 and 19:15. No adults who are not converted will be allowed to enter the millennial kingdom. The judgment here is not a final judgment, but is preparatory to establishing the kingdom of righteousness and peace, of which many Scriptures speak.

The passage, while not dealing specifically with amillennialism or postmillennialism, clearly gives these views no support whatever. The postmillennial dream of a gradually improving world is not revealed here. Instead, Christ comes to a world that is basically anti-Christ and worshiping a man satanically empowered. A judgment like this does not fit into the amillennial interpretation either, because there is no basis here for concluding this to be a judgment of all men living and dead. It is quite different than the judgment of the great white throne (Rev 20:11-15), which takes place in space, whereas this judgment takes place on earth.

Although the question of whether Christ will come for His church before the tribulation (the pretribulational view) or at the time of His second coming to earth (the posttribulational view) is not dealt with in this passage, the implications are clearly in favor of the pretribulational view. If the rapture and translation of the church occur while Christ is coming from heaven to earth in His second coming to set up His kingdom, and the church meets the Lord in the air, it is obvious that this very act would separate all the saved from the unsaved. Under these circumstances, no judgment of the nations would be necessary subsequent to the second coming of Christ, because the sheep and the goats would already be separated.

The implication of this passage in Matthew is that no rapture of living saints occurs at the time Christ comes to set up His kingdom. This implies that there is a time period between the rapture and the time Christ comes to set up His kingdom, during which a new body of saints, both Jews and Gentiles, is created by faith in Christ.

Furthermore, when these saints are judged, they are not given new bodies, but enter the millennium in their natural bodies, in keeping with the millennial predictions of Scripture which describe the saints as bearing children, building houses, and otherwise having a natural life (Is 65:18-25).

A proper exegesis of this passage, accordingly, tends to support both the premillennial and the pretribulational point of view, even though this is not the main purpose of this prophecy. It is an interesting fact that posttribulationists generally ignore this passage in their treatment of the rapture question, and that amillenarians who attempt to harmonize it with their

point of view ignore the fact that the passage does not state
what they read into it.

Taken as a whole, the Olivet discourse is one of the great
prophetic utterances of Scripture and provides facts nowhere
else given in quite the same way. In it, Christ, the greatest
of the prophets and the master Teacher, described the end
of the age as the climax of the troubles of earth in a great
tribulation. The time of unprecedented trouble will be terminated by the second coming of Christ. The saved and the unsaved will be separated, and only the saved will enter the
millennial kingdom. This is the final word, which Matthew
brings in answer to the leading question of this first gospel,
concerning the fulfillment of the prophecies of the Old Testament of a glorious kingdom on earth. Matthew states clearly
that while Christ, in His first coming, suffered and died and
was rejected as both King and Saviour by His own people,
He will come again and, in triumph, will bring in the prophesied kingdom literally, just as the Old Testament prophecies
had anticipated. There is postponement but not annulment
of the great prophecies of the kingdom on earth.

It is clear that the disciples did not understand these prophecies at the time. In the few days that followed, they were
to witness the death and then the resurrection of Jesus Christ.
They were to ask again the question of when the kingdom
would be brought in on the day of the ascension of Christ
(Ac 1:6). As further revelation was given in the writing of
the New Testament, and the disciples pondered the words that
they had not understood before, they gradually comprehended
the truth that Christ was first coming for His own in the rapture of the church, but then that there would be a fulfillment
of the predicted time of trouble. This, in turn, would be
climaxed by the second coming of Christ and the establishment of the kingdom. Not one prophecy will be left unfulfilled when history has completed its course and the saints
are gathered in the New Jerusalem in the new heaven and
the new earth.

PART NINE

THE DEATH AND RESURRECTION OF THE REJECTED KING

26

Jesus' Last Hours Before Crucifixion

FINAL ANNOUNCEMENT OF HIS COMING DEATH, 26:1-5

HAVING CONCLUDED His comprehensive answer to the disciples' questions concerning the end of the age, Jesus returned to the consideration of the impending events (cf. Mk 14:1-2; Lk 22:1-2). He said to His disciples, "Ye know that after two days is the feast of the passover, and the Son of man is betrayed to be crucified" (Mt 26:2). Lenski observes that this notation concerning the time indicates that Jesus was speaking on Tuesday of the last week and that Matthew's account of that Tuesday begins in 21:23 and extends through 26:5.[1]

Liberal scholars try to make the most of what they believe is an inaccuracy here.[2] Part of the problem is that Mark 14:1-2, in the parallel account, adds also "and of unleavened bread," referring to the seven-day feast which followed the Passover. All this, however, is much ado about nothing, because, although the expression "after two days" may have more than one interpretation, it clearly connotes that two days or more would elapse before the Passover would occur. The Passover also used unleavened bread, and if more than two days elapsed before the Feast of Unleavened Bread, which follows the Passover, there would be no real error in fact. The practical point is that they were faced with the final betrayal and crucifixion of Jesus.

There is no record of the disciples' comment on this, but Matthew records that even as Jesus was speaking, the chief priests, the scribes, and the elders of the people had assembled in the palace of the high priest Caiaphas, plotting to take Him when the people would not be around to prevent it. It is possible that they had in mind waiting until after the Feast of Unleavened Bread, which would be ten days later, when the pilgrims would have begun returning to their homes, but Jesus said, "after two days." And so it was. The early arrest of Jesus was to be made possible by the betrayal of Judas Iscariot. Only hours separated Jesus from the cross on Calvary.

JESUS ANOINTED FOR BURIAL, 26:6-13

During these last days before His crucifixion, Jesus stayed in Bethany on the eastern slope of the Mount of Olives, probably residing with Lazarus, Mary, and Martha. The incident, recorded here in Matthew and in Mark 14:3-9 and more in detail in John 12:1-8, occurred in the house of Simon the leper. While some have taken this as another name for Lazarus or possibly for Lazarus' father, there is no reason it should not be another home, for Jesus had many friends in Bethany. In any event, Lazarus, Martha, and Mary were there. Matthew and Mark omit any reference to them, but John states plainly that Lazarus was there, that Martha served, and that it was Mary who anointed the feet of Jesus (Jn 12:1-3). Matthew and Mark, likewise, do not give the exact date and apparently are not reciting events in their strict chronological order. John, however, specifies that the event took place six days before the Passover. If the Passover was on Friday, then Lenski may be right that this supper took place on Saturday evening after the Sabbath had ended.[3] The whole chronology of the week leading up to the crucifixion is debatable, and some place the crucifixion on Wednesday or Thursday instead of the traditional date of Friday, which is assumed here.

As they were reclining about the table in the cool of the evening, Mary took an expensive alabaster box containing a precious ointment, which John describes as "a pound of ointment of spikenard, very costly" (Jn 12:3), and anointed Jesus. Matthew 26:7 and Mark 14:3 refer to the anointing of only His head. John adds that she also anointed His feet and wiped His feet with her hair (Jn 12:3). The fragrant perfume permeated the entire house.

This amazing act of devotion coming from Mary, who had sat at Jesus' feet and perhaps more nearly than any other really understood that He would die, aroused criticism from the disciples. John mentions that it was Judas Iscariot who spoke up and asked why the ointment had not been sold for three hundred denarii and the proceeds given to the poor (Jn 12:4-5). John observes that Judas Iscariot said this not because of his concern for the poor but because he was a thief and was the treasurer of the twelve (v. 6). It is possible that the other disciples were also indignant, for Matthew and Mark both picture more than one of the disciples participating in the criticism (Mt 26:8; Mk 14:4). Jesus, perceiving the genuineness of Mary's devotion, rebuked His disciples saying, "Why trouble ye the woman? for she hath wrought a good work upon me" (Mt 26:10). He went on to say that they would have the poor with them always, and Mary had done this by way of preparing His body for burial. He predicted, "Wheresoever this gospel shall be preached in the whole world, there shall also this, that this woman hath done, be told for a memorial of her" (v. 13).

The loving and sacrificial act of Mary has many connotations. While the disciples were slow to accept the repeated prophecies of His death, Mary seems to have comprehended it at least in part. Although she was not as active as the disciples or in a place of leadership, and though she did not serve as Martha had done, sitting at the feet of Jesus had given her insight into spiritual things which many in their busy lives never achieve. Undoubtedly, the precious ointment had been a treasure held in the family for some time, and the reckless abandon with which she dedicated it to the anointing of Jesus was not a senseless extravagance but an act of supreme devotion. That Jesus permitted it without rebuke was to Judas Iscariot the final evidence that led him to question that Jesus was indeed the Messiah, and the verses which follow record his covenant to betray Jesus.

JUDAS SEEKS TO BETRAY JESUS, 26:14-16

When Judas went to the high priest (cf. Mk 14:10-11; Lk

22:3-6), Jesus had already cleansed the temple, as He had done it on Monday morning, and they were eager to find some way by which they could lay their hands on Him privately. Nothing is said concerning how they bargained back and forth, but they agreed on thirty pieces of silver. The price was not high, as it was the same as the fine for killing a slave accidentally (cf. Ex 21:32), but Judas was all too willing to sell the King of kings for the price of a slave. No doubt, the money was immediately weighed out to him, fulfilling Zechariah 11:12 precisely, as Judas was not going to take the risk of betraying Christ and then going penniless. He knew all too well that if he did not carry out his bargain, the money would have to be returned, as the Jews could have had him arrested at any time. Matthew records, "And from that time he sought opportunity to betray him" (26:16). The time was going to come earlier than even the chief priests had thought possible.

LAST PASSOVER, 26:17-25

Matthew gives only a brief account of the preparations for the last Passover which Jesus celebrated with His disciples (cf. Mk 14:12-16; Lk 22:7-13; Jn 13:1-12). The parallel passages describing the preparation of the Passover in Mark and Luke give more details. The time was apparently Thursday, presuming that there were no events recorded for Wednesday and that Friday was the day of crucifixion, as most expositors have held. The two disciples, designated to find the place under the special instructions which Jesus gave them, were Peter and John, according to Luke 22:8. The rest of the disciples were not to know the place until that evening, when they would be led there by Jesus Himself.

No explanation is given for the somewhat secretive way in which preparations for the Passover were made. Jesus, of course, knew that the chief priests and scribes were plotting to arrest Him and that Judas had agreed to betray Him. The other disciples also were somewhat aware of the dangers of His being in Jerusalem, especially at night away from the crowds. Accordingly, the plan to keep the place completely secret from Judas and the rest of the disciples, except Peter and John, was necessary to avoid premature arrest and interference with the events of the evening.

None of the accounts indicate the name of the owner of the house, though apparently he was someone who recognized Jesus and was a disciple. Speculation is useless as to the identity of this man, and even the location is unknown, although visitors to Jerusalem today are often shown a traditional site for the Last Supper. The Passover was to be a hallowed occasion for Christ and the disciples, their last night together after more than three years of association, a night never to be forgotten.

The account of the Passover itself is recorded not only in Matthew but in Mark 14:17-21 and Luke 22:14-30. Luke includes in the middle of his account the institution of the Lord's Supper. John 13:1-12 records the incident of Christ washing the disciples' feet.

Matthew records that when evening (probably Thursday) came, which after sundown was actually the beginning of Friday, Jesus sat down with His twelve disciples. The verb *sat down* actually means to recline or to lie down. They lay on couches arranged around a table which was low enough to permit them to feed themselves while reclining. There was probably a long table with the disciples arranged in a U shape around one end with the other end acting as a serving table. The traditional picture of Jesus and His disciples seated about a table is inaccurate. The record of the situation in the various gospels indicates there had been some contest among them concerning who would sit close to Jesus.

Judging by the conversation between Jesus, John, Peter, and Judas, John, the youngest disciple and the one whom Jesus loved, was on one side of Jesus. It may be that Judas Iscariot was on the other, and that Peter, ambitious for one of these places, ended up on the opposite side of the table. In any case, Peter does not seem to be close to Jesus (Jn 13:24). The spirit of contest among them as to which should be the greatest (Mt 18:1-4; Mk 9:33-37; Lk 9:46-48), which had been going on for six months, and which Jesus had previously rebuked, was again evident at the Last Supper and was the occasion of the demonstration by Jesus of washing the disciples' feet.

While none of the accounts in the four gospels give all the details, it is obvious that Matthew is providing only a concise summary. The extended discourse of Jesus in John 15-17 is not mentioned by Matthew. The events in Matthew, Mark, and Luke are treated topically and not necessarily in order chronologically. From Matthew's point of view, the important point was the betrayal of Jesus by Judas, and this is what he introduced immediately into the narrative of the last Passover.

It is probable that most of the Passover feast was observed before Judas was identified. After washing the disciples' feet and making introductory comments, the order of events was probably this: (1) Jesus gave thanks and they drank from the cup; (2) the bitter herbs were introduced, symbolizing their rigorous life in Egypt; (3) Jesus introduced the unleavened bread and the lamb which had been killed and roasted according to the instructions, as well as any other sacrificial meat; (4) Jesus ate the bitter herbs, and the others followed suit; (5) Jesus mixed the wine and the water for the second cup, which, in an ordinary home situation, would occasion the son asking the meaning of the Passover feast and the father explaining; (6) they sang the Hallel, Psalms 113 and 114 and then they drank again from the cup; (7) Jesus ceremonially washed His hands, then taking two cakes of bread, went through the ceremony of breaking one, laying it on the unbroken bread, blessing the bread, wrapping the broken bread with herbs, dipping in the juices of the roasted lamp, and eating of the meat; (8) the rest joined Him in eating the food that had been prepared.

While it is not possible to pinpoint the time when Judas was exposed, Lenski is probably right that it occurs at this point.[4] The Passover celebration was normally concluded by the drinking of a third cup, the singing of Psalms 115-118, and then one or more drinks from the cup. The conclusion would be singing from Psalms 120-137. Whether all these details were followed by Jesus, the Scriptures do not make clear. It was probably at the end or near the end of the Passover that Judas was identified and the Lord's Supper was instituted.

It must have been a great shock to the disciples, in the context of this hallowed feast, for Jesus to have said, as He did in Matthew 26:21, "Verily I say unto you, that one of you shall betray me." Matthew records that they all were extremely sorry and asked the question, "Lord, is it I?" Judas himself apparently was strangely silent for a time. In answer to the question of the other disciples, Jesus affirmed simply, "He that dippeth his hand with me in the dish, the same shall betray me" (v. 23). The whole incident must be interpreted as a gracious attempt on the part of Jesus to make Judas realize his terrible sin and turn from it before it was too late. That he would reject His pleas and harden his heart is all too evident in the words of Jesus in verse 24, "The Son of man goeth as it is written of him: but woe unto that man by whom the Son of man is betrayed! it had been good for that man if he had not been born."

Up to this time, Judas had not been identified clearly. According to John 13:21-26, Peter motioned to John, who was leaning on Jesus' bosom, to ask who it was. John was informed, according to John 13:26, "He it is, to whom I shall give a sop, when I have dipped it. And when he had dipped the sop, he gave it to Judas Iscariot, the son of Simon." Peter and John accordingly knew that Judas was the betrayer.

Whether this prompted Judas to ask the question is not revealed, but according to Matthew 26:25, "Then Judas, who betrayed him, answered and said, Master, is it I? He said unto him, Thou hast said." If Judas was immediately to one side of Jesus, it is possible that the other disciples did not hear. The Scriptures do not indicate whether any heard the conversation between Jesus and Judas. Matthew does not record Judas' response, but John 13:27-30 indicates that immediately after the conversation and his identification by receiving the sop, Judas went out into the night. Jesus had said to him, "That thou doest, do quickly" (Jn 13:27).

The question had apparently arisen in Judas' mind whether Jesus actually knew that he had plotted against Him. Judas was torn between faith and unbelief, but with the cunning

of a heart that is desperately wicked, he reasoned that if Jesus
was indeed the Messiah, his betrayal of Him would not be
effective. On the other hand, if He were not the Messiah and
He were crucified as He had predicted, Judas at least would
be ahead thirty pieces of silver. With the crooked reasoning
of the natural mind, Judas concluded that he could not lose.
His problem was that while he wanted to follow a King who
would reign gloriously, he did not want to follow a crucified
Saviour.

INSTITUTION OF THE LORD'S SUPPER, 26:26-30

Probably at this point in the sequence of events, after Judas
left, the Lord's Supper was instituted, something new and
additional to the Passover feast. All the gospels record the
event (Mk 14:22-25; Lk 22:17-20; Jn 13:12-30). Further
instruction is given by Paul in 1 Corinthians 11:23-34. It was
while they were involved in eating the major portion of the
Passover feast that this special ceremony was introduced.

Engaging the disciples' attention, Jesus took the ceremonial
bread and after prayer broke it, giving pieces to the disciples
with the instructions, "Take, eat; this is my body." Following this, He also took the cup, and, again giving thanks, He
gave the cup to them saying, "Drink ye all of it." He then
explained the ceremony in Matthew 26:28, "For this is my
blood of the new testament, which is shed for many for the
remission of sins." The new ceremony, instead of relating to
the lamb slain in Egypt, now was referring to Christ as the
new Passover Lamb, the one who would be slain on the
cross. Although it was a new ceremony, it was also their last
meal together, and He concluded the introduction of the
Lord's Supper with the words of verse 29, "But I say unto
you, I will not drink henceforth of this fruit of the vine, until
that day when I drink it new with you in my Father's kingdom." Here He was referring to the millennial kingdom,
when Christ will return to the earth with His resurrected disciples and participate once again in the earthly scene. There
is no indication anywhere that wine will be drunk in heaven.
Concluding with the final hymn of the Passover feast, they

left the upper room and went to the Mount of Olives.

The ceremony of the Lord's Supper has been a point of controversy in the history of the church. Of the bread and the cup, the Roman church holds to transubstantiation, that the elements actually are transformed into the body and blood of Christ. The Lutheran church, historically, has held that while the bread remains bread and the wine remains wine, it is actually invested with the character of the body and blood of Christ, and that partaking of one is the same as partaking of the other.[5]

Calvin held that the Lord's spiritual presence was in the elements but not His physical presence.[6] Zwingli suggested that they were merely symbols and represented the body of Christ.[7] The controversy cannot be settled, but many have concluded that Zwingli was probably right and that the bread and the cup become the body and blood of Christ no more than Jesus became a vine because of His words, "I am the true vine." These are figures of speech, although wonderfully eloquent in their meaning. The important point is to partake of Christ in reality, not physically. The truth is that the believer is in Christ and Christ is in the believer in a wonderful, organic union of eternal life.

JESUS' TEACHING ON THE WAY TO THE GARDEN, 26:31-35

As the group walked from the upper room toward the Garden of Gethsemane at the foot of the Mount of Olives, Jesus delivered His final teachings to His disciples, recorded mostly in the gospel of John (13-17). Matthew records Jesus' prediction in 26:31 that all the disciples would forsake Him on that fateful night; "Then saith Jesus unto them, All ye shall be offended because of me this night: for it is written, I will smite the shepherd, and the sheep of the flock shall be scattered abroad." The word translated "shall be offended" is a Greek word from which we get the word *scandal,* with the meaning here of causing one to stumble.

The events of the evening were to be too much for all the disciples, and Matthew records in 26:56 that they all "forsook him, and fled." Jesus called their being offended a fulfillment of prophecy, as recorded in Zechariah 13:7, "Smite the shepherd, and the sheep shall be scattered."

Jesus, however, also had anticipated His resurrection (Mt 26:32) and that they would meet again in Galilee. Actually, of course, Jesus met His scattered disciples first in Jerusalem before they all went to Galilee. Peter had been previously informed, according to John 13:38, that he would deny Jesus, but apparently Peter could not believe it, and here again, Matthew 26:33 records Peter's renewed conversation with Jesus on this point and with the same warning from Jesus in verse 34 that Peter would deny Him before morning. The other disciples joined in their profession of faithfulness to Jesus even unto death (v. 35).

JESUS IN GETHSEMANE, 26:36-46

Having left the city of Jerusalem, and having crossed the Kidron Valley, Jesus was now at the foot of the Mount of Olives. They had come to a place called Gethsemane, meaning "oil press," probably located in a grove of olive trees for the purpose of pressing oil from the olives. Visitors today are shown a place called Gethsemane at the foot of the Mount of Olives. There is no way to identify the place accurately. In a parallel account in Mark 14:32-42, Gethsemane is also named, but in the account in Luke 22:39-46, it is called simply the Mount of Olives. John 18:1 calls it a garden beyond the Brook Kidron.

Asking eight of the disciples to sit down, Jesus took Peter, James, and John, and they went farther into the garden. These three, who seem to form the inner circle, had been with Him on the mount of transfiguration (Mt 17:1-9; Mk 9:2-13; Lk 9:28-36), had seen the girl raised at the house of Jairus (Mt 9:18-25; Mk 5:35-43; Lk 8:40-56), and were apparently the three from whom Jesus could most expect sympathy and understanding in this hour.

These three disciples perceived that Jesus was greatly agitated. A comparison of Matthew's description with that of Mark and Luke emphasizes the fact that Jesus was experiencing great sorrow and inner struggle such as the disciples had never before witnessed. He said to them, "My soul is exceeding sorrowful, even unto death: tarry ye here, and watch with me" (Mt 26:38). This did not mean that Jesus was in danger of dying on the spot, but it did mean that He was in extreme inner conflict. In this hour, He desired the sympathetic understanding of the three disciples. However, He went a little farther into the garden, away from even the three, and there began to pray (v. 39).

Many have commented on this experience of Jesus and have attempted to enter into the struggle which is revealed in the threefold prayer, and to discuss the contrast between Jesus in His agony and the sleepy disciples. While many truths can be derived from a study of this passage, the overwhelming impression is one of the loneliness of Jesus in His hour of crucifixion.

G. Campbell Morgan describes the progression of Jesus away from the multitude and toward the loneliness of the cross. Jesus first had left the multitude in order to be with His disciples in the upper room. There Judas had forsaken him. He went with the remaining eleven to the entrance to the Garden of Gethsemane. There, He had left eight of the disciples and took the faithful three with Him into the inner garden. Then He had left the three and retired to pray. The incidents relating to the whole scene emphasize the loneliness of Christ as He took upon Himself the sins of the whole world.[8]

As Christ retired from even His closest three disciples, Matthew records that He "fell on his face, and prayed, saying, O my Father, if it be possible, let this cup pass from me: nevertheless not as I will, but as thou wilt" (v. 39). Luke 22:41 states that He "kneeled down"; it is probable that He kneeled first, and then, in the process of His prayer, sank down until He was completely on His face on the ground. Hebrews 5:7 is the commentary on this prayer, speaking as it does of "strong crying and tears." This was an hour of supreme agony on the part of Jesus.

He addressed His prayer to "my Father," claiming Their intimate eternal relationship. The clause, "if it be possible," and the petition, "let this cup pass from me," indicate the natural desire of Jesus' human heart to avoid the supreme issue that was before Him. No man, in sinful and mortal flesh, can understand the conflict in the holy soul of Jesus who had never experienced the slightest shadow of sin and had never known any barrier between Himself and the Father. Now upon this holy One had come the hour when He would bear all the terrible sin of the world—past, present, and future—and would experience being the sin offering forsaken by the Father.

The human desire to avoid such an issue is not incompatible with the immutability of the divine nature. While this presents no theological problem to anyone accepting the full humanity as well as the full deity of Christ, at the same time, it offers no basis for men to understand the agony of Jesus. It is clear that whatever the desire of the human nature may have been, the will of Jesus was always without wavering to do the will of the Father.

After His first prayer and petition, Jesus returned to the three disciples, who probably were very near, and found them asleep. Matthew records that He addressed His words to Peter, and Mark 14:37 adds "Simon." The address, however, was in the plural, "What, could ye not watch with me one hour?" In the hour of Christ's supreme need, Peter, who had affirmed that he would die with His Lord, could not even keep awake. Recognizing the limitations of the human flesh, Jesus exhorted them, "Watch and pray, that ye enter not into temptation: the spirit indeed is willing, but the flesh is weak" (Mt 26:41). Christ did not question their desire to stay alert, but their will was not equal to the occasion.

Leaving the disciples a second time, He prayed, "O my Father, if this cup may not pass away from me, except I drink it, thy will be done" (v. 42). This time, the condition is stated in the negative, which may indicate a progression in His prayer and a recognition that the cup could not pass away. Returning to the three disciples, He again found them sound asleep. Leaving them a third time, He prayed again, repeating the same words as in the second petition.

Luke 22:40-44 records only one of the three petitions, probably the last of the three, and indicates that Jesus withdrew "about a stone's cast" from the three disciples. Luke records, however, the appearance of an angel from heaven to strengthen Him as He continued praying, and that His agony was so great that "his sweat was as it were great drops of blood falling down to the ground" (vv. 43-44). Short of death itself, Jesus could not have been in more agony of soul.

Coming back to His disciples for the third time, He found them again asleep, and to them He said the sad words, "Sleep on now, and take your rest: behold, the hour is at hand, and the Son of man is betrayed into the hands of sinners" (Mt 26:45). Many have tried to analyze this statement of Jesus as being sarcastic or cutting. It probably was said in sad recognition of His own loneliness. Jesus said, in effect, that they should take their rest, for He knew that in a few moments, their rest would be interrupted, and a sleepless night was ahead of them all.

Matthew does not indicate that any time elapsed between verses 45 and 46, but probably there was a brief interval. Then Jesus, awakening them for the third time, said, "Rise, let us be going: behold, he is at hand that doth betray me." The agony of Gethsemane was behind Him. The brutality of His arrest, beating at the hands of the soldiers, and the crown of thorns were ahead, but even this was just the prelude to the cross itself.

Betrayal and Arrest of Jesus, 26:47-56

As Jesus was awakening His disciples, the crowd led by Judas was seen approaching the garden. In the parallel accounts of Mark 14:43-50; Luke 22:47-53; and John 18:3-11, it is apparent that this was a large company of possibly several hundred people, including the chief priest and elders, a motley crowd which had been gathered by Jewish leaders to assist them, and may have included the two hundred Roman soldiers assigned to the use of the Sanhedrin.

Lenski points out that the fact that they carried short swords would identify the Roman soldiers, and the clubs would identify those hired as temple police. Some also carried torches and lanterns.[9] The size of the company indicated

the apprehension of the Jewish leaders that, even at such
a late hour in the night, the pilgrims who thronged Jerusalem
might interfere with the arrest of Jesus. The importance of
the event to the chief priests and scribes is indicated by their
presence on the night of the Passover for the occasion of
Christ's arrest.

Judas kept his sordid bargain with the Jews, and, in keeping with the prearranged plan to identify Him with a kiss, he
came out of the multitude to Jesus and said, "Hail, master,"
and kissed Him (Mt 26:49). His respectful address was the
extreme in hypocrisy, and his kiss expressed, as no other
means could possibly have done, his wicked unbelief, which
rejected the evidence that Jesus was indeed the Messiah. In
his heart, he was done with the whole concept that Jesus was
the King and that he would reign with Him. The Greek verb
translated "kissed" indicates that he kissed Him again and
again, so that in the darkness, all would see and understand.

The fact that Christ permitted him to do it was in keeping
with His purpose to be submissive to the will of God, even unto
the death on the cross. But for Judas himself, it was also the
last attempt of Jesus, even in this hour, to let Judas repent
of his sin and unbelief. Jesus addressed Judas as "friend"
which is translated from the Greek *hetaire* meaning friend or
associate, but in contrast to *phile,* which would have meant
a beloved friend. There was no hypocrisy in Christ's words,
and He asked searchingly, "Wherefore art thou come?"

Why, indeed, would one who heard the matchless sermons
of Jesus and witnessed hundreds of miracles turn away from
such a wonderful person? Such is the hardness of the human
heart and the blinding of satanic influence that one who had
every reason to trust in Christ and had been blessed as no
unsaved man had ever been blessed, would persist in his hardness of heart and unbelief. Judas, like Pharaoh of old, had
gone beyond the point of no return.

Only John records the conversation between Jesus and
those who had come to arrest Him (18:4-9). According to
John's gospel, Christ asked the question, apparently after
He had already been identified by Judas, "Whom seek ye?"
When they answered, "Jesus of Nazareth," Jesus replied, "I

am he." John records that after Jesus said, "I am he," that "they went backward, and fell to the ground." Apparently, there was a momentary display of divine power, a final witness to Judas who betrayed Him, to the disciples who were to flee from Him, and to the crowd that was filled with hatred for Him. Jesus then told them again that He was the one that they sought and then added that they should let the disciples go their way.

It is at this point that Matthew picks up the story and records the incident of Peter smiting a servant of the high priest. Only John identifies the disciple and gives the name of the servant, Malchus (Jn 18:10). By the time this was recorded in John, Peter was already dead.

Jesus had told them in the upper room that the time had come when one not having a sword should sell his garment and buy one, and they replied that they had two swords, which the Lord said were enough (Lk 22:36-38).

When it became apparent that Jesus was about to be arrested, Peter, with sudden courage, drew his sword and struck at the servant of the high priest, no doubt intending to hit him on the top of the head and kill him. He missed, however, and the sword cut off the ear of the servant and probably hit the armor covering the shoulder. If Peter had killed the servant, it is possible that he would have been crucified at the same time as Jesus. To him, however, Jesus addressed the words, "Put up again thy sword into his place: for all they that take the sword shall perish with the sword" (Mt 26:52). The time would come when Peter would die as a martyr for the faith, but this was not the hour, nor was the sword the way by which he should serve Christ.

To make it plain that Jesus needed no defender, He told Peter that all He needed to do was to pray to the Father and He would be given twelve legions of angels. A Roman legion consisted of from three thousand to six thousand men, and therefore, twelve legions was a company far in excess of the multitude that had gathered against Jesus.

It was not, however, the will of God that Jesus should be so rescued, and Jesus posed the question, "But how then shall the scriptures be fulfilled, that thus it must be?" (26:54).

Complete submission to the will of God and to the path that led to the cross is evident in the words of Christ.

To the multitude who had gathered, Jesus addressed the biting words, "Are ye come out as against a thief with swords and staves for to take me? I sat daily with you teaching in the temple, and ye laid no hold on me" (26:55). He was reminding them that the force that was gathered here was not because He would resist arrest but because the chief priests and the scribes feared the retaliation of those who had put their trust in Him. Matthew adds, "But all this was done, that the scriptures of the prophets might be fulfilled." This was the will of God.

At this point, fear overtook the disciples, and Matthew records sadly, "Then all the disciples forsook him, and fled." Jesus was indeed alone in this tragic hour, but out of the tragedy would come salvation and restoration even for those who had forsaken Him and fled. The majestic person of Christ may have impressed some of those in the multitude that arrested Him. Who knows whether some of them may not have been included in the multitude who became His followers on the day of Pentecost and afterward?

TRIAL OF JESUS BEFORE CAIAPHAS AND THE SANHEDRIN, 26:57-68

Having arrested and bound Jesus as a dangerous prisoner, they led Him away, according to Matthew's account, to Caiaphas—the high priest—and the Sanhedrin. A parallel account is given in Mark 14:53-65. John mentions that Jesus first had a brief trial before Annas (Jn 18:13-23) and that Annas had sent Him to Caiaphas (Jn 18:24). Matthew and Mark do not mention the trial before Annas, and Luke does not mention either of these trials. The whole procedure was highly illegal, as they were not to hold trials like this at night.[10]

The purpose of these preliminary trials was to find a legal basis on which Jesus could be condemned to death. Matthew 26 indicates that they sought false witnesses, but they could not get even the false witnesses to agree, until finally they found two that agreed, as Matthew quotes them in 26:61, "This fellow said, I am able to destroy the temple of God, and to build it in three days." Even this, however, was not a sufficient ground for condemnation.

In desperation, the high priest addressed Jesus saying, "Answerest thou nothing? what is it which these witness against thee?" (v. 62). Jesus, however, did not answer until the high priest said to Him, "I adjure thee by the living God, that thou tell us whether thou be the Christ, the Son of God" (v. 63). At this official and direct question, Jesus responded, "Thou has said: nevertheless I say unto you, Hereafter shall ye see the Son of man sitting on the right hand of power, and coming in the clouds of heaven" (v. 64).

It is strange that the high priest was unable to produce any witnesses to confirm his charges, as Jesus had freely claimed His deity and Messiahship, but the words of Jesus were all the high priest needed. Jesus not only claimed to be "the Christ, the Son of God," but He added that He would sit at the right hand of God and come in clouds of heaven as the predicted Messiah. This clear claim of deity prompted the high priest to tear his clothes and say, "He hath spoken blasphemy. What think ye?" The crowd answered, "He is guilty of death" (vv. 65-66).

The issue was clear enough. If Jesus were not all He claimed to be, indeed He was guilty of death, according to the Jewish law. What the chief priests and the scribes ignored was the fact that Jesus had not only made the claim but He had fully supported it by the very credentials and miracles which the Old Testament had attributed to Him.

Then, contrary to both Jewish law and Roman law, they abused Him. "Then did they spit in his face, and buffeted him; and others smote him with the palms of their hands, saying, Prophesy unto us, thou Christ, Who is he that smote thee?" (vv. 67-68). This cowardly abuse of Jesus was not limited to servants; the text indicates the Sanhedrin itself lowered its dignity to participate. Tasker is too kind when he states, "It would seem highly improbable that such an august body would have demeaned themselves by such undignified behaviour."[11] They hated Jesus and delighted in this opportu-

nity to hurt Him. In all this abuse, Jesus was silent. He was
ready to answer sincere questions of faith but not the slanted
questions of unbelief.

PETER'S THREE DENIALS, 26:69-75

Peter, who had followed Jesus into the high priest's court
at a safe distance and had gone in to sit with the guards
(26:58), hoped that no one would notice him. However, he
was drawn to the scene as if by a magnet and wanted desperately to know what would become of Jesus. Parallel accounts of his denial are found in Mark 14:66-72; Luke
22:54-62; and John 18:15-18, 25-27. The three denials
recorded by Matthew were probably interrupted by some of
the other incidents.

The first to detect Peter's identity was a maid who accused, "Thou also wast with Jesus of Galilee" (Mt 26:59).
But Peter was loud in his denial. Peter then went out into the
porch, where another maid saw him and accused him, "This
fellow was also with Jesus of Nazareth" (v. 71). This time,
Peter denied more emphatically and even denied with an
oath that he did not know Jesus. Mark 14:68 records that
after the second denial, the cock crowed. The third denial
came some time later, which Luke refers to as after "about
the space of one hour" (Lk 22:59). The third denial came
when the crowd itself said to Peter, "Surely thou also art
one of them; for thy speech [betrayeth] thee" (Mt 26:73).

At this third accusation, Matthew records, "Then began he
to curse and to swear, saying, I know not the man" (v. 74).
It was then that the cock crowed the second time. Matthew,
Luke, and John record only this crowing of the cock, but
Mark records that the cock crowed twice, "And the second
time the cock crew. And Peter called to mind the word that
Jesus said unto him, Before the cock crow twice, thou shalt
deny me thrice. And when he thought thereon, he wept"
(Mk 14:72). Luke records that at this point, "The Lord
turned, and looked upon Peter" (Lk 22:61). It was the
look of Jesus that caused Peter to remember the prediction of

Jesus that he would deny Him thrice. Peter, who thought he was willing to die for his Lord, now faced the bitter truth that in the hour of testing, he had failed.

Jesus Delivered to Pilate, 27:1-2

No DOUBT REALIZING that the trials before Annas and Caiaphas in the night were illegal both in the way they were conducted and in their outcome, the chief priests and elders reviewed their case against Jesus at a meeting held the next morning. Mention of this is made in the other gospels (Mk 15:1; Lk 23:1; Jn 18:28). The problem was not only the illegality of the trial, but the fact that the Jews did not have the authority to put Jesus to death. This could only be done by an order from a Roman ruler. Accordingly, at the close of this third trial before a Jewish authority, Jesus was bound and led away to be delivered to Pontius Pilate, the governor, for the first of the three trials before Roman rulers. Before proceeding with the account of the trial of Christ, Matthew records the remorse of Judas.

Judas Repents Too Late, 27:3-10

The sad end of Judas Iscariot, recorded only in Matthew in the gospels, is mentioned by Luke in Acts 1:16-19 in connection with the election of Matthias as his successor. According to Matthew's account, when Judas found that Jesus had been condemned to die, he repented of his act and attempted to return the thirty pieces of silver to the chief priests and the elders. Apparently, Judas had not believed that the arrest of Jesus would lead to His condemnation, or perhaps he was confronted now with his wicked betrayal of Jesus. In his conversations with the chief priests he said, "I have sinned in that I have betrayed the innocent blood" (27:4). While his feelings concerning the claim of Jesus to be the Messiah may still have been mixed with unbelief, he knew that Jesus was not worthy of death. The priests, however, were quite unconcerned and threw the problem back at him. This encounter with the chief priests and elders may have been before Caiaphas' palace, as Lenski suggests.[1]

Upon being spurned by them, however, Judas went to the temple and hurled the silver into the sanctuary (Gr. *naos*), meaning the entrance to the holy place. He then went out and hanged himself. Acts 1:18-19 describes the horrible deed in detail. The chief priests, confronted with what to do with this blood money, decided it could not be put in the treasury but could be used to buy a potter's field in which to bury strangers. This they did; and according to Matthew, the field became known as "The field of blood," or, as Acts 1:19 calls it, "Aceldama." The whole transaction reflected on the one hand the casuistry of the Pharisees and their indifference to their crime, and on the other hand, the despair of Judas, for whom there seems to have been no road to forgiveness, even though he had remorse.

Matthew notes that this was a fulfillment of "that which was spoken by Jeremy the prophet, saying, And they took the thirty pieces of silver, the price of him that was valued, whom they of the children of Israel did value; And gave them for the potter's field, as the Lord appointed me" (27:9-10). The reference to this as a quotation from Jeremiah has caused difficulty to expositors, as it is actually a quotation of Zechariah 11:12-13. How can this apparent discrepancy be explained?

Probably the best explanation is that the third section of the Old Testament began with the book of Jeremiah and included all that followed. Just as the first section was called the law, after the first five books, and the second section was called the psalms, although other books were included, so the third part began with Jeremiah, and the reference is related to this section of the Old Testament rather than to the book of Jeremiah. The references sometimes cited in Jeremiah, such as 18:2-12 and 19:1-15, do not correspond sufficiently to justify the quotation.[2]

In Zechariah 11:12-13, the thirty pieces of silver are paid to dispose of Israel's shepherd. In Matthew, the actual ful-

fillment is found in that the price was paid to dispose of
Jesus, the true Shepherd of Israel. Obviously, Matthew is
referring to the idea in Zechariah rather than to the precise
wording.

TRIAL BEFORE PILATE, 27:11-26

The other gospels, in their description of the trial before
Pilate, include some details not given by Matthew (cf. Mk
15:2-15; Lk 23:2-25; Jn 18:28—19:16). As Luke 23:6-12
indicates, Pilate, after a preliminary hearing of the case and
on learning that Jesus was of Galilee, as a friendly gesture,
sent Him to Herod, who was in Jerusalem at the time. Herod,
after encountering complete silence from Jesus, sent Him back
to Pilate to be judged. Jesus had three Roman trials, first before Pilate, then before Herod, and then again before Pilate.
Matthew, Mark, and John combine the two trials before
Pilate.

According to Luke 23:1-2, the trial began with various
accusations being leveled against Jesus, including that He
perverted the nation, forbade to give tribute to Caesar, and
claimed that He was a king. It is at this point that Matthew
begins his record because of the special interest in the gospel of Matthew in Jesus Christ as King.

Pilate asked Jesus, according to Matthew 27:11, "Art thou
the King of the Jews?" Jesus replied, "Thou sayest," in other
words, affirming that it was true. The full conversation between Jesus and Pilate is recorded in John 18:33-38. From
John's account, it is evident that Pilate explored fully the
possibility that Jesus was a king who might threaten his rule
and satisfied his mind that there was nothing to the charge.
His conversation with Jesus ended up with the philosophical
question, "What is truth?" According to John 18:38, Pilate
at this time declared Jesus innocent in the words, "I find in
him no fault at all."

After Jesus was pronounced innocent, the chief priests and
scribes renewed their vehement accusations, in reply to which
Jesus was completely silent. As Lenski points out, this is the
second important silence of Christ, the first being in Matthew

26:63 and the third in John 19:9.[3] Pilate marveled that Christ could keep silent under the circumstances. The fact is that after Pilate pronounced Him innocent, Jesus was under no obligation to answer the Jews further; and, if more investigation was required, it was up to Pilate to reverse his former judgment and continue the examination. It was in the course of further accusation by the chief priests and the scribes that Pilate learned that Jesus was from Galilee and used this as an occasion to refer the whole matter to Herod.

When Jesus was later sent by Herod back to Pilate, a plan occurred to Pilate to get out of his problem. According to Matthew 27:15, it had been the custom for many years to release a prisoner whom the people would choose on the occasion of the feast. Pilate picked the worst possible prisoner, Barabbas, who, according to Mark 15:7, was guilty of insurrection and murder. (There is an interesting play on words here, as *Barabbas* means "son of the father." Barabbas was released instead of Jesus who was the true Son of the Father.) Pilate, assured that Jesus was popular with the people and that the plot against Him was connived by the Jewish leaders, thought the people would choose Jesus rather than Barabbas and thus relieve him of the problem of making a final judgment. Matthew 27:18 notes that Pilate knew that the chief priests had delivered Jesus to him because of envy.

While in the process of discussing this, the wife of Pilate sent him a message which said, "Have thou nothing to do with that just man: for I have suffered many things this day in a dream because of him" (v. 19). There has been much speculation as to who Pilate's wife was and what the background of this incident could have been. The simplest explanation is that she had such a dramatic dream that she felt compelled to share it with her husband, with whom, no doubt, she had discussed Jesus on previous occasions. As Tasker points out, Pilate's wife was concerned at the possibility of an innocent man of prophetic character being killed unjustly.[4]

Meanwhile, however, the chief priests and elders had been busy persuading the people to ask for Barabbas and to request that Jesus be killed. To Pilate's amazement, when the question was posed to the people, they asked for Barabbas to be released. In his astonishment, he asked, "What shall I do then with Jesus which is called Christ?" He hoped for a punishment short of death. They replied, "Let him be crucified" (v. 22).

Pilate was now occupied not only with the justice in the case but how he could reasonably sentence a man who had not been convicted of any real crime. Accordingly, he asked again, "Why, what evil hath he done?" But the people cried all the more, "Let him be crucified." Unquestionably, they were influenced by the chief priests and elders.

Pilate, then, under great pressure lest there be an insurrection against him which would be damaging to his reputation, publicly took water and washed his hands before the multitude saying, "I am innocent of the blood of this just person: see ye to it." Remarkably, in the same chapter, Jesus is pronounced innocent both by Judas and by Pilate (vv. 4, 24). The people recklessly responded, "His blood be on us, and on our children." How tragically these words seem to have been fulfilled in the destruction of Jerusalem and the slaughter of several hundred thousand Israelites on that occasion.

Having reversed his earlier judgment that Jesus was innocent, Pilate now released Barabbas, scourged Jesus, and delivered Him to be crucified.

JESUS MOCKED AND SCOURGED, 27:27-32

According to Matthew and Mark, Jesus was taken by the soldiers into the common hall, the praetorium, which was thronged with Roman soldiers. There, they stripped Him and mocked Him by putting on Him a purple robe and a crown of thorns. The indignities included being spit upon and being repeatedly beaten on the head. A parallel account is given in Mark 15:16-20, but Luke says only that Pilate delivered Jesus "to their will" (Lk 23:25). The fullest account is found in John 19:1-16, where the actual order of events which took place is given.

Putting the accounts together, it seems that Pilate himself observed and supervised this abuse of Jesus. His motivation was to degrade Him and to make His claim as a King of the Jews to be ridiculous. It is probable that Pilate hoped by this means to get off without actually having to order the crucifixion of Jesus. While Matthew introduces this idea of crucifixion in 27:26, John 19:16 makes clear that the order for crucifixion came at the end of the mockery rather than at the beginning. Matthew is simply recording the facts without necessarily giving the order of events.

That Jesus was submissive to this entire procedure is the measure of His total submission to the will of God. Here, the Lord of glory, capable of destroying anyone who put a hand upon Him, allowed Himself to be abused in this painful and humiliating way. Although the Scriptures are graphic, even they state only the essentials. The prophet Isaiah anticipated this when he stated in Isaiah 52:14, "His visage was so marred more than any man, and his form more than the sons of men." Jesus was beaten about the head and the body until He was almost unrecognizable.

Few incidents in history more clearly illustrate the brutality in the desperately wicked heart of man than that which was inflicted on Jesus the Son of God. The mockery of the crown of thorns, painful as well as humiliating, His being stripped naked in front of the large crowd; the mockery of the purple robe, intended to represent a kingly garment; His being spit upon and beaten over the head repeatedly as well as the mocking worship testified to the unbelief and sordidness of the actors in this situation. It was only after enduring all of this in complete silence, except for the conversation between Christ and Pilate recorded in John 19:8-11, that Jesus was finally led away to the crucifixion.

As the custom was, the accused had to bear His own cross. Luke 23:26-32 records some of the incidents that occurred on the way to Golgotha. Because of Christ's suffering, He was too weak to carry the cross Himself; and Simon of Cyrene, who is identified in Mark 15:21 as the father of Alexander and Rufus, was forced to carry the cross for Jesus. Some believe he was black, not of Jewish background. The hour had come for the Lamb of God to die for the sins of the whole world.

JESUS CRUCIFIED, 27:33-44

The account of Matthew and the parallel accounts in the other gospels (Mk 15:22-32; Lk 23:33-43; Jn 19:17-24) need to be combined to give the full account of the incidents that occurred at the crucifixion leading up to His death. The order of events seems to be as follows:

1. The arrival at Golgotha (Mt 27:33; Mk 15:22; Lk 23:33; Jn 19:17)
2. The offer of the wine mingled with gall (Mt 27:34; Mk 15:23)
3. The act of crucifixion between the two thieves (Mt 27:35-38; Mk 15:24-28; Lk 23:33-38; 19:18)
4. The first cry from the cross, "Father, forgive them" (Lk 23:34)
5. The soldiers taking the garments of Jesus, leaving Him naked on the cross (Mt 27:35; Mk 15:24; Lk 23:34; Jn 19:23)
6. The Jews mocking Jesus (Mt 27:39-43; Mk 15:29-32; Lk 23:35-37)
7. The conversation with the thieves (Mt 27:44; Mk 15:32; Lk 23:39-43)
8. The second cry from the cross with the words, "Today shalt thou be with me in paradise" (Lk 23:43)
9. The third cry, "Woman, behold thy son!" (Jn 19:26-27)
10. The darkness which overtakes the scene on Calvary (Mt 27:45; Mk 15:33; Lk 23:44)
11. The fourth cry, beginning, "My God, my God" (Mt 27:46-47; Mk 15:34-36)
12. The fifth cry, "I thirst" (Jn 19:28)
13. The sixth cry, "It is finished" (Jn 19:30)
14. The seventh cry, "Father, into thy hands I commend my spirit" (Lk 23:46)
15. The Lord dismissing His spirit by an act of His own will (Mt 27:50; Mk 15:37; Lk 23:46; Jn 19:30)

Matthew notes that Golgotha is "a place of a skull," which is what *Golgotha* means, apparently from the idea that the hill Calvary looked something like a human skull. The hill above the garden tomb discovered by Gordon has a skull-like appearance from the side. The top of the hill is now a Muslim cemetery, and there is a convenient tomb which is identified as the tomb of Jesus at the foot of the hill in the garden. Positive identification of this site, of course, is impossible today.[5]

Matthew records Christ's refusal to drink the sour wine mingled with a drug, which would have tended to dull His senses and make the cross easier to bear. Matthew simply records His crucifixion without going into details, as the crude spikes were driven through His hands and His feet, and the entire cross was set up by being placed in a hole in the ground.

The soldiers took His garments, tearing them in four pieces so that each soldier could have a part, but they cast lots for the coat, which was a woven garment, as John 19:23-24 explains. Matthew regards this as a fulfillment of the prophecy of Psalm 22:18. Textual evidence seems to indicate that this was added to Matthew's gospel, but that in John 19:24, it is properly included.[6] In any case, the prophecy was fulfilled.

The event of His crucifixion, as stated in Mark 15:25, reckoned according to Jewish time, was the third hour, or 9:00 A.M., or, as mentioned in John 19:14, the sixth hour, according to Roman time, actually meaning after 6:00 A.M., or early in the morning.

According to John 19:19, Pilate himself had ordered that the accusation made against Jesus should be nailed to His cross; and Matthew records this as, "THIS IS JESUS THE KING OF THE JEWS" (27:37). The wording in each gospel varies, and the title itself was written in Hebrew, Greek, and Latin (Jn 19:20). Putting the accounts together, the full inscription was, "This is Jesus of Nazareth, the King of the Jews." All the accounts contain the phrase, "The King of the Jews," which was the substance of the accusation. Pilate intended this as a rebuke to the Jews, but at the same time it was a testimony to the person of Christ.

Mention is also made of the two thieves who were crucified on either side of Jesus. Only Luke 23:39-43 describes the conversion of one of the thieves. Matthew records the mocking of the crowd and the chief priests and scribes and elders, as they challenged Christ to come down from the cross, if He were indeed the Son of God who had said that He could destroy the temple and build it in three days.

How tragically true it was, as recorded in Matthew 27:42, "He saved others; himself he cannot save." It was not that He lacked power; it was because it was the will of the Father that He should die. The mockery accurately fulfilled the anticipation of Psalm 22:6-13. Tasker notes there were three classes of mockers: (1) "Ignorant sinners"; (2) "religious sinners"; (3) "condemned sinners."[7] The tragedy was not that one was dying on the cross, but that the people beheld Him in hardness of heart and wickedness of unbelief.

JESUS DIES ON THE CROSS, 27:45-56

The closing events of the life of Jesus as He died on the cross are recorded in all gospels (Mk 15:33-41; Lk 23:44-49; Jn 19:30-37). Matthew records that from the sixth hour, or noon in Jewish reckoning, there was darkness over the land until the ninth hour, or 3:00 P.M. This darkness seems to have begun after the third cry of Christ on the cross in which He put His mother, Mary, under the care of John (Jn 19:26-27). It was in this period of darkness that Jesus became the sin offering and, as such, was forsaken by God the Father. Matthew records the fourth cry of Jesus on the cross as being spoken in a loud voice: "Eli, Eli, lama sabachthani? that is to say, My God, my God, why hast thou forsaken me?" (27:46). Matthew's account uses the Hebrew for "My God," *eli,* but "lama sabachthani" is Aramaic, the spoken language of the Jews. Mark changes the Hebrew *eli* to *eloi,* which is Aramaic. The petition of Jesus is, of course, the quotation of Psalm 22:1, although the gospels do not mention it as a fulfillment.

The cry of Jesus has been variously interpreted, but it seems clear that God had judicially forsaken Jesus on the cross in contrast to the fact that He had strengthened Him in the garden of Gethsemane. Here Jesus was bearing the sins of the whole world, and even God the Father had to turn away as Jesus bore the curse and identified Himself with the sins of the whole world. When Jesus actually died, He commended Himself back into the Father's hands.

Those who heard Jesus utter this cry mistook the word *eli* for *Elias,* and thought that He was calling for Elijah. Matthew records that one of them took a sponge, filled it with sour wine, and put it on a reed, in order to bring it to the lips of Jesus, to enable Him to speak more clearly. The rest of the observers, however, said that he should let Jesus alone to see whether Elijah actually came to save Him. While they observed, according to Matthew, "Jesus, when he had cried again with a loud voice, yielded up the ghost" (27:50). Luke 23:46 records that Jesus said: "Father, into thy hands I commend my spirit." John records simply that Jesus said, "It is finished" (Jn 19:30). Jesus had lived as no man has ever lived, and He died as no man ever died. Having completed His act of sacrifice, He dismissed His spirit by an act of His will. As He had stated earlier, in John 10:18, in regard to His life, "No man taketh it from me, but I lay it down of myself. I have power to lay it down, and I have power to take it again."

At the moment of His death, a number of awesome things took place. An earthquake occurred, and the heaving ground brought fear to those who observed. According to Matthew 27:51, the heavy veil of the temple, which separated the holy of holies from the holy place, was torn in two from the top to the bottom. As the divine commentary in Hebrews 10:19-22 signifies, the death of Jesus opened the way for ordinary believers to go into the holy of holies, where formerly only the Jewish high priests could go.

Although not immediately known to those who witnessed the scene of Christ's death, Matthew also records an event not mentioned elsewhere in the Bible: "And the graves were opened; and many bodies of the saints which slept arose, and came out of the graves after his resurrection, and went into the holy city, and appeared to many" (27:53). As a careful reading of this account reveals, the raising of the bodies of the saints, although mentioned here, actually occurred after the resurrection of Jesus. This event is nowhere explained in the Scriptures but seems to be a fulfillment of the feast of the first fruits of harvest mentioned in Leviticus 23:10-14. On that occasion, as a token of the coming harvest, the people would bring a handful of grain to the priest. The resurrection of these saints, occurring after Jesus Himself was raised, is a token of the coming harvest when all the saints will be raised.

The centurion, impressed by the darkness and the earthquake, although he probably was not informed of the tearing of the veil of the temple, according to the Scriptures, feared greatly, saying, "Truly this was the Son of God" (27:54). Although he had witnessed many executions, there never before had been one like this.

Matthew comments that many of the women who had followed Christ were beholding this from a distance. Among them were Mary Magdalene, Mary the mother of James and Joses, and the mother of Zebedee's children. No doubt, with the coming of evening and the knowledge that Christ had died, they went sorrowfully to their homes.

BURIAL OF JESUS, 27:57-61

Ordinarily, there was little ceremony in connection with those crucified, and their bodies would be thrown into a shallow grave or even on a refuse heap. The problem of what to do with the body of Christ was quickly solved, however, by the intervention of Joseph of Arimathaea. The account given in all four gospels (Mk 15:42-47; Lk 23:50-56; Jn 19:38-42) indicates that he was a wealthy and influential man, a member of the Sanhedrin (Lk 23:51), and one who had been secretly a disciple of Jesus (Jn 19:38). He went boldly in to Pilate, although this involved ceremonial defilement for a Jew during the feast, and requested the body of Jesus. Mark 15:44-45 records Pilate's surprise that Jesus was already dead, his inquiry from the centurion to verify the fact, and his permission to Joseph.

Matthew and the other gospels record the details of His

burial. In the custom of the Jews, He was wrapped in clean linen cloth, and His body was placed in a new tomb hewn out of the rock. The stone door was rolled before the opening of the tomb, as they completed the act of burial. Matthew records that the two women, Mary Magdalene and "the other Mary," identified in Mark 15:47 as "mother of Joses," watched the burial. John 19:39-40 adds that Nicodemus, who first encountered Jesus in the incident recorded in John 3, participated in the burial, bringing myrrh and aloes of about one hundred pounds, the spices being used to saturate the linen cloths in which the body of Jesus was bound. John also records that the place of burial was in a garden.

The entire burial operation was done with some haste, because the Sabbath, which began at sundown, was already beginning (Mk 15:42; Lk 23:54; Jn 19:42). The Sabbath following the Passover had a special meaning, leading as it did to the seven-day Feast of Unleavened Bread.

SEALING OF THE TOMB, 27:62-66

Only Matthew records the incident of the chief priests and Pharisees coming to Pilate the next day, which was Saturday, and requesting that the tomb be sealed to keep the disciples from stealing the body of Jesus and then claiming that He was risen from the dead. It is most interesting that the chief priests and Pharisees, who were unbelievers, remembered the prediction of Jesus that He would rise again after three days, while this truth does not seem to have penetrated the consciousness of the disciples in their sorrow. With Pilate's permission, the Jews sealed the stone, which had closed the tomb's door, and set a watch of soldiers to be sure there was no interference with the tomb.

The temple soldiers were not used for this purpose, as their jurisdiction was only the temple area. A regular detachment of Roman soldiers was sent to watch the tomb. Pilate had said to them, "Make it as sure as ye can," and so they did. Stealing the body of Jesus was an impossibility, but chief priests, and Pharisees, and all the power of the Roman government

28

The Resurrection and Final Words of Jesus

APPEARANCE OF JESUS TO THE WOMEN, 28: 1-10

THE RESURRECTION OF JESUS on the first day of the week is detailed in all four gospels (Mk 16:1-14; Lk 24:1-49; Jn 20:1-23). The probable order of events was as follows:

1. Appearance to Mary Magdalene when she returned after a preliminary visit of the women to the tomb (Mk 16:9-11; Jn 20:11-18)
2. Appearance to the women who had been to the tomb and were bearers of the message of the angels (Mt 28:8-10)
3. Appearance to Peter on the afternoon of the resurrection day (Lk 24:34; 1 Co 15:5)
4. Appearance to the disciples on the road to Emmaus (Mk 16:12; Lk 24:13-32)
5. Appearance to the ten disciples on the evening of the resurrection day, Thomas being absent (Lk 24:36-43; Jn 20:19-25)
6. Appearance a week later to the eleven, Thomas being present (Jn 20:26-31; 1 Co 15:5)
7. Appearance to seven of the disciples beside the Sea of Galilee (Jn 21:1-14)
8. Appearance to about five hundred brethren as well as the apostles (Mt 28:16-20; Mk 16:15-18; 1 Co 15:6)
9. Appearance to James, the half brother of Jesus (1 Co 15:7)
10. Appearance on the day of ascension from the Mount of Olives (Mk 16:19-20; Lk 24:44-53; Ac 1:3-12)

Matthew records that "Mary Magdalene and the other

Mary" came "to see the sepulchre" (28:1) early that resurrection morning. There were other women, however, including Salome (Mk 16:1). The women were the same group that had beheld the burial of Jesus and therefore knew where the tomb was. Mary, the mother of Jesus, apparently was not with them.

Mark 16:3 records their question, as they approached the tomb, concerning who would roll away the stone. Upon arrival at the scene, there was a great earthquake, and an angel descended from heaven and rolled back the stone. Matthew describes him, "His countenance was like lightning, and his raiment white as snow" (28:3).

The Roman soldiers were paralyzed with fear, but the angel said to the women, "Fear not ye: for I know that ye seek Jesus, which was crucified. He is not here: for he is risen, as he said. Come, see the place where the Lord lay. And go quickly, and tell his disciples that he is risen from the dead; and, behold, he goeth before you into Galilee; there shall ye see him: lo, I have told you" (vv. 5-7). Luke 24:1-8 gives further details on the message of the angel and indicates that the women entered into the tomb, but the body of the Lord was gone. Matthew records, "They departed quickly from the sepulchre with fear and great joy; and did run to bring his disciples word" (28:8).

The account concerning Mary Magdalene would indicate that she saw the stone rolled away but did not linger long enough to understand the full meaning of it, and informed Peter and John simply that the tomb was empty. It was on her second visit to the tomb that Jesus first appeared to Mary Magdalene. She, who sought Jesus most earnestly, was honored to be the first to see the resurrected Christ. Matthew records the second appearance to the other women as they also had left the tomb in order to tell the disciples, and records that the women "held him by the feet, and worshipped him" (v. 9). Jesus instructed them, as the angel had also mentioned in verse 7, to tell the brethren to go into Galilee, where they would see Jesus. However, He appeared to them that evening and apparently again a week later before the Galilee appearances occurred. For Matthew, the Galilean appearance was the climax of Jesus' ministry. It was there that Christ witnessed to many outside of Judaism, an anticipation of His worldwide witness.[1]

REPORT OF THE SOLDIERS, 28:11-15

Just as Matthew alone records the request of the priests and Pharisees, the watch by the soldiers at the tomb, so Matthew alone records the outcome following the resurrection of Christ. Some of those guarding the tomb went to the chief priests and reported what had happened. It is astounding, as Lenski points out, that the chief priests heard of the resurrection of Jesus before the disciples.[2] The result was that they gave a bribe, described by Matthew as "large money," to the soldiers and instructed them to report that the disciples had stolen the body by night while the soldiers slept. They also promised the soldiers that if it reached the Roman governor's ears that they would protect them and persuade the governor not to punish them.

Under Roman law, the soldiers could be put to death for failure to do their duty, as was done to the soldiers who were watching Peter (Ac 12:19). The soldiers, glad both for the money and for the protection, did as they were instructed and started the rumor among the Jews that the body of Jesus had been stolen.

The dishonesty and lack of integrity on the part of the scribes and Pharisees, when confronted with the fact of the resurrection of Jesus, all too frequently are found in other forms of unbelief. Liberal scholarship today shows the same incredible blindness to the facts and tends to give credence to any criticism of the scriptural record more than to the Scriptures themselves. The unbelief of the scribes and Pharisees is shown here in all its stark wickedness, and their stooping to bribery and lies shows the extremity into which they fell. As Lenski notes, the very soldiers who were ordered to prevent the fulfillment of the prophecy of Christ's resurrection were the first witnesses of it.[3] It is possible that some were beneficially influenced and may be numbered among those who did come to Jesus in the early days of the church, as recorded in Acts.

The story of the soldiers, of course, was obviously false. How could they know that the disciples stole the body if they were actually asleep? So often the truth is more reasonable than the theories seeking to contradict the truth. The three thousand at Pentecost who believed Peter's message concerning the death and the resurrection of Christ no doubt had investigated the story, had seen the empty tomb, and were fully persuaded that the facts as presented by Peter were the truth. The story served to bolster those, however, who, for various reasons, did not want to believe in Jesus, and Matthew reports the story was still common at the time he wrote the gospel.

JESUS' MEETING WITH HIS DISCIPLES IN GALILEE, 28:16-20

The closing verses of Matthew's gospel record Christ's meeting with the eleven disciples in Galilee, prophesied in 28:7, 10. This is not clearly identifiable with any other appearance of Jesus. The appearance recorded in Mark 16:15-18, though often considered the same as this appearance in Matthew, could just as well fit the meeting on the second Sunday night, recorded in John 20:26-31. Sometimes also, the reference in Matthew 28 is linked with 1 Corinthians 15:6, where Jesus is said to have appeared unto more than five hundred brethren at once. The meeting mentioned in 1 Corinthians, however, may be another appearance of Jesus not found anywhere else in the gospels. The fact that "some doubted," that is, were not sure the person they were seeing was Jesus, as mentioned in Matthew 28:17, might indicate that there was a larger crowd than just the eleven.

Lenski argues that the one hundred and twenty which met in Jerusalem in Acts 1:15 were a smaller company, and, because of the many converts in Galilee, a group of five hundred there would be understandable.[4] The meeting in Galilee has a prominence in Scripture because it was mentioned three times before, in Matthew 26:32; 28:7, 10. Just as the mountains of Galilee had been the scene of some of Christ's great messages, such as the Sermon on the Mount, and had been the scene of His transfiguration, Galilee was a fitting place for a last meeting with a large group of His disciples.

The fact that "some doubted" is at first glance a problem, but it seems to indicate only a preliminary reaction as to whether or not this was indeed Jesus, not doubt concerning His resurrection. This doubt was soon dispelled, as Jesus spoke saying, "All power is given unto me in heaven and in earth. Go ye therefore, and teach all nations, baptizing them in the name of the Father, and of the Son, and of the Holy Ghost: Teaching them to observe all things whatsoever I have commanded you: and, lo, I am with you alway, even unto the end of the world. Amen" (28:18-20). Only Jesus could speak such words, and it must have brought reassuring faith to all who were there. As Criswell states, "The commission is mandatory, not optional. High mountains, deep oceans, wide deserts, starvation, shipwreck, death are not to be excuses for not going! We are to preach the Gospel to every creature."[5]

In keeping with the theme of Matthew's gospel, presenting Jesus as the King who was rejected but who will return to reign in majesty and power, these words were the final orders of the King concerning what should go on in His absence. He began by reaffirming His power or authority, both in heaven and in earth. On the basis of this authority, they, as His representatives, were to teach all nations. This was much wider than the purpose of Jesus in relation to Israel. Now the world-wide results of His death and resurrection must be publicized. As they recognized believers by the act of water baptism in the name of the Triune God, they were to instruct them concerning the obedience required by their faith in Jesus Christ as Saviour and Lord.

In commanding them to observe "whatsoever I have commanded you," Jesus was not referring to all His teachings in general, some of which were interpretative of the Law of Moses and were under the older dispensation, but to what He had commanded them as the believers who would be members of the church which was His body. Specifically, in using the word *commanded,* He was recalling the new commandment which He had given them in the upper room and the particular instructions that applied to the disciples in the organic union, symbolized by the vine and the branches. His presence with them, captured in the statement "ye in me,

NOTES

INTRODUCTION

1. Cf. Henry Alford, *The Greek Testament,* 1:25-27. For a good recent discussion of this problem, see Donald Guthrie, *New Testament Introduction,* 3d ed. Rev. pp. 33-34.
2. R. C. H. Lenski, *The Interpretation of St. Matthew's Gospel,* p. 17.
3. W. F. Albright and C. S. Mann, *The Anchor Bible,* Vol. 26, *Matthew,* p. CLXXXIII.
4. Willoughby C. Allen, *A Critical and Exegetical Commentary on the Gospel According to S. Matthew,* in the International Critical Commentary, p. xiii.
5. William R. Farmer, *The Synoptic Problem,* pp. vii-x.
6. Lenski, p. 19.
7. Allen, pp. x1-1xii. For a conservative discussion of *Q* materials, see Guthrie, pp. 143-57.

CHAPTER 1

1. W. Graham Scroggie, *A Guide to the Gospels,* pp. 260-61. Scroggie notes that of the 1068 verses in this gospel, 387 whole verses and parts of 23 other verses, 410 in all, are peculiar to it, which is more than a third of the whole gospel.
2. Cf. R. C. H. Lenski, *The Interpretation of St. Matthew's Gospel,* pp. 30-33.

CHAPTER 2

1. R. C. H. Lenski, *The Interpretation of St. Matthew's Gospel,* p. 57; W. C. Allen, *The Critical and Exegetical Commentary on the Gospel According to S. Matthew,* pp. 11-12.
2. Allen, ibid.
3. Alfred Plummer, *An Exegetical Commentary on the Gospel According to S. Matthew,* p. 14.
4. Richard Glover, *A Teacher's Commentary on the Gospel of Matthew,* p. 14.
5. Lenski, p. 81.
6. Flavius Josephus, *Wars of the Jews,* 1:33. Cf. also Lenski, p. 83.

CHAPTER 3

1. R. V. G. Tasker, *The Gospel According to Matthew,* Tyndale Bible Commentaries, p. 46.
2. R. C. H. Lenski, *The Interpretation of St. Matthew's Gospel,* p. 101.
3. Ibid., pp. 99-103.

CHAPTER 4

1. R. C. H. Lenski, *The Interpretation of St. Matthew's Gospel*, p. 141.
2. R. V. G. Tasker, *The Gospel According to St. Matthew*, p. 52.
3. Lenski, p. 139.
4. Ibid., p. 150.
5. Tasker, p. 52-53.
6. Lenski, pp. 153-54.
7. Tasker, p. 53.
8. Lenski, p. 171.

CHAPTER 5

1. William Kelly, *Lectures on the Gospel of Matthew*, p. 104.
2. R. V. G. Tasker, *The Gospel According to St. Matthew*, p. 59.
3. Kelly, p. 7.
4. R. C. H. Lenski, *The Interpretation of St. Matthew's Gospel*, p. 180.
5. Kelly, p. 106.
6. Arthur W. Pink, *An Exposition of the Sermon on the Mount*, p. 13.
7. Many independent works on the Sermon on the Mount have been published, most of them making spiritual applications of these general truths to Christians living today. Of these, volumes such as *Studies in the Sermon on the Mount* by David Martyn Lloyd-Jones, and *The Sermon on the Mount* by James Montgomery Boice are helpful, and *The Sermon on the Mount* by F. B. Meyer is a classic. Most expositions, however, content themselves with spiritual application and present application, and do not consider each verse contextually in its relation to the doctrine of the kingdom. While good application is common, precise interpretation is rare.
8. Tasker, p. 59.
9. D. Martyn Lloyd-Jones, *Studies in the Sermon on the Mount*, 1:151-52.
10. G. Campbell Morgan, *The Gospel According to Matthew*, p. 56.
11. Morgan, p. 58.

CHAPTER 6

1. William L. Pettingill, *The Gospel of the Kingdom*, p. 68.
2. H. A. Ironside, *Expository Notes on the Gospel of Matthew*, p. 63.
3. R. V. G. Tasker, *The Gospel According to St. Matthew*, p. 76.

CHAPTER 7

1. G. Campbell Morgan, *The Gospel According to Matthew*, p. 71.
2. R. V. G. Tasker, *The Gospel According to Matthew*, p. 80.
3. Morgan, pp. 75-76.
4. Tasker, p. 82-83.
5. H. A. Ironside, *Expository Notes on the Gospel of Matthew*, p. 83.
6. Ibid.

CHAPTER 8

1. On this whole matter, see R. V. G. Tasker, *The Gospel According to Matthew*, p. 87.
2. G. Campbell Morgan, *The Gospel According to Matthew*, p. 82.
3. Cf. Tasker, p. 95.

CHAPTER 9

1. W. H. Griffith Thomas, *Outline Studies in the Gospel of Matthew*, p. 129.
2. H. A. Ironside, *Expository Notes on the Gospel of Matthew*, p. 109.
3. R. V. G. Tasker, *The Gospel According to St. Matthew*, p. 100.
4. William Kelly, *Lectures on the Gospel of Matthew*, p. 217.

CHAPTER 10

1. R. V. G. Tasker, *The Gospel According to Matthew*, p. 106.

CHAPTER 11

1. R. C. H. Lenski, *The Interpretation of St. Matthew's Gospel*, p. 425.
2. G. Campbell Morgan, *The Gospel According to Matthew*, p. 111.

CHAPTER 12

1. G. Campbell Morgan, *The Gospel According to Matthew*, p. 124.
2. R. C. H. Lenski, *The Interpretation of St. Matthew's Gospel*, p. 461.
3. R. V. G. Tasker, *The Gospel According to Matthew*, p. 133.

CHAPTER 13

1. R. V. G. Tasker, *The Gospel According to St. Matthew*, pp. 134-35.
2. *Zondervan's Pictorial Dictionary*, S. V. "Tares." *Unger's Bible Dictionary*, pp. 1144-45.
3. C. H. Spurgeon, *The Gospel of the Kingdom*, p. 104.
4. R. C. H. Lenski, *The Interpretation of Matthew's Gospel* (Minneapolis, 1943), p. 528.
5. Ibid., p. 530.
6. Richard C. Trench, *Notes on the Parables of Our Lord*, pp. 102-10.
7. Lenski, p. 547.
8. While Protestants generally have held that Mary had children by Joseph subsequent to the birth of Jesus, Roman Catholics have denied this, as the brothers and sisters could have been children of Joseph's by an earlier marriage, or could even be cousins. Most Protestants find no problem in Mary having other children.

CHAPTER 14

1. For more details, see R. C. H. Lenski, *The Interpretation of St. Matthew's Gospel*, pp. 555-57.
2. For discussion on the route across Galilee, see R. V. G. Tasker, *The Gospel According to St. Matthew*, pp. 144-45.

CHAPTER 15

1. Cf. R. C. H. Lenski, *The Interpretation of St. Matthew's Gospel*, pp. 581-83.
2. Edwin W. Rice, *People's Commentary on the Gospel of Matthew*, p. 162.

CHAPTER 16

1. Edwin W. Rice, *People's Commentary on the Gospel of Matthew*, p. 163.
2. W. F. Albright and C. S. Mann, *The Anchor Bible*, Vol. 26, *Matthew*, p. 195.
3. R. C. H. Lenski, *The Interpretation of St. Matthew's Gospel*, p. 626.
4. Rice, pp. 168-69.
5. H. A. Ironside, *Expository Notes on the Gospel of Matthew*, p. 206.
6. R. V. G. Tasker, *The Gospel According to St. Matthew*, p. 161.

CHAPTER 17

1. R. V. G. Tasker, *The Gospel According to St. Matthew*, p. 167.
2. W. A. Criswell, *Expository Notes on the Gospel of Matthew*, p. 103.
3. R. C. H. Lenski, *The Interpretation of St. Matthew's Gospel*, pp. 654-55.
4. Ibid, pp. 655-56.
5. Ibid, pp. 662-63.
6. John F. Walvoord, *The Revelation of Jesus Christ* (Chicago: Moody, 1966), pp. 178-80.
7. G. Campbell Morgan, *The Gospel According to Matthew*, p. 224.
8. Ibid, p. 226.
9. Tasker, p. 169.

CHAPTER 18

1. H. A. Ironside, *Expository Notes on the Gospel of Matthew*, p. 222.
2. W. H. Griffith Thomas, *Outline Studies in the Gospel of Matthew*, p. 268.
3. W. A. Criswell, *Expository Notes on the Gospel of Matthew*, p. 107.
4. R. C. H. Lenski, *The Interpretation of St. Matthew's Gospel*, pp. 696-97.
5. Ibid., p. 708.
6. W. C. Allen, *A Critical and Exegetical Commentary on the Gospel of S. Matthew*, p. 199.
7. Lenski, p. 712.

CHAPTER 19

1. G. Campbell Morgan, *The Gospel According to Matthew*, p. 236.
2. R. C. H. Lenski, *The Interpretation of St. Matthew's Gospel*, pp. 727-28.
3. Richard Glover, *A Teacher's Commentary on the Gospel of Matthew*, p. 218.
4. Lenski, p. 755.
5. Ibid.

CHAPTER 20

1. Cf. R. C. H. Lenski, *The Interpretation of St. Matthew's Gospel*, p. 767.
2. G. Campbell Morgan, *The Gospel According to Matthew*, pp. 244-45.
3. Ibid.
4. W. A. Criswell, *Expository Notes on the Gospel of Matthew*, p. 117.
5. Lenski, p. 796.

CHAPTER 21

1. R. V. G. Tasker, *The Gospel According to St. Matthew*, p. 197.
2. Cf. R. C. H. Lenski, *The Interpretation of St. Matthew's Gospel*, p. 811.
3. Ibid., p. 813.
4. G. Campbell Morgan, *The Gospel According to Matthew*, p. 255.
5. Cf. Tasker, pp. 201-2; also Lenski, pp. 825-26.
6. Lenski, p. 825.
7. W. C. Allen, *A Critical and Exegetical Commentary on the Gospel of Matthew*, pp. 225-26.
8. Lenski, p. 835.
9. W. A. Criswell, *Expository Notes on the Gospel of Matthew*, p. 125.

CHAPTER 22

1. G. Campbell Morgan, *The Gospel According to Matthew*, p. 263.
2. W. A. Criswell, *Expository Notes on the Gospel of Matthew*, p. 126.
3. Morgan, pp. 269-70.
4. R. V. G. Tasker, *The Gospel According to St. Matthew*, p. 213.

CHAPTER 23

1. Cf. R. V. G. Tasker, *The Gospel According to St. Matthew*, p. 217.
2. Richard Glover, *A Teacher's Commentary on the Gospel of Matthew*, p. 259, 263-65.
3. W. A. Criswell, *Expository Notes on the Gospel of Matthew*, p. 129.

CHAPTER 24

1. Alan Hugh M'Neile, *The Gospel According to St. Matthew*, p. 343.
2. Ibid.
3. G. Campbell Morgan, *The Gospel According to Matthew*.
4. Ibid., p. 286.
5. Alfred Plummer, *An Exegetical Commentary on the Gospel According to S. Matthew*, pp. 330, 332.
6. H. A. Ironside, *Expository Notes on the Gospel of Matthew*, pp. 313-18.
7. Morgan, p. 286; Plummer, p. 332.
8. William Kelly, *Lectures on the Gospel of Matthew*, p. 442.
9. Ironside, p. 322.
10. For fifty reasons why the church will not go through the tribulation, see John F. Walvoord, *The Rapture Question*, pp. 191-99.
11. Cf. Kelly, p. 451; Arno C. Gaebelein, *The Gospel of Matthew*, 2:213-14.
12. Morgan, p. 286; Willoughby C. Allen, "A Critical and Exegetical Commentary on the Gospel According to S. Matthew" in *International Critical Commentary*, p. 259; R. V. G. Tasker, *The Gospel According to St. Matthew*, p. 227.
13. R. C. H. Lenski, *The Interpretation of St. Matthew's Gospel*, p. 951.
14. Gaebelein, 2:214-15.
15. William F. Arndt and F. Wilbur Gingrich, *A Greek-English Lexicon of the New Testament*, p. 153.
16. John Calvin, *Commentaries on the Catholic Epistles*, ed. and trans. John Owen (Edinburgh, 1855), p. 189.
17. Martin Luther, *Table Talk, Luther's Works*, 54:427.
18. Hugh Thomson Kerr, Jr. ed., *A Compend of Luther's Theology*, p. 245.

CHAPTER 25

1. Cf. G. Campbell Morgan, *The Gospel According to Matthew*, pp. 280-95; A. C. Gaebelein, *Gospel of Matthew*, pp. 225-27.
2. Cf. R. V. G. Tasker, *The Gospel According to Matthew*, p. 233.
3. W. F. Arndt and F. W. Gingrich, *A Greek-English Lexicon of the New Testament*, p. 811.
4. R. C. H. Lenski, *The Interpretation of St. Matthew's Gospel*, p. 988.
5. Tasker, p. 238.
6. Henry Alford, *The Greek New Testament*, 1:254.
7. A. H. M'Neile, *The Gospel According to St. Matthew*, p. 369.

CHAPTER 26

1. R. C. H. Lenski, *The Interpretation of St. Matthew's Gospel*, p. 1002.
2. Cf. W. C. Allen, *A Critical and Exegetical Commentary on the Gospel According to St. Matthew*, pp. 266-67.
3. Lenski, p. 1005.
4. Ibid., p. 1017.
5. Ibid., pp. 1026-31.
6. John Calvin, *Institutes of the Christian Religion*, 2:641-711.
7. On the contrast of Zwingli's and Luther's views of the Lord's Supper, see Albert H. Newman, *A Manual of Church History*, 2:312-13.
8. G. Campbell Morgan, *The Gospel According to Matthew*, pp. 300-303.
9. Lenski, pp. 1046-47.
10. Cf. Lenski, p. 1056.
11. R. V. G. Tasker, *The Gospel According to St. Matthew*, p. 255.

CHAPTER 27

1. R. C. H. Lenski, *The Interpretation of St. Matthew's Gospel*, p. 1078.
2. Ibid., pp. 1082-83.
3. Ibid., p. 1085.
4. R. V. G. Tasker, *The Gospel According to St. Matthew*, p. 260.
5. Lenski, pp. 1105-6.
6. Ibid., p. 1108; Tasker, p. 264.
7. Tasker, p. 265.

CHAPTER 28

1. Cf. R. V. G. Tasker, *The Gospel According to Matthew*, p. 271.
2. R. C. H. Lenski, *The Interpretation of St. Matthew's Gospel*, p. 1161.
3. Ibid.
4. Ibid., p. 1167.
5. W. A. Criswell, *Expository Notes on the Gospel of Matthew*, p. 166.

BIBLIOGRAPHY

Albright, W. F. and Mann, C. S. *The Anchor Bible*. Vol. 26, *Matthew*. Garden City, N. Y.: Doubleday, 1971.

Alford, Henry. *The Greek Testament*. Vol. 1. Chicago: Moody, 1958.

Allen, Willoughby C. "A Critical and Exegetical Commentary on the Gospel According to St. Matthew." In *International Critical Commentary*. 3d ed. Edinburgh: T. & T. Clark, 1907.

Arndt, William F. and Gingrich, F. Wilbur. *A Greek-English Lexicon of the New Testament*. Chicago: U. Chicago, 1957.

Boice, James Montgomery. *The Sermon on the Mount*. Grand Rapids, Mich.: Zondervan, 1972.

Calvin, John. *Commentaries on the Catholic Epistles*. Trans. and ed. John Owen. Grand Rapids: Eerdmans, 1948.

———. *Institutes of the Christian Religion*. Vol. 2. Trans. John Allen. Philadelphia: Presby. Brd. of Chr. Ed., 1936.

Constitutions of the Holy Apostles. Vol. 7, *The Ante-Nicene Fathers*. Ed. Alexander Roberts and James Donaldson. Buffalo, N.Y., 1886.

Criswell, W. A. *Expository Notes on the Gospel of Matthew*. Grand Rapids, Mich: Zondervan, 1961.

Farmer, William R. *The Synoptic Problem*. New York: MacMillan, 1964.

Gaebelein, Arno C. *The Gospel of Matthew*. 2 vols. New York: Our Hope, 1910.

Glover, Richard. *A Teacher's Commentary on the Gospel of Matthew*. Grand Rapids: Zondervan, 1956.

Guthrie, Donald. *New Testament Introduction*. Downers Grove, Ill.: IVP, 1971.

Ironside, Henry Allen. *Expository Notes on the Gospel of Matthew*. New York: Loizeaux, 1948.

Kelly, William. *Lectures in the Gospel of Matthew*. 5th Amer. ed. New York: Loizeaux, 1943.

Kerr, Hugh Thompson, Jr., ed. *A Compend of Luther's Theology*. Philadelphia: Westminster, 1943.

Lenski, R. C. H. *The Interpretation of St. Matthew's Gospel*. Minneapolis: Wartburg, 1943.

Lloyd-Jones, D. Martyn. *Studies in the Sermon on the Mount*. 2 vols. Grand Rapids, Mich: Eerdmans, 1959.

Luther, Martin. *Table Talk: Luther's Works*. Vol. 54. Trans. and ed. Theodore F. Tappert. Philadelphia: Fortress, 1967.

Meyer, F. B. *The Sermon on the Mount*. Grand Rapids, Mich.: Baker, 1959.

Morgan, G. Campbell. *The Gospel According to Matthew*. New York: Revell, 1929.

M'Neile, Alan Hugh. *The Gospel According to St. Matthew*. London: MacMillan, 1955.

Newman, Albert Henry. *A Manual of Church History*. Vol. 2. Chicago: American Bapt., 1931.

Pettingill, William L. *The Gospel in the Kingdom*. Findlay, Ohio: Fundamental Truth, n. d.

Pink, Arthur W. *An Exposition of the Sermon on the Mount*. Swengel, Penn.: Bible Truth Depot, 1950.

Plummer, Alfred. *An Exegetical Commentary on the Gospel According to St. Matthew*. London: Robert Scott Roxburghe, 1909.

Reese, Alexander. *The Approaching Advent of Christ*. London: Marshall, Morgan & Scott, n. d.

Rice, Edwin W. *People's Commentary on the Gospel of Matthew*. Philadelphia: Amer. S. S. Union, 1887.

Scroggie, W. Graham. *A Guide to the Gospels*. London: Pickering & Inglis, 1948.

Spurgeon, C. H. *The Gospel of the Kingdom*. London: Passmore & Alabaster, 1893.

Tasker, R. V. G. *The Gospel According to Matthew,* Tyndale Bible Commentaries. Grand Rapids: Eerdmans, 1961.

Tenney, Merrill C. *Zondervan's Pictorial Dictionary*. Grand Rapids: Zondervan, 1963.

Thomas, W. H. Griffith. *Outline Studies in the Gospel of Matthew*. Grand Rapids: Eerdmans, 1961.

Trench, Richard C. *Notes on the Parables of Our Lord*. New York: Appleton, 1851.

Unger, Merrill F. *Unger's Bible Dictionary*. Chicago: Moody, 1957.

Walvoord, John F. *The Rapture Question*. Grand Rapids: Zondervan, 1957.

The Works of Flavius Josephus. Trans. William Whiston. Philadelphia: Porter & Coates, n. d.

SCRIPTURE INDEX